The Exiles

ALSO BY *Albert J. Guerard*

THE PAST MUST ALTER

THE HUNTED

MAQUISARD

NIGHT JOURNEY

THE BYSTANDER

Criticism:

ROBERT BRIDGES

THOMAS HARDY

ANDRÉ GIDE

CONRAD THE NOVELIST

The Exiles

A Novel by *Albert J. Guerard*

THE MACMILLAN COMPANY, NEW YORK

FIRST PRINTING

PRINTED IN THE UNITED STATES OF AMERICA

Library of Congress catalog card number: 63-8967

For Lundie

1

THE WHIM, yet not entirely a whim, that brought
Manuel Andrada blundering into my life . . .

Last spring I was looking for something to write about,
when the Villamayor "case"—the Villamayor outrage—
again popped into mind. It has had a way of popping in
and out, because of my slender personal connection with
it. *Justo de Villamayor*, poet, historian and lamentably unsuccessful statesman. I had been down there, in what I
shall call "Santa Isabella," at the time of his first abduction, though I understood nothing about this then. Later,
I became curious concerning Villamayor's second and
more lasting disappearance. Why, I asked myself (now
that the big weeklies and even the liberal ones had forgotten that murky affair)—why not do a "serious" article
on Villamayor and his writings, and on the enigma of his
few weeks in the Santa Isabella Cabinet? It was time to
look at the matter calmly. Three years had passed since
his brief and futile gesture of resistance to total authority
and since his sudden and violent removal from office.
Eight months after that occurred the second disappearance, which the world soon began to forget. Brutalities
succeed brutalities, the single incident is lost in the mass.
Too many exiles have disappeared, after all; one cannot
remember everything.

Once before I had thought of writing about Villa-mayor, but had turned to something else. Then last spring, during a weekend in New York (where so many dark faces remind one of Cuba, of Puerto Rico, of "Santa Isabella") I thought of him again. This time I went to the Consulate of that parched land without even telephoning for an appointment. That was my whim. I think I wanted, if only out of curiosity, to catch them unawares. I wondered how they would react to the name of their shadowy victim, twenty-five months after his second disappearance. Would they not reasonably suppose this one small incident in the country's long chronicle of violence would by now have been forgotten . . . especially since nothing was ever "proved"?

I had to wait for more than an hour in the small windowless anteroom, under the scornful stare of the receptionist at her antique switchboard. I had given her my name and said I was interested in writing about Santa Isabella; that was all. In the Consulate of any other country I suppose I would have been made welcome. But Santa Isabella had at last accepted the fact that all publicity, unless solicited and paid for, would be bad. On one wall of the anteroom was a faded poster inviting winter vacationists. There were modern buildings above a curving sea—*The Jewel of the Caribbean . . . Relax in the Sun.* The discolored poster must have gone back ten years or more to the time when tourists did flock there, after the building of the two luxury hotels. On the opposite wall was the inevitable large portrait of the nation's guardian and ruler: The Protector. In this one he wore evening clothes and a broad jeweled sash that looped over one shoulder: still another decoration conferred by the nation's eager gratitude. The civilian clothes and sickly

smile were intended to beguile American businessmen,
welcome them to the "Paradise of Investors."

During my hour and more of waiting, four or five small
dishonest-looking men in tight brown suits appeared,
spoke to the receptionist, and entered the Consul's office.
In time they reappeared. They glanced at me with dis-
approval.

Then I was received by the commercial attaché, one
Eufemio Rodriguez, a small bulky man whose eyes di-
verged oddly. He looked up when I came into the room,
then back at his papers. I was not asked to sit down. "Yes,
what is it you want?" But when I asked my blunt question
—*"What is the official attitude of your government toward the memory of Villamayor?"*— the swarthy head
and diverging eyes rose slowly, both to me and to the wall
behind me. There, of course, was another portrait of The
Protector: this one in the splendid uniform of general-
issimo. It appeared Eufemio Rodriguez was keeping one
distrustful eye on me while the other eye looked to The
Protector for guidance.

The voice issuing from this fat watchful man was a
querulous feminine whine.

"And you say you are a journalist? Please let me see
your credentials."

"I'm a free lance, I don't have any credentials. I want
to do a magazine article on Villamayor. On his writings
especially."

Eufemio Rodriguez folded his hands patiently. The
puffy fingers stirred.

"You journalists distort everything. But now there is
nothing left to distort. Villamayor is dead and forgotten."

"Then your government's attitude . . ."

"My government has no attitude toward Villamayor.

Why should it have an attitude? It is commonly said he was a poet and historian of great though squandered gifts. My personal opinion is that he was a dilettante. But there is nothing more to be said about the late Justo de Villamayor. You would do well to find a better subject for an article."

The dark head went back to the papers; I was being dismissed.

"Did Villamayor leave anything behind? Any books or articles that haven't been published?"

The dissociated eyes rose more quickly this time, to me and to the portrait behind me.

"Writings? You think there are unpublished writings?"

"I thought you would know."

Eufemio Rodriguez examined me. He was silent for what seemed a very long time.

"We have no cultural attaché in New York. As for myself, I am not interested in the arts and literature. My task is to facilitate fruitful commerce between our two great democracies." He indicated with his fat hands the desk covered with pamphlets, statistics, documents. "I have no time to spend on a dilettante writer of frivolities. A writer who is, moreover, dead. Santa Isabella lives for the future, not the past. For the reinvigoration of the economy. . . ."

Again I was being dismissed. But just as I reached the door the whining voice arrested me:

"Why did you think there were unpublished writings?"

"Writers usually leave something behind. I thought there might be talk among the exiles . . ."

"I have no communication with exile scum," Eufemio Rodriguez said. "The deserters of the faith. Have you ever visited my country, Mr. Clive?"

"Yes, three years ago."

"Why not write about the touristic attractions, and the beautiful capital city?"

"I'm more interested in Villamayor."

Eufemio Rodriguez sighed.

"And why? I repeat: you journalists distort everything. Always you exaggerate. So you were in Santa Isabella three years ago?" Eufemio Rodriguez calculated rapidly. Yes, he must have reasoned, I was there at the time of the "incident." The fingers went on fluttering. "Very well: leave your address with the girl. I will speak to one of my compatriots who is interested in the arts and literature. For me, none of that is of importance. But my friend will call you if there is anything new to be said . . . about the writings of the late Villamayor."

I gave the girl my address: my impersonal Boston room in a chrome-and-glass apartment building overlooking the river—my room where, two weeks later, Manuel Andrada would find me. Was he summoned all the way from Santa Isabella as a result of my unexpected question? Or had he already set out on a blundering quest of his own? About this, as about many other matters, I shall probably never know.

So in any event it began, whimsically and innocently, five months ago: the ridiculous adventure. A serious article on Villamayor the intellectual rebel, the revolutionary *malgré lui* . . . I went back home to do research on this man of letters whose last days had taken such a melodramatic and sinister turn. Every morning I went to the library, and followed Villamayor through the files. And every afternoon in my rooms I sat at a neat metal desk thrust against a wall made entirely of glass. I could stare down on the pale strip of grass bordering the water and on the traffic of the Drive. Or I could watch the spitting rain. On one side of my desk were Villamayor's own four books. On the other were my folders: *Education, Politics, Personality*. There was a thick folder titled *The Disappearances*, containing my speculations, also my notes on the sensational articles of two and three years ago. I had everything neatly organized. And there through the long dull spring afternoons I worked, fatuously confident my article was taking shape, and that I—a casual journalist, resident of Santa Isabella for a little over a month—that I could discover the political secret and define the personality of this devious man, this slightly disreputable victim.

Meanwhile, in the two weeks before Andrada arrived, my "credentials" on file in the capital city were presumably examined. They must have been (because of my father? because of my small inherited investment?) found satisfactory. Certainly Manuel Andrada when he came— he too intensely interested in the "unpublished writings" —seemed to expect my cooperation.

So it began with my whim, and with that unannounced call at the Consulate. It began with the well concealed alarm of one Eufemio Rodriguez. And now, these five months later, I sit naked and sweating at this other "desk" (a vermin-pitted and stained table with a great crack running through it) . . . working on this longer narrative. On this "novel," I suppose it must be called, since a novel can be anything. And it seems to me five years not five months have passed, since Andrada entered my life. Now I sit (a towel around my neck) in my room with its sagging precarious balcony overlooking a broiling portside square. The swarm of a feverish seaport, a hundred degrees in the October shade, and the foul odors of an estuary. A seaport very different from the clean

Ciudad Santa Isabella: the clean, the orderly, the deadly. And here I "work." I sit and dream too: of the night to come and of languid hours in a café, of the sounds and odors of midnight. And always weaving into my thoughts are the newsboys' cries and the cries of the *gaseosa* and lottery salesmen. I work, I try to write. Outside, a policeman leans against the peeling yellow dockside installation, smoking. He scratches at his groin, delicately, as if to seek out the individual culprits. Another policeman is at work on his teeth. And always the newsboys' cries. Beggars stagger across the square to seek the protection of shade; the long afternoon burns. But evening will come at last, with its charcoal odors and its voices in the darkness, plaintive as doves, then suddenly strident.

A sagging bus roars across the square, scattering newsboys and beggars and *gaseosa* salesmen.

And again I begin to write. *Justo de Villamayor, the victim, was the son of a wealthy rancher. . . .* But there are no neat folders now. My desk and floor and bureau are covered with papers, time charts, outlines, scribbled speculations. For I have been overwhelmed by the oddities and complexities of this affair. Stuck pinned to the wall are the insistent questions I come back to—*Why did Villamayor bury himself for so many months? Why was V. so patient with Julieta? Did he expect to be killed?* And many more such questions.

The papers and outlines and unanswered questions, this still unwritten novel, litter my half of the room. At the other end, away from the window and balcony, is the less intellectual disorder a seventeen-year-old girl can create: the pomades and brushes, the eyeshadow and powders and ointments, and ubiquitously the scatter of romantic magazines and comic books. The great billowing snowy petticoats (the pride of her young life, my latest gift paid for from the inherited "golden trickle") hang on hooks in the musty dark above our sagging unmade bed. She never leaves herself enough time to make it. And even in her absence a rank perfume emanates from one dark corner as from an oily animal crouching there: a drugging, sickly sweetness. In an hour she will be back, and my "work" for this day will be done. Will she kiss me or spit at me with scorn? One can never know in advance.

But that is no matter. For she (my slim lithe dark replica of Manuel Andrada's best love) has no place in this story of political gratifications, passions, defeats . . . this story in which even death seems to take on the character of farce. My companion of the snowy petticoats has indeed no place in it. But neither, for that matter, have I. I stumbled into the historical enigma of Villamayor three years ago, during my month in Santa Isabella, when I really saw and understood nothing. Then again last spring I rushed into it, acting on my whim. After that I "went along" and watched and listened, and for some weeks played my writer's role of a bland neutrality. Yes, I watched but that is nearly all. I accomplished no heroic actions during the months that have intervened; and the one absurd death was not mine. Am I in fact only this grave, slightly puzzled voice: this interlocutor, this northern intruder on the sincerity of their political passions? Yes: only the teller of a tale.

As for the girl—whom I took such pains to seduce—, and to "court" even; whom I enticed to my room and sagging bed with such difficulty, only to discover very soon she had been assigned to me by an uneasy police bureaucrat, to report on my activities . . . someday she and I may have our turn to step to the forefront of a narrative. But not now. For the present I must write this other story—which is the story of Justo de Villamayor and the long shadow he cast: of the Villamayor who collected mad disciples against his will, of the Villamayor whom Andrada pursued. Yes: most of all the chronicle of these two, of Andrada and Villamayor, and the collision of their two worlds, the absurd collision of their loyalties. And even that, of course, is not the "whole story." For behind them both, behind the tall immortal Villamayor and the squat, most obscure Andrada, lies the parched corrupted brutalized inescapable fatherland: the "Santa Isabella" where both were born, some twenty years apart.

I HAVE seen only photographs of the statue of Villamayor. For I had left the city of The Protector before it was erected: before it was thrown up, rather, in the roughest plaster and as a sop to popular indignation over the disappearance of the man himself. The State, which could not tolerate Villamayor the dabbler in politics, was willing to honor the writer. The sculptor even did his work of appeasement under the public's eye. The skeletal ribs of the armature appeared and grew more and more human even as speculation continued, secretly of course, concerning the perishable body of the historian and lyric poet. There was no time for marble or bronze.

And there it doubtless still stands in cracked and peeling plaster on the Avenue of the 30th of May, under the scrawny browning palms, facing the thin breakwater and the soiled angry sea. Villamayor wears the flowing robes of a Minister of State. The rough plaster model has even caught the peculiar twist and torment of his face and neck—as though The Maker had given that face a mali-

cious wrench in the instant before birth. The sunken eyes
are noncommittal. But one hand is raised as in exhortation;
the other rests on an open book. The back is turned, a
little scornfully, on the wide avenue and the silent city.
The pose might suggest a theorist's aloofness and detachment from political realities.

The plaster model was thrown up to placate an enraged
opinion: a kind of resistance that was no longer supposed
to be possible in Santa Isabella. Still, the small statue might
also be regarded as a final insult to Villamayor. For his is
but one of twenty or so statues—these others of forgotten
generals and obscure relatives of The Protector, scattered
among the sickly palms and the obelisks. It is a little more
than lifesize but much smaller than the other statues,
which are already in final marble or bronze. Villamayor
seems almost an excrescence: small and futile in the burning solitude of that Avenue, in the white Caribbean glare.
The wide walks are empty. And few drivers venture on
this curving Avenue where eight cars could go abreast.
But every afternoon at five the Avenue is closed to the
public while The Protector takes his ritual bath in the
sea, under the poised submachine guns of his bodyguards.
Or perhaps it is a mysterious rite of pollution? The city
is spotless, as everyone knows; the most modern methods
for disposal are used. Yet there always blows, deeper than
the acrid odor of salt, a smell of sewage from the sea.

The base of the statue is doubtless yellow with urine,
while the statue itself must attract the pellet droppings
of gulls. *Justo de Villamayor, historiada y poeta.* The dates
indicate that the poet, historian and dabbler in politics
died more than three years ago, at the age of forty-five.
But who could have confidently said where or when, in
the absence of a corpse? The first disappearance occurred

in a particular year, hour and day. During the siesta Villa-mayor was hustled brazenly from his office in the Ministry of Education before the dazed eyes of a few secretaries and one guard, down the marble steps faintly resisting, and into a small truck that vanished north up the empty Avenida Coronel Martinez. The truck was followed by four buglike gray cars of the secret police, refurbished Volkswagens, their abnormally high thin antennae waving dangerously. The Government thus said as openly as possible that no such political deviations, not even the mildest, would be tolerated. After three days the *Diario del Caribe* made a curt announcement of an "unexplained kidnapping" and of Villamayor's presumed death.

The wholly unexpected public demonstration of rage—the first such demonstration in years, as Villamayor's speeches had been the first Cabinet dissent—caught the security forces off guard. For hours under the sullen eyes of police on horseback a crowd in black filed back and forth in front of the Ministry, then marched to the Cathedral. This is the historical event I saw yet did not see, for I did not know what I was looking at. Actually, the protests went on for days, and led to that hasty erection of the statue in temporary plaster form. The Nation would honor its dead. Obituary articles were prepared, generous to a fault, speaking of the skeptic's place in history.

However, Justo de Villamayor did not die under the blows of his first captors. Some months later he appeared in Mexico City, crippled, and leaning on a cane, having suffered many broken bones. How he got there, with whose aid or forbearance, was unknown. But alive he certainly was, as The Protector's Consul-General must have reported with alarm. The tormented thoughtful face was twisted no further than before from a normal axis.

The discovery was reported joyfully in the *Diario* and in the *Prensa Libre*. The nation's chief cultural ornament had survived and was resuming his literary activities during a brief sojourn in Mexico. He was the guest of a fellow historian and notorious socialist: Alonso Moreno. There followed a controversy in the papers concerning the premature statue, with its incorrect terminal date. The casting into final form would certainly be put off. Should the living Villamayor, distinguished poet but dubious political theorist and moralist, be allowed to stand among the honored dead? A subtle campaign of vilification began. But before it could get very far, and before any move was taken to demolish or remove the plaster model, Villamayor had disappeared again. He vanished quietly from Mexico City, perhaps to enjoy the company of a female secretary, one Julieta Aparicio. For she herself vanished the day after he did. And what does "vanished" signify? Were they both victims of The Protector's love of order, or were they only seeking an immoral solitude? This time there was little public speculation. Emotions were already exhausted, and there had been no visible violence. The affair was too small, after the first days, for New York or even Miami papers. It was not until much later that I heard (from Manuel Andrada, in fact) of postcards from Villamayor sent to Alonso Moreno from several provincial cities in Mexico . . . prior to the deeper silence that ensued.

So I never saw that plaster likeness of Villamayor: only poor photographs of the "provisional" unveiling, with the unsmiling Protector in attendance, surrounded by his nephews and his generals. But I have seen The Protector himself more than once, in his waxen flesh and with his dead calm eyes: the "Great Catholic Gentleman," the Reinvigorator of the Economy. Three years ago, while

Villamayor was in office in fact, I was down there for a month. I was even permitted once to attend The Protector's slow, dignified, as it were symbolic descent into the sea. I was down there, trying to sell my shares in the Azucarera San Tomás, and all the time I was blind to the political drama played behind the city's bland surface. I thought I knew the city . . . and I think I do know it now. Yes, I have known that low-built city of silence as one knows the still interior of a dream. Ciudad Santa Isabella. The empty streets pass shuttered houses flush on the sidewalk into a drab infinity of adobe and withered palm. But there is a policeman with a white baton at every intersection, to direct the sparse traffic. Only half a dozen cars pass in an hour; people stay at home. Here few dare to wander on Sundays in the well kept public gardens and admirable Zoo or in the famous Horticultural Institute. Lulling popular music is piped above the empty walks. The international fairgrounds, now the seat of government buildings, is a dry solitude. Not even *their* vigilance can keep down the weeds and marsh grass encroaching on the official buildings and on the two vast empty luxury hotels overlooking a scorched sea.

(And it is, for all their efficiency, a land where mishaps occur, grotesque public ones, worthy of the Japanese. This is one thing I have learned from my study of the nation's recent history. Dignitaries are always being tumbled from overcrowded reviewing stands. Or they come to grief on the too highly polished floors of official ballrooms. Once a papal nuncio was drenched when a welcoming government tender overturned. And once too a nephew of The Protector was gored by a bull at a showing of cattle imported from Texas to improve the breed. I mention him as I think of another cretin nephew of The

Protector, the President of the Republic in fact, who presided sleepily at the first meeting of the Cabinet attended by Villamayor. The poet's initial outburst was absent-minded: Villamayor was only following the habits of a lifetime. But even after an hour the Nephew failed to understand fully that the new Minister of Education was daring to oppose an important Government decree. Only the astonished faces of the others at last put him on guard.)

This then is the city of the browning palms: Ciudad Santa Isabella. For one long hot month I lived there in a white underfurnished apartment near the Cathedral with a houseboy who once each day, I assume, reported on my activities to the police. Actually he had very little to report. For I had gone down there in all innocence to try to sell those few shares in the Compañiá Azucarera San Tomás . . . the golden trickle inherited from my father, who had acquired it in the mid-thirties as a personal favor from one of The Protector's associates. (He had gone down early in the savage reconstruction days, the "Period of Rectification," and had built one handsome curving railroad bridge over a ravine . . . a bridge in which the then youngish Protector took great pride. The most modern bridge in all Latin America! I have seen photographs of that bridge in the government's rotogravure albums: a small curving span and tracks vanishing into a tunnel. The mouth of the tunnel is fringed by ferns and grasses.)

I was unable to sell those shares, which are never traded on a public market. And I daresay I shall be possessed of them for the rest of my life. The golden trickle: the rush of liquid golden sugar solidified to neat sacks of white and transformed again to the trickle of gold, silver, dividends, some two thousand dollars a year. . . . Each morning for

ten days I consulted with a lawyer on the Calle Obregón
concerning these shares. He could not hide his uneasiness.
Eventually through him I was received by a smiling name-
less high official in the white Ministry of Commerce who
threw up his hands. *Sell shares in the Compañia Azucarera
San Tomás!* That, he remarked, would be foolish as well
as illegal. Had I no idea how warmly I was to be congrat-
ulated on possessing the shares, since high dividends would
be paid eternally? And how many foreigners of "modest
means" were permitted the honor of taking part in a
national enterprise of reinvigoration owned in large part
by one of The Protector's beloved nephews? I was told I
need never worry about my investment in the progressive
Nation . . . this investment my "illustrious father" was
permitted to make in recognition of the railroad bridge.
I could visit the sugar mill, if I wished, then go home with
my "spirit at ease."

I remained another two weeks. It was because of this
that I witnessed (no, stared blankly at) the silent procession of protest over the abduction of Villamayor. I
stayed down in Santa Isabella because that apartment was
paid for for a month. I was enjoying the terrible heat in a
drugged languid way. Moreover I had my small pleasures,
the good rum and the hotel pools, and the various dark
sullen girls that the houseboy thrust into my bed. I remained curious, too, concerning this sleepy town where
my dead father had spent a few months of his life: this
town on the surface so silent and orderly, yet notorious
throughout the hemisphere for its long chronicle of violence and torture. In the first days I was made uneasy by
the ubiquitous police, and by the fact that I was regularly
and even openly followed. But I soon discovered my fol-
lowers wanted to be "friends"; they begged for cigarettes.

So the photographs of The Protector in every shop window came to seem harmless and at last ridiculous. I made a few friends among the scatter of Americans, but met no one who had known my father. Also I came to know quite well, or so I thought, a wizened sickly journalist who wrote monthly brochures in English celebrating The Protector's economic achievements. *A Paradise for Investors.* . . . (Not a paradise for me, who could not sell those shares!) This man assured me, almost casually, that all the stories of torture and oppression were the inventions of communists and exiles. The Protector was really a "good sort," traduced by the envious.

I was very nearly ready to believe him. For I myself saw no violence. I dare say I was languishing by one of the empty hotel pools, in the peaceful hot afternoon, at the very hour Villamayor was hustled from his office in the Ministry of Education, and into the small truck. It was not days or months but three years later that I apprehended the vivid details: the "four buglike gray cars," for instance.

Three days later I did read the *Diario*'s brief report of an unexplained kidnapping and of Villamayor's presumed death. The Minister of Education had disappeared. But my eye was not then trained to detect, between these lines, what would be evident to all educated citizens of Santa Isabella, to all but the most naïve: that this was the Government's frank acknowledgment of its complicity and a blunt warning against similar deviation. I dare say I glanced at this article, then turned to the sports page. Late that afternoon, standing at a dark bar off the Cathedral square, one of those bars open to the street, I chanced to look out into the blue dusk and saw the long silent procession of men and women in black. They moved very

slowly toward the Cathedral, while policemen on horseback watched. There were also police cars at the mouths
of alleys. But I stared at all this uncomprehending: quite
unable to distinguish this most audacious act of political
protest from an ordinary procession of mourners. The
historical moment. . . . A few days later (still only
dimly aware of the great political drama that had been
played during my month in the city) I went home, after
a stopover in Port-au-Prince.

There may have been some uneasiness at the very end
because I had stayed so long, and because I did at last ask
a few questions. *What did the procession mean? Why so
many police? Why wasn't it reported in the papers?* The
sickly American journalist, when I asked him these questions, simply nodded and went on his way. On the last
afternoon of my stay in the city I walked along that wide
empty seaside avenue where the statue of Villamayor
would presently rise. To a native it would have seemed
tempting fate to walk in such an emptiness; and so it
would seem to me now. And in fact I was not alone on
that vast boulevard where eight cars might have driven
abreast. A pick-up truck with lettering in English—
DR. SCHOLL'S FOOT POWDER—shot by me again and again
before hurling itself into side streets: the only car I saw
during all that time. The mad act of walking in that heat
when all other visitors ride must have given the services
of security some pause. My month's "record" must have
impressed them with its innocence, though. I was allowed
to leave Santa Isabella undisturbed.

Still I have often dreamed of that truck advertising a
product popular throughout this area subject to scaled
and rotting feet. And I have often had the illusion too
that it would be impossible to leave The Protector behind.

Would I not have my small stake in his success and survival (the "golden trickle") for the rest of my days?

Be that as it may: I had no idea what had happened "under my nose," or while I lay basking by the pool and quietly drinking in bars. What had happened was a half-conscious impulse to radical reform, almost to "revolution"—an impulse that proved abortive. And even back in New York and Boston three years ago, I did not learn very much. The accounts in the weeklies were sparse and generally inaccurate. In fact I did not speculate seriously on this tenebrous affair until Villamayor disappeared for the second time, some eight months later. And I did not begin to penetrate its subtleties until last spring, when I decided to write about it, and made my whimsical call at the Consulate. So it was not down there in the incandescent city of the browning palms but under the cold gray staining skies of the northern one, and in the cellars and stacks of a university library, that I began to make some order of these events.

Last spring . . . which already seems years ago. I read through Villamayor's own books quickly, skimming the poems, puzzling out the theories of history. And I was reading everything I could find in the various Mexican journals hostile to The Protector . . . when Manuel Andrada found me. He was Santa Isabella's response to my reawakened curiosity, and to my abrupt questions concerning the unpublished writings. His arrival marked the real beginning: marked my initiation, some three years late, to the political realities of Santa Isabella.

EVERYTHING was strange about his coming. It was a warm Saturday afternoon and many tenants were away. Somehow he got by the doorman and to the elevator without ringing. He did not wait to be asked in. Instead he walked into my apartment (finding me without shoes) holding a slip of paper with my name and address: a feverish apparition, stocky, in a coarse brown winter suit. My name had been supplied, he told me, by the commercial attaché of his Consulate in New York: one Eufemio Rodriguez. I thought of that bulky man of the fat fluttering fingers and divergent eyes. Could this creature be the compatriot interested in "the arts and literature"? He looked more like a prize fighter. And he brought the very breath of Santa Isabella into my room, with his harsh stare and peasant wariness. His black hair might have been cut by following the edge of a bowl, except for the deep sideburns.

He bowed and introduced himself but would not sit down. Instead he looked with alarm at the chair I pointed to—a thing of orange canvas hooked to fragile steel supports, and sinking almost to the floor. He was also startled by my one wall that was only glass.

"Manuel Andrada," he said again. "I represent the National Library."

He stood his ground in the center of the room: a scarred burning little man. He had been sent north, he said, to recover a "national property." He leaned forward as he spoke, rocking on black cardboard shoes pointed and small as daggers at the toes. The brown suit was drawn abominably tight with odd bulges near the armpits and a ballet dancer's crotch. And the scar! A thick white gash

ran above the right eye for half an inch, then cut down
through the brow. A knife thrust directly at the eye in
mortal anger must have struck the skull and been repelled
by its savage hardness. Knowing Andrada as I have come
to know him, I can imagine the bending of that knife and
the staring fright of his assailant. The two bulges, small
misplaced female breasts, signified first a revolver and
second a wallet containing the many documents necessary
for survival in Santa Isabella. All the certificates, all the
dispensations and indulgences of a whimsical absolute
power.

In time I would have my opportunity to know the
contents of that wallet. And in time too my long view of
Señor Andrada would change. His "soul changed," as he
once put things. But so too did mine, and I came to feel
something other than scorn. Last spring, though, it was
this impression of a man burning he chiefly made, as he
rocked on those cracking shoes, a slow burning of the
flesh from within. He looked thirty-five but was actually
twenty-eight, only a year older than I. The skin glowed
dry and tight over sharp cheekbones.

Manuel Andrada stared at my feet as he talked. He
repeated himself several times, having memorized his
speech. He had been sent to recover the "national property" which also concerned me: certain manuscripts of
little commercial but great patriotic value. They belonged
in the National Library and Archives of Santa Isabella.
There would doubtless be poems and perhaps other works
by the late Villamayor.

"You too are interested in the writings, Señor Clive.
You will sympathize with my mission. You know the
aspirations of my country, and its splendid cultural tra-
ditions."

It was almost the last time he said "Señor." Thereafter, perhaps because he thought this was the American custom, perhaps as a claim to intimacy, he would say "Nicholas Clive." He continued to look down, distressed by my bare feet.

"I was given your name, you are writing for a magazine. It is said you write about Justo de Villamayor. You believe there are unpublished writings. Therefore I come to you, there is no one else to help me. . . ." And in the same somber tones: "I do not understand your country, Nicholas Clive. It is my first trip away from the homeland. Your customs bewilder me."

At once, as though to punctuate or discredit these remarks, he coughed: a short disreputable cough. A bark. He coughed without putting his hand to his mouth, almost without moving his lips.

Again he refused to sit down. But he assured me we would "collaborate fruitfully." He extracted from the enormous wallet a long package of dollar bills, the elongated bills of another era. He had come prepared, he said, to purchase these national treasures. They would be published by the National Library itself.

I was much amused. I sat down, even though he would not. He continued to stand above me rigidly, in the manner of a schoolboy on trial. The crude haircut and burnished cheeks gave his face an Indian cast.

"Are you offering me that money? I don't have any manuscripts."

"I did not expect you to. But we will work together to find them, Nicholas Clive! You are writing about Villamayor, yes? You are known to be a friend of our progressive though misunderstood country. You have been there."

"I've been there all right. I'm afraid that doesn't make one a friend. I was glad enough to get out."

The tightly bound shoulders stirred impatiently. Manuel Andrada was very surprised. And I in turn was surprised to learn how large and favorable my "file" evidently was, in the secret cabinets of Santa Isabella.

"You wanted to leave! But how can that be, Nicholas Clive? You are an owner of many shares in the *Azucarera San Tomás*. A small fortune. Moreover, you had two luxurious rooms with private bath on the Calle Conde when you visited us three years ago. Yes, and mistresses. You have known our city and its benefits. Consider too The Protector's plan for National Reinvigoration."

"I've considered it," I said. "What manuscripts do you think there are?"

"Nothing is known with certainty. On this question there exist many rumors, concerning what Villamayor wrote. It has been said there was a book on political affairs. Also it is said he was writing the story of his early years. And can we not believe he was writing more poems? Yes, certainly more poems. The inspired poet cannot keep silent."

I was fully convinced Andrada had not read a line of Villamayor. (In this I turned out to be wrong: every schoolboy in Santa Isabella must memorize many of his lines.) I was also convinced Andrada had never been inside the National Library he claimed to represent. He had his stilted way of speaking, as though everything had been committed to memory. But otherwise he had all the manner of the government bullyboy, the brute body and badly fitting suit, and the wary fanatic eyes. I had seen his like many times down there, accompanying the taxi drivers on their rounds.

His mission, as regards any manuscripts of Villamayor, would be to suppress or destroy them.

"What have you found so far?"

"Nothing. After five days in your country—still I accomplish nothing! I do not know where to start. In fact I have been much discouraged."

He continued to stand, embarrassed, in the center of the room.

"So Eufemio Rodriguez sent for you, and then sent you to me?"

"Señor Rodriguez? I did not meet him until yesterday. In New York I had to wait four days for his return. Permit me to explain my bewilderment on arriving in such a place in search of the lost writings of a man who died no one knows where. Who am I to undertake such a mission? I found myself unequipped. I found myself in the city of New York without preparations or instructions. I descended from the airplane. . . ."

And suddenly he began to wave his stubby arms, recapitulating that first bewilderment. I suspect he had not dared to say these things to Rodriguez, commercial attaché of the Consulate, a man unforgiving of weakness. But he could not withhold them from me: the nightmare experience of his first hours and days in New York. He had already assumed that much intimacy between us, and became very talkative. Even the New York hotel room had bewildered him, with its small translucent packages and bags and cloths. For most of that first evening he sat entranced by the television set with its many channels, each conveying new information on American life. He found himself harboring new desires. But that was not all. Later (when I came to know him better) Andrada confided that he had not dared to use his toilet on that first night. When after hours of indecision he broke the cellophane that tightly covered it, and lifted the lid, he was dismayed by an unearthly violet glow.

The next morning he got lost in the subway, and spent hours in the labyrinth beneath Times Square.

"It is all a madness for one who comes unprepared." Andrada looked about him at the unfriendly modern furnishings, and at my shelves of subversive-looking volumes. "I have spent a great deal of my money. And there is so much to learn, I buy many of the magazines."

"There's also Villamayor's published work," I put in. "I suppose you read that too?"

He ignored my question in favor of certain lonely meditations.

"If I fail, I will deserve punishment."

The simple statement, bearing all the weight of a dim unquestioned autocracy, disarmed me. Suddenly I felt sorry for this poor foolish instrument of obscure and malign power. And I was curious to know what more they had told him about me. I offered him a drink.

He accepted at once, and with a shy grin: a great gold tooth appeared. His lip curled up as though on purpose to reveal it. And now he was even willing to sit down. He took the one straight chair in the room, and faced me with his short legs just touching the floor. I would not realize until later what importance he attached to the offer of a drink, this "first act of friendship." That was what he came to call it.

"I'm surprised you came to Boston. Wouldn't Villamayor's friends be in New York, rather? Or in Miami?"

"Boston is a center of the arts and literature. . . . I think Villamayor must have lived here for a time. There was a postcard from Villamayor to his friend Alonso

Moreno, saying he hoped to visit Boston." Andrada looked at me fixedly, a black intimate stare. "Furthermore you were here, Nicholas Clive. I knew there was someone here with a knowledge of our country and our literature who would be willing to help me. A friendly collaboration. You have your article on Villamayor to write, I procure the manuscripts."

"I'm not sure I like the idea too much. What else did they tell you about me—besides my 'mistresses'? And my shares in the Azucarera?"

"Your father built one of the first of our noble bridges. That was during the dark hour of the reconstruction, the heroic but dark hour. He came to us when others refused, fearful they would not be paid."

"He was just an engineer," I said. "It was strictly professional."

"And you, Nicholas Clive. You are a journalist of distinction. How many articles have you written for magazines? Almost thirty, I believe. Yet you have not written one unfriendly article about Santa Isabella. Many of your compatriots do."

"I haven't written about Santa Isabella at all. So how exactly was I supposed to help you?"

Manuel Andrada leaned forward confidently.

"Ah, excellent! We begin to collaborate. Very well—I suggest you speak to American writers. The late Villamayor was a poet and historian of international fame. Who else would know more about his unpublished writings? Yes, and you could talk to some of the exiles from our country who live in Boston. I have a few names. You could find more, you could establish a list. . . ."

"Why don't you talk to them yourself?"

Manuel Andrada stared.

"They are evil creatures, malcontents and grudge-bearers who have betrayed the national honor by exile and treason. They have fouled the nest. It would be impossible for me to see them, at least at the first. Moreover, they would not trust me."

I turned impatiently away. By leaning far back I could see the thin Saturday crowds along the river. The men were in shirt sleeves; a few carried coats over their arms. It is against the law, in Santa Isabella, to carry a coat over one's arm. Too much might be concealed.

"I don't think you're looking for manuscripts at all. What is it you really want? Who?"

"But of course we want the manuscripts! Justo de Villamayor though misguided was the greatest of our poets. Anything from his pen belongs to the rich national heritage. He was a statesman as well as a man of letters. He had an important public life."

"He didn't have much chance for statesmanship, did he? How long was he in the Cabinet? Three weeks?"

"Twenty-six days," Andrada said. Once again he coughed sharply without covering his mouth. "Then he left us."

"That's an interesting way of putting it. He 'left you.' There were a good many broken bones when he turned up in Mexico."

Andrada looked away from me. The lip curled up once more to reveal the great gold tooth, but this time in anxiety or dismay.

"An unsolved mystery, I know nothing of such matters. I am a little man, an unpolitical observer. I represent the National Library." He took out the bulky wallet: a slow and cumbersome procedure. "Perhaps you distrust me?"

"Perhaps."

Yet I felt a curious desire to know him better, this burning little man. He handed me a letter in Spanish and English, identifying him as an emissary of the Ministry of Education and as Envoy Extraordinary of the National Library. He also gave me a card with his name. Lettered at the bottom was his Boston address: a small and sordid hotel, one of the oldest, located near the North Station. The graystone front was blackened by the smoke of half a century's trains, now long extinct, and by an intricate latticework of fire escapes. I have seen men slink into that hotel clutching their paper bags, and emerge blinking in the barred light of day.

The official letter with its blue typescript crowded to the margins evoked a roomful of sweating black faces in the city of torture and corruption. How many emissaries of the Ministry of Education, I wondered, carry such bulky revolvers? I was reluctant to become involved. But Andrada broke in on my hesitations:

"So, now you have examined my document. You see, Nicholas Clive? You were wrong to distrust me! You must prepare for collaboration. Please tell me—have you yourself heard of any manuscripts of Villamayor? The Library is prepared to pay a good price."

"I'm just writing an article about him," I said. "I really don't know anything yet. It was I who went to Eufemio Rodriguez for advice. I didn't expect him to come to me."

"It is the National Library that sent me, not Eufemio Rodriguez. Well—Rodriguez said you spoke of Villamayor's unpublished writings. That is why I thought you had already made discoveries. We are interested in the same things, Nicholas Clive. Therefore it will be fruitful to collaborate. You know the writers and intellectuals . . ."

"Not so many. And I don't know your exile circles at all. I wouldn't know how to begin."

"You can learn! Are you not an experienced journalist? I repeat: I have names and addresses."

"I don't think I want them. I might as well tell you I don't have much use for The Protector. In fact, I don't like anything about him."

Andrada's coarse hands flew up in protest.

"Then you don't know him, Nicholas Clive. You don't know him! Doubtless you have been listening to the rumor-mongering of riffraff and to the snarlings of exile scribblers. I assure you all are liars. The Protector is the savior of our country."

The patriotic indignation and eloquence floated from him effortlessly. I wanted to get him back to the point.

"What happened to Villamayor after he disappeared from Alonso Moreno's?"

Andrada frowned.

"This too is an obscure matter. He disappeared in the company of a woman. No doubt there were sexual activities."

"You don't think he was helped to disappear? Given another little push?"

"Of all this I know nothing." The manner of Andrada was more than ever that of the guilty schoolboy attempting to summon arguments in his defense. For the moment he simply did not know how to cope with my skepticism. So he stood up and held out his dark hands; the sick grin returned. "I go now, it is enough for the first meeting. But permit me to thank you, Nicholas Clive. It was a friendly act to ask me to sit down, and to offer me refreshment. You are the first to have shown kindness. Yes, the first to show the hospitality I expected in a sister republic."

Hospitality? I took Andrada to the door with a determination to be rid of him at once. My article could do without his help. Hospitality? Had there been some, obscurely, in the fact that I was in my rooms to be found by him on this vacant Saturday afternoon? Or that my life had been such as to surrender certain innocent details for permanent record in the dusty files of a security office in Santa Isabella? Even "mistresses," two rooms and a bath. . . . I told Andrada I didn't think I could be very helpful.

I tried to dismiss him, yes. And yet I found it impossible to say the words that would have disposed of him forever. I did, at his clumsy insistence, keep his card.

HE was back two mornings later, not at all discouraged by my resistance. Had I not offered him a drink? Moreover, the very fact that he had sought me out established, in his mind, some claim . . . even a claim to friendship. He thrust himself on me and would not be thrust away.

He would have made a wonderful salesman, Manuel Andrada. For there would have been no getting him out, once his foot was in the door. There he would have stood with the preposterous, hideous product (say the gilt-embossed encyclopedia, or the statue of Christ that glows by night)—burning with his belief, undiscouraged by insult and denial, waiting not only for the inevitable order but to be offered a cup of coffee. Yes: in a very literal sense Andrada simply "moved in." In the next days he used my name in the most diverse places, and shook off all my denials. He seemed to think I had no right to refuse to "collaborate." Mine was the "designated name"—the name given him by competent authorities—and that should have been an end to it.

So he was back two mornings later. Once again he must have slipped by the doorman. I had spent the night with a friend (another girl who, luckily, has no place in this story) and got back to my rooms about nine. I found Andrada crouched outside my door in the polished hallway, sitting on his heels in the immemorial jungle posture. All about him was the scatter of my Sunday *New York Times*. He had been engrossed in the accounts of engagements and marriages, and had circled with pencil several photographs of brides-to-be.

I told him I was tired, and could not invite him in. I was not going to discuss Villamayor or anything else at nine o'clock on a Sunday morning.

"I can understand that you are tired, Nicholas Clive. You didn't come back last night."

"You waited?"

"Until two o'clock. After that I walked to my hotel beset by temptation. You are Catholic?"

"No. I'm nothing."

He seemed greatly disappointed.

"That is terrible—to say that you are nothing. But if you are not Catholic, Nicholas Clive, you cannot help me now. I did not come to discuss Villamayor. No. I want the name of a priest who speaks Spanish for purposes of confession."

"What's wrong with your English?"

"It will not do for confession. There are things to be said, certain things I have done . . ."

"I don't want to hear about them," I said. I began to gather my newspaper.

"But now that I am here, Nicholas Clive—shall we not discuss our plans?"

"I'm too tired. And next time why don't you telephone me?"

"The telephone is impersonal. I prefer to come myself."

"Well, please don't. Wait till I call you."

But he was not to be got rid of as easily as that. Early Monday afternoon a girl phoned from the college library to ask about a Señor Andrada. He had presented his credentials as Envoy Extraordinary of his National Library, and requested the "usual privileges." As a rule they would have been extended. But something in the manner of the envoy—it is easy to think of several things—aroused the suspicions of the secretary to whom he was referred. The anxiety, even the fright, not just the suspicions. I could imagine her trying to keep her smiling presence of mind even as she measured the scarred little man who had entered her office unannounced, the coarse brown suit buttoned tight with inexplicable bulges near the armpits. When she spoke of a possible delay, Andrada at once offered me as a reference. I was a graduate of the college, a responsible citizen. Moreover, I was a man known for my interest in Latin-American affairs. I would vouch for his good name and for the fact that he was here on a "cultural mission."

I don't know how or where it was conveyed to Andrada that his request had been denied. Perhaps he was reminded of the Public Library and its rich facilities. But the very next afternoon he used my name again: this time in attempting to establish credit at one of the large department stores. Ordinarily I would have heard nothing of this for days. But the manner of the applicant must have seemed to call for urgent action; and I was again approached by phone. The audacity of a man who lived in that hotel applying for credit, that particular way station on skid row, must have struck the interviewer as preposterous. The day after that it was a doctor, who sounded distinctly worried. It was not a question of credit this time; a doctor with that accent would demand cash. I could hear in the background a continuous rumbling of trucks. No, the worry must have been something else. No doubt Andrada came to this doctor with a variety of tropical complaints, or to make some unspeakable demand. I had been listed as the person to call in the event of an emergency. But I cut off the doctor's inquiry by saying that I was in no sense a friend.

Andrada was amusing enough. Still I had already reached the conclusion this poor eccentric would be useless to me, so far as an article on Villamayor was concerned. And he could only get me into trouble. So several times in the next days I thought of writing him to insist that he stop giving me as a reference. But before I had done so he used my name in an even dingier quarter: with one of the shyster lawyers who hang around the night court. It was after one in the morning when the lawyer phoned. This time Andrada (dragged into court screaming of "diplomatic immunity") had been arrested after a fight with two sailors on a downtown street, one of whom he had sent to the hospital, and for carrying a concealed weapon. The many documents in Spanish could not save him from a night in jail, and he had less than twenty dollars in hand. Would I consent to appear on his behalf? And would I also use my influence "as a journalist" to keep his name out of the newspapers? I suppose Andrada dreaded having his mishap come to the attention of Eufemio Rodriguez, that stern servant of The Protector.

I refused, of course. And yet I was fairly sure even this would not discourage the "emissary of the National Library." He had attached himself to me and nothing was going to cut him loose. Still, I could not have a madman bandying my name about. So the next afternoon I went down to that squalid hotel blackened by a half-century of trains. And as he had come unannounced to me, so I went to him.

He was fully dressed when he opened the door, except for the coat of the bulging armpits. Yet he had been lying on the bed. I had heard, as he left it quietly, the protest of ancient springs. He nodded to me without surprise, as though I had come by appointment, and precisely on time. It was an inside room with its one window facing a wall. But the first thing I saw was The Protector's lumpy and waxen stare, the dead face above garish epaulets. It was an immense framed poster placed strategically to protect the rumpled bed and its occupant. It would be the first thing Andrada would see in the dim morning, together with the large brass crucifix just above his feet. The Protector looked down unwinking and noncommittal on this small patriotic subject lost and bewildered in a foreign city of many vices and temptations—who on his second night (the outraged room clerk told me later) had asked in one breath for the "zone of the brothels" and for a Spanish-speaking priest. That was after his first violently repudiated attempt to pick up a girl on the street.

That too I heard about later. But I did, seeing his room for the first time, achieve a sudden insight. The poster and crucifix, the grim unadorned revolver broken open on the dresser, the little man himself still pathetically confident—I thought I could reconstruct, seeing the room, the harsh Catholic childhood in a baked provincial town, the frightened scurrying past the first and then second confessional box, and the years of iron deprived adolescence in some Costanza or Villahermosa or Santa Rosa and at last the capital city, the move there under the severe regard of a perhaps widowed mother. Actually, the child Manuel Andrada had always lived in the capital city. He had been one of the truly poor at the cathedral gates: a shoeshine box in his hand, watchful, carefully discriminating the successful from the unsuccessful, determining soon to be not a soldier but a "man useful to the government," chauffeur perhaps for one of the larger police cars of that time or even a policeman himself, even a secret agent.

The Protector dominated one wall. Another wall was covered with half-naked girls from magazines, a third with travel folders in English on the charms of Santa Isabella. There were several pictures of a hotel swimming pool. A gnawed loaf of dark bread was on the bedside table, together with a stack of magazines. There was also an antiquated television set.

"I knew you would come, Nicholas Clive. I have been waiting with impatience."

"I came to tell you not to use my name again. As a reference or for any other reason."

"Please sit down, Nicholas Clive. There is such a disorder, I don't know what's wrong with me. I had to use your name, it was the only name I had. The lawyer would not trust me." He stared at me stolidly. "I am so bewildered, I do not understand your institutions. I come here, a simple man, a representative of the National Library . . ."

"Oh yes, the Library. That's how you got into the fight with the sailor? Perhaps you were discussing the Library?"

Andrada went to the bed and sat down. He was very small there. The intense scarred unsmiling face peered up at me: an animal at the edge of its hole.

"I was looking for women. I wanted sexual gratification."

"So you tried the sailors instead?"

"I only wanted to ask for the zone of the brothels. Sailors would know. But one of them hit me before I could ask. Then I had to defend myself."

One could see that too: the stragglers on that narrow street after the bars were closed and all the theaters dark, as Andrada stalked burning and alone. I could imagine his timid then sudden swerve and approach: his unintelligible pleas to the sailors, with the dark craving face thrust up; the foreign-sounding murmur, perhaps a claw on the sailor's sleeve, and the indecent female swellings near the armpits. The outraged sailor must have struck out at once . . . only to find himself moments later slumped and bleeding against a wall.

"Defend yourself? Yes, of course. And have you found the 'zone of the brothels'?"

"I think there is no such zone. And yet the city is full of irregularities. Yes, even this hotel. There are many women of evil habits. One came to my room, but would not stay. She took my money then gave it back to me. In fact she threw my money on the floor and rushed out of the room. I wonder why that was?"

"Maybe she didn't like The Protector's face."

Andrada stared at me, puzzled.

"Actually, it is not such women I want. I want to meet the others."

"What others?"

"Ordinary American women. These."

He picked up the bedside stack of magazines and riffled through it, discarding the dozen or so magazines of nude models and starlets in bikinis, and the larger magazines of female confession, until he reached those encouraging lonely-heart correspondence. He had studied the promises of bright nurses and schoolteachers, of wealthy virgins of a certain age.

"Have you written to any?"

"I have written to several women. There has not been time for answers."

"I trust you didn't give them my name as a reference."

"Of course not." He stared at me in bewilderment. "I only describe myself, my personality and my interests."

"I see, your interests." For the moment I had quite forgot Andrada's "mission." "And how about Villamayor and his manuscripts? Is that still one of your interests?"

He looked down at the floor.

"I know, I know. I am ashamed, I too betray the trust. I have not left the room all day. Yes, I have been afraid to go out. I would get in trouble again."

"Well, if you don't go out . . ."

"I knew you would come, Nicholas Clive. I am helpless without you." Suddenly he sprang from the bed and faced me. "Listen: there were letters to Alonso Moreno, after Villamayor disappeared from Mexico City. I think he must have come to the United States again. Yes, no doubt even to Boston. Perhaps very near to us exist precious manuscripts that belong to the national heritage."

"How do you know about the letters?"

"It is part of The Protector's task, to keep watch on his children abroad. There are informations."

"I see. Then you don't work for the National Library, really?"

"Who said I did not? This information was given me before I left, to help me in my search. Listen, I am going to give you the names of the evil ones. I want you to see them. I have made a new list."

He handed me a sheet, at the top of which my own initials stood in large letters. There were four names under the same address, a street near the North Station.

"But that street's gone! The whole area is condemned. Nobody can live there. They're tearing down the buildings."

"You are wrong, Nicholas Clive. There are many empty spaces, yes. But four of the traitors meet there. There is a Committee of Liberation, a silly thing. But I think they would know of Villamayor and of his work. They are there. I have seen the names on the small glass box near the door."

The place was only a few blocks away. I knew that row of empty brick houses, black inside, the furnishings and even the glass gone from many of the windows. Behind these houses was a desolation of broken brick and plaster rubble, with one narrow building still rising out of it.

"Tell me—why do you really want Villamayor's man-uscripts?"

"The National Library requires . . ."

"Forget the Library. I doubt that you've ever been in it."

For a moment I thought Andrada would spring at me. The hunched body straightened, the feverish angry head thrust forward. The curving scar was pointed like a weapon.

"Why do you insult me, Nicholas Clive? In what way have I harmed you?"

"I don't want to give you the chance. Listen: why do you want the work of a man who died in exile? Wasn't he too 'one of the evil ones'?"

"I have told you: Villamayor was an artist, a man of letters, he is part of the national heritage. He is respected even by his political enemies. One can despise his political ideas yet respect the art. But these men are riffraff."

The poster hung above us in the still room: the glazed stare intolerant of criticism.

"Did Villamayor write something attacking the good Protector? Is that what you're after?"

Andrada glanced over his shoulder at the waxen, disapproving face.

"It is possible. Many of Villamayor's ideas were mistaken."

"In fact that's the whole point, isn't it? There's some manuscript The Protector is afraid of?"

"The Protector afraid of scribblings? What an idea! The Protector is afraid of nothing!" Andrada paced to his blank window and back. "There are only rumors, Nicholas Clive, we don't know what writings there are. Poems, essays, the story of his life, perhaps even a romance. . . . Who knows? Anything from Villamayor's pen would be precious. But then—there may be nothing at all. Perhaps all has been lost."

"But you don't think so?"

"Truly I do not know. That is why you must help me." He pointed to the list of names. "You have your own article about Villamayor to write, Nicholas Clive. Is not this a good place to begin?"

I told him I would think it over. I did keep the list.

LOOKING back after these long months, I find it hard to explain the exact nature of my reluctance. The possibility of a subversive manuscript, and of crude attempts to discover and suppress it, and the notion that the forgotten victim could still speak from beyond the grave—what better material could one hope to stumble on, for the enlivening of an article on Villamayor? But the truth is that I had not thought in terms of a "lively" article. Villamayor was dead; the time for melodrama was past. My plan had been to write a serious historical essay, a "psychograph" so to speak, based entirely on Villamayor's own writings and on the writings of others about him. In fact I had never thought of further interviews after that first one at the Consulate in New York. But here now was history threatening to become flesh . . . if only in the burning flesh of a singularly naïve and patriotic agent who walked the streets with a bulky revolver, got himself arrested for assault and battery, and even traveled with a huge portrait of the dictator. And who now proposed that I interview exiles plotting The Protector's overthrow. I had the sense that my life had been suddenly and not so quietly invaded.

All the same I did, out of curiosity, go to the address Andrada had given me: the gaunt three-story brick building, the last still standing in that emptiness. The whole area was being cleared for a housing development. There were steps rising absurdly from a street that had ceased to exist, but the front door had been torn away. And there I saw the four names—Peralda, Reynosa, Gutierrez, Sánchez (a fifth name had been crossed out)—penciled near the small typed card: *Committee for Democratic Liberation*. (Whatever other resources the Committee may have had for the overthrow of The Protector, it needed a new typewriter ribbon.) I wondered what had happened to the fifth member of the Committee—self-exiled in outraged disagreement or excommunicated by the four others? And even as I waited—uncertain, tempted against better judgment to go into the thing after all—the door opened, and a lean hand reached out for a bottle of milk. For a moment the dark stooping figure was framed in the yellow light, suddenly unmoving and alert as his eyes caught mine looking up.

He took in the bottle quickly, then; we both at the same moment turned away. I had been in contact with a revolutionary exile!

I DID not hear from Andrada for almost a week. Then he was arrested again. This time it was for molesting ("assaulting" would again have been more exact) a woman in a large chain drugstore not a block from the Common. The woman had gone there for lunch. The lawyer who reached me by telephone was much amused by the claims of his excitable client. Would-be client, that is. It seems Andrada had only done what he had seen done many times, successfully, in motion pictures and on television. He had described his conduct as "quite normal and pleasant." The lawyer, still laughing, evoked the small somber figure in the brown winter coat walking the long line of summery female backs, their faces addressed to the soda-

fountain and the mirrors—the secretaries and salesgirls
and filing clerks at the end of their lunch hour. And I
could see Andrada hesitate, then move slowly up and
down the line in embarrassment, pausing now and then
in his shyness to consider and fondle some object without
seeing what it was, whether tube or paste or cream, remedy for headache or remedy for insomnia. He would have
stared unblinking at the vast shelf of deodorants.

Then it appears he made his choice, made it abruptly
and propelled himself toward the woman's back. He addressed the silken back in a low embarrassed murmur:
"*tonight . . . cinema . . . entertainment . . . affection
. . . refreshment . . . hotel.*" Evidently the woman did
not know Andrada was speaking to her, and went on
munching her sandwich. But he stood his ground obstinately, the hard jaw and slashed forehead and eyebrow
poised just above her shoulder. And began to rub her back
with the slow circular motion which, he had read, was
sexually exciting.

The woman did understand, then; understood at least
something. She turned and began to scream. It was, she
later told the police, like seeing a face in a nightmare:
the burning face and maniacal unsmiling eyes only inches
from hers, while the arm reached now quite around her
and continued to rub her back.

She went on screaming. Andrada, frightened, aware of
the white faces turning aghast and outraged on nearby
stools, used his free hand to reassure her. "*It is nothing.
It is only for pleasure!*" he shouted, himself panic-stricken
now, holding her arm as with a claw. When the police
arrived a minute or so later the employees of the drugstore
had not yet been able to separate them. They were rolling
on the floor. It was then—still entangled now with this

spitting fury of a woman, the two of them rolling as in combat or twin epileptic seizure—that Andrada (seeing the police at hand for the second time in a week) began to bellow my name. His coat had been ripped down over one shoulder, exposing the butt of the revolver obscenely. His cheek was bleeding; circumstances were beyond his control. And now the police again!

So he called out my name; it was the only name that occurred to him at this moment of crisis. I was, after all, his "only friend" in Boston.

Half an hour later, when things were calmer, Andrada explained to the lawyer what I could do for him: at the very least identify him as the representative of a friendly foreign country, in Boston on a "cultural mission." Andrada had only five dollars in his pocket, no wallet, or identification. Perhaps I would, this time, go bail for him? Or the lawyer could telephone authorization to Andrada's hotel to admit me to his room, where I would find six hundred one-dollar bills in the ventilating shaft near the bed. The lawyer wanted to know whether I would at least guarantee his own small retainer.

I think the lawyer expected me to refuse. But by now the thing had gone so far beyond ordinary outrage—Andrada's absurd bouncing back to me—that common-sense objections no longer held. So I said I would look for the money in the ventilating shaft. I was willing to engage myself at least this far for the sake of seeing Andrada's room at my leisure.

The room clerk might well have let me go to the room, authorization or no. He was an intent worried man in his sixties, thin and bald, with bulging blue eyes, who in his time had seen most of the forms of poverty and vice pass through his hotel. But he didn't know what to make of Manuel Andrada.

"I'll go along with anything, if you'll get him out of here. I'm not particular. But your friend pushes things pretty far."

"How?"

"I'd say he's got an arsenal up that ventilating shaft, not just money." The clerk leaned very close to me. "He leaves the transom open. You can hear him moving around there in the dark. Why doesn't he turn on the light? And that isn't all. You know what he does to women?"

"What?"

"I don't know. But I saw this one come shooting down the stairs white as a sheet, she'd only been up there a couple of minutes. And she wasn't one to be particular."

He limped up to the room with me, mumbling complaints all the way. (It was then he told me of Andrada's outrageous demand as in a single breath for the "zone of the brothels" and for a Spanish-speaking priest.) But he would not go inside the room, and went quickly back downstairs. He did not want to be involved.

My own involvement was intense as I stood in that musty room, with the objects around me and even the smells of another man's life. And I had the eerie sense of being back in the city of sick palms, with the dead waxen face watching me. They were part of the same evil: the magnified stern face on the poster, and the faint yet rich smell of oil for the cleaning of guns. Suddenly I too felt an odd impulse to turn out the light, and grope about in the dark room.

I found (besides the envelope with the money) much that I had expected to find: especially the thickening pile of girlie and lonely hearts magazines. But there was other evidence of the little Andrada's yearning for a fuller social life. One drawer contained clippings from the travel pages of newspapers, with certain features of the

resorts thickly underlined in pencil: *Invigorating Sports
. . . Evening Entertainment . . . Congenial Companionship Guaranteed.* There were even two scented and
purplish envelopes, the letters removed, from an un-
heard-of Ohio town. By burrowing a little farther I
discovered what I had cruelly hoped for: Andrada's
statement of his own attributes and needs, for publication
in one of the magazines, or perhaps for file with a "club"
—*"Young Spanish-speaking poetic gentleman knows also
English seeks knowledge and friendship of young beautiful Catholic girl of patriotic sentiments."* In the same
drawer were many scratched-out variants of the same
declaration. One (beginning *"Handsome gentleman of
Latin-American origin, rich . . ."*) was defaced, humbly,
by a large penciled cross. Others, in imitation of those he
had seen in the magazines, made wild claims of interest
in "all outdoor sports."

In a second drawer I found a small black notebook
which contained (with a few addresses and much else)
certain comments on myself. It was a shock to come upon
my name. *"Clive es un hombre de bién, y muy human-
itario."* I was a man of good heart, good feelings; therefore I would, at last, recognize the injustice I was doing
him. Also I was an "honest man," but I stubbornly refused
to admit the achievements of The Protector. I ran through
the notebook quickly for comments on Villamayor. But
I found only one. It was succinct enough: *"Su inteligencia
y su falta de religión han perjudicado la personalidad de
Villamayor."* Which had done more to ruin that character
—the intellect or the lack of faith?

The notebook was an extraordinary mixture of odds
and ends, full of Andrada's discoveries about American
life and of admonitions to himself. There were several

pages devoted to television shows he had watched, with notes on what he had learned from each concerning American customs and manners. It was not necessary (the envoy from the National Library had learned) to hold open the automobile door for a young lady to descend; she is expected to open it herself. But for love, the notebook observed, it is necessary to have a pleasing personality and also to give erotic pleasure. *"También es necesario dar placer."* That too was succinct!

The light thrown on Manuel Andrada's character and temper was enormous: on the dusky character formed by an iron and deprived childhood, in the white Caribbean glare. There were hurriedly copied standard prayers, and naïve prayers of his own for companionship, health, success. There was even a long enumeration, in schoolboy outline, of the many things the people owed to The Protector, in this anniversary year of his rule. *The schools, the protection of the police, the fine Horticultural Gardens, the luxury hotels.* . . .

But the last page of the notebook, facing the back cover, was a reminder of a different kind, a page cut and pasted from a book on professional method. It too had its place in the picture, together with the small arsenal I did indeed find—not in the ventilating shaft with the money but under the mattress: the two switchblade knives and the supplementary revolver, a small .25.

. . . there are invisible weapons, which are very efficient. Here are some of them: Ladies' hatpins, five or six inches long. Or a wrist-knife, strapped to your wrist with the hilt downward. A knife worn around the neck on a thong or cord. A small revolver, held up your sleeve by rubber bands or in a shoulder-holster. A stiletto with a nine-inch blade, no wider than three-quarters of an inch at its broadest, and double-edged for its full length. Be sure it has a hilt guard on the haft. This instrument you should grasp solidly, placing the ball of the thumb along the flat of the blade. You use it with a twist of the wrist, stabbing upward and inward, under the lower rib towards the heart, or aiming at the spinal cord to sever it. . . .

Other useful weapons are hammers—either to smash a man's skull or hit him between the shoulder blades to stun him; cheese-cutters—the wires with wooden handles you see in grocery stores—which are handy for strangling people; fish lines, for strangling too. . . .

I knew that book; I had read it while in the army. And now my first impulse was to laugh. Would any *bona fide* agent of Santa Isabella have needed to cut out that page? It seemed to me the page belonged with Andrada's television dreams of successful love. And yet it is not easy to laugh when alone, or standing under The Protector's portrait. Those cold instructions could not so easily be dismissed. I turned off the light, on a whim, and the room went dark except for a faint yellow at the transom; objects dissolved. Then I might truly have been back in my room in the city of the soiling palms. I was trembling, yet felt myself at home.

Suddenly I realized that I intended to watch Manuel Andrada, at least for a time, and perhaps even to help him. The whole thing was too amusing to be given up, with my life in Boston so uneventful. And who better than this political innocent—this fiery and devoted little patriot—could instruct me in the nature of the tyranny that had bred him? That had corrupted him since early childhood? My article on Villamayor, I realized, was taking on new dimensions.

so I went down there after all, no longer so outraged because he had used my name. And the first thing I heard, when I reached the jail was, in fact, my name. The thick desperate voice echoed down stone corridors, the accent more foreign than usual. It shouted that I would arrive at any moment to bail him out and to establish his own good name. For that was what poor Andrada must have begun to care about most of all: what Eufemio Rodriguez and those behind him would think, as his cultural "mission" led to one misadventure after another. Now, locked up for the second time in a week, he was at the edge of hysteria. And even before I saw him (listening to the frenzied shouts) I knew he would be clenching the bars of the cell door in the ancient posture of exasperation and despair, while his cell mates looked on angrily: *he will come, Nicholas Clive will come, he will speak for my character. A young man of promise, a journalist, you must know him, he is known in the right places, Nicholas Clive. He has enjoyed the hospitality of my country, he has seen the fine avenues and cafés, the unexcelled climate, the women of pleasure, he will come. A journalist, a man of ability, an investor in important enterprise. Nicholas Clive had his own apartment, his fine apartment in The Protector's city, two rooms and private bath, he owes us all this debt. He has seen my documents, Nicholas Clive, he will defend me, he will come. . . .*

The crescendo chant went on against a rising tide of *Shut ups*. He screamed out my name again.

Then we were face to face. The screaming died away: not stopped but died away until he had whispered *Nicholas Clive* a final time. He fixed me with the brown unwinking animal stare of one who refuses to be beaten off.

"So you have come."

He was still breathing heavily, but the crazed look was gone.

"Yes, I brought the money."

"And you will help me find Villamayor's manuscripts?"

I in my turn watched him very closely.

"Or Villamayor himself?"

"What do you mean, Nicholas Clive?"

"Don't you think I know—that you think Villamayor is still alive?"

2

THUS I DISCOVERED, face to face with the fiery little Andrada, the decision I had already made. And discovered too my surmise, my conviction really, that Villamayor had again survived.

But for Señor Juan Peralda (teacher of languages at a junior college for girls, chairman of the Committee for Democratic Liberation) no such hope or doubts existed: Justo de Villamayor was dead. He was the "late Villamayor," occupying already his large place in Santa Isabella's literary history and his small one in her political chronicles. *"De mortui nihil nisi bonum."* These were among Peralda's first words on the subject of Villamayor. "It may be said the late poet and historian's intentions were good, however vacillating the political will. I speak of course as one who was compelled to watch these events from a distance."

The headquarters of the Committee was also Peralda's one-room dwelling, where the four men received me. It was a feminine room of worn chintz curtains, delicate thin-legged chairs, and a small rose sofa covered with mimeographed documents. On one chair were many copies of a brochure, "The Crimes of the Protector." Above the sofa were the textbooks of a teacher of Spanish, and a shelf of classics much repaired by Scotch tape. The bed covered in a faded and tasseled rose fitted exactly into a narrow closet which must have been at least six feet deep. It suggested a wall grave into which a coffin had been slid. At night only the head of Peralda the teacher of languages would be visible, or only his upturned feet.

The four men watched me with mistrust. Reynosa was a linotypist and Gutierrez a hotel cook. Sánchez, who did not speak, could have been a longshoreman or retired boxer. All three looked familiar enough, the very faces of "democratic liberators" I had seen in Miami bars and in newsreels, passionate and discouraged faces. Peralda himself was a small precise man with gray hair imperfectly rinsed to brown. His light gray suit had been crudely refitted. A sweet odor of burned coffee, a familiar Santa Isabella smell, emanated from his person.

Peralda greeted me a little pompously, holding out his left arm stiffly. The right sleeve hung slack. He must have suspected I was from the FBI or CIA, and he was determined to establish the Committee's innocence at once. He handed me copies of a mimeographed newsheet.

"We are only theorists of liberty working for peaceful change. The committee violates no laws."

I could see at a glance that many of the articles were devoted to attacking rival Committees of Liberation in New York. No doubt he was right: all this was innocent enough. I assured Peralda that I didn't like The Protector any more than they. My sympathies were all with Justo de Villamayor, on whom I hoped to write an article.

"We know nothing about the late Villamayor," Peralda said. "Why do you come to us?"

"I'm trying to see as many of your compatriots as I can."

Peralda shrugged his thin shoulders.

"Villamayor was almost unknown in the United States. I cannot believe an American magazine would publish an article about him, now that he has been dead three years."

"He was known in literary circles," I said. "And there's the matter of these odd disappearances. Why didn't they kill him the first time. And what happened to him when he disappeared in Mexico?"

"We have no idea. Perhaps this time they succeeded."

The tired unsmiling faces watched me; no one sat down.

"Did you know him personally?"

"I? After all, I am a humble man. An assistant professor of languages. . . ."

There followed a consultation in Spanish so rapid that I lost the thread of argument. It concerned, of course, my motives. Peralda, Reynosa and Gutierrez all talked at once, while the stolid Sánchez watched. In the end they decided to take me at my word: I was a journalist not an investigator. I realized how right Andrada had been not to want to come himself.

I was to receive, as it turned out, a professorial lecture: just such a lecture as Peralda might have given to a roomful of sleepy girls. I had expected to ask questions. But suddenly he began to pace the room with rapid dainty steps.

"So. Very well: we are to write an article on the late Justo Vicente de Villamayor, historian and poet. We must therefore consider the formation of his character, that is the way to begin. He was the son of a very rich planter three generations from Spain and of a mother of French birth."

Peralda articulated with care. Lecturing, he stalked past the dull stares of Sánchez, Reynosa and Gutierrez, perhaps dreaming of scholarly congresses. *The précis of a life,*

much of it misspent, in spite of the love of freedom. . . .
Much of what Peralda related I had already learned from
the biographical dictionaries—the adolescent years divided
between the father's ranch and the Colegio, the stimulat-
ing years spent in France in "literary circles," the later
journeys abroad for writing and research. Peralda had
actually known Villamayor, as he presently admitted. And
yet he saw him as a romantic figure of a distant past, a
Byron or Victor Hugo of fantastic adventures and good
fortune. I detected an undertone of envy. Shouldn't he
too (teacher of Spanish at a junior college for the less
gifted) have been the son of a rich planter and a mother
of French birth? Shouldn't he too have had his *wanderjahre* in Europe, and won international renown?

Peralda lectured in the academic present tense. This
seemed to consign Villamayor still more deeply to the past.

"Even at the Colegio, where he came from Paris at
fourteen, Villamayor finds at once a circle of admiring
friends. He passes his vacations on the ranch. And the
young man of twenty: he too is drawn alternately to his
two homes. The Villamayor of the ranch is taciturn, a
silent young man, brooding and poetic. But the Villamayor
of the city! He is a lover of conversation and women, a
gay blade with much wealth. After a day of writing and
study he plunges into an evening of unbridled pleasure.
Remember too the young Villamayor has a golden tongue,
and the manners of the rich. He is a charmer. Many
women love him, perhaps also many men." The powdered
teacher of languages stared at me somberly, as though
announcing a profound discovery. "It is not difficult to be
lovable, when one is very rich. And when nothing you
touch turns to dust."

I broke in to say that I found his analysis most interest-

ing. But I could see no sign, in all this, of the Villamayor
who became a symbol of political independence in his
mid-forties: the Minister of Education for twenty-six
days.

"You must wait, everything in its time—though I
assure you even the dilettante of the Paris years hates The
Protector and his coarse brutality! But we must speak
first of the *wanderjahre*. This is the second point to be
made by your essay: Villamayor is a Europeanized man.
He has an ironic and French temperament. And now he
is torn not between the ranch and the city, but between
France and the ruined homeland. He loves his life in Paris
and on the Riviera. Remember he is still very rich! Nothing is beyond his grasp! Yet always he feels deeply an
obligation to return home. He is guilty with regard to
those who live under the oppression."

It was obvious the *wanderjahre* had long preoccupied
Peralda, exiled in a bleak Boston. He told of how the young
Villamayor lived the "life of a prince": dining at Maxim's
and the Tour d'Argent. He attended balls in provincial
châteaux.

"Yes, he has his luxurious apartment, doubtless off the
Champs-Elyseés, and his villa on the Côte d'Azur. His
mistresses come from the nobility. There are motor cars
and actresses. Yet all this time he is also leading the life
of a young intellectual struggling for recognition. Villamayor sits at the Closerie des Lilas and the Deux Magots.
. . . No doors are closed to him, he finds a sympathetic
audience of his peers. Yes, he has also the Left Bank."

And now Peralda (pacing delicately before me and the
members of his committee) evoked a decayed but charm-
ing room on the Rue Jacob. There the young Villamayor
engages in passionate discussions of theory with other

writers. There are girls in black sweaters and berets, whose hair falls to their shoulders.

I found Peralda most amusing. But he was, after all, wasting my time. I broke in to ask whether he had ever been to Paris.

"Why do you ask? I know the city well from books and photographs."

"I mean Villamayor's Paris sounds rather complicated. Was he having all this at the same time? Not just the two apartments but the girls in berets as well as the mistresses from the nobility?"

Peralda shrugged his shoulders eloquently.

"Why not? There were times when this man had everything. He would give up nothing, he would sacrifice none of his desires. And he was strong though of small stature, a man of physical skills. Did I mention that he was a champion swordsman at the Colegio in his youth? That he had two apartments at the same time is quite probable. I think of him as a man of great erotic capacities: women will not leave him alone. No doubt there are times when unsatisfied he gives himself to debauchery with women of the streets. Anything is possible when you are rich. . . . And he travels. In those years he goes everywhere: Madrid, Rome, Palermo, Aix-les-Bains."

"Aix-les-Bains?"

"It is a resort. And in these same years, you understand, his great intellectual development takes place. The spirit is transformed. Yes, Europeanized. There is a certain subtlety and refinement of spirit developed that makes action difficult. *L'immobilisme des savants*. . . . He is inhabited by contradictory yearnings."

I was persuaded, by now, that Peralda knew Villamayor not at all. The sybarite and Don Juan of his fantasies would never have consented to become Minister of Education, nor have concerned himself with The Protector's crimes. Why should he even have returned from France? It all seemed most improbable. Peralda himself was improbable enough . . . as a worker for "democratic liberation."

But a few minutes later (after more nonsense about the *wanderjahre*, and a sunlit villa on the Côte d'Azur) he suddenly stopped his pacing.

"What I say sounds to you unlikely? It is essentially true, though perhaps a little exaggerated. You are right, I have not been to Europe, I must depend on what I have read. And yet I know that what I say of Villamayor is true."

"How do you know?"

"Because I knew him. I met Villamayor in 1949 in Mexico. It does no harm to reveal this, now that the poet is dead. We were engaged in the same terrible fiasco of Puerto Limón."

"You were in that!"

I remembered that abortive invasion of Santa Isabella well enough to be astonished. A small fleet of old planes, eight to be exact, had been gathered in Yucatán for the overthrow of The Protector, with pilots recruited in Miami. For the soldiers there were months of training in malarial swamps. On the invasion day the planes left at different times, since they had very different cruising speeds. But only one seaplane reached its destination, a bay near Puerto Limón. Several planes were forced down by a tropical storm on an island just off the Mexican coast. One escort plane reached Havana, one never got off the ground at all. Of those who landed from the seaplane, a few were imprisoned. The bodies of the others were hacked to pieces after a running fight with small arms. Two of the invaders killed each other by mistake.

"Yes, in a sense I was in that invasion, as was Justo de Villamayor. I was in one of the planes forced down on that island, and I was interned by the Mexican police. But the Mexicans didn't do this." With a deft movement he lifted the slack right sleeve to reveal a stump ending in a wrinkled cone where the wrist should have been. A pointed finger of flesh, almost a weapon. "Unluckily my name became known after the internment. They found me in Mexico City. One evening I was run down by an automobile on a wide and empty avenue. The driver broke my leg but he did not want to kill me, he wanted other names. He took me into the car. But I refused to speak. Later that evening they extracted my fingernails, and an infection resulted."

There was nothing I could say. The sharp but wrinkled cone beneath a slack sleeve, pointed as an accusation. . . . It is one of the particularities of Santa Isabella that it leaves its defacing mark on nearly everyone. What brutalities, I wondered, did the clothes of Reynosa and Gutierrez conceal? The effeminate Peralda of the powdered face and curling hair was a true revolutionist after all.

"And Villamayor was there?"

"He was fortunate. He was in the one plane that never left the ground, because of engine troubles. Thereafter he was not arrested or interned. It is even possible The Protector's agents never found out he was involved. I at least did not surrender his name. But now that he is dead: *de mortui.* . . . One can say, yes, that Villamayor did what he could on that historic occasion."

"It's hard to imagine Villamayor in an invasion. Your wavering intellectual, your lover of pleasure . . ."

"He was not a weakling," Peralda said. "Remember he was a champion swordsman at the Colegio. As for Puerto Limón—his participation was kept secret during the months of planning. He gave us money from the first. And he was to have been one of the political leaders, if an insurrection had occurred in Santa Isabella, after the invasion. This was what was planned in Mexico. First the invasion, then the insurrection, beginning with a student strike and defections in the army. The political leaders were to come later. But then at the last minute Villamayor insisted on coming with us. He felt an obligation to do so. But later he told me was horrified by what happened."

"Later?"

"We met once more in Mexico City, some months after the disaster. We exchanged only a few words. But he talked with great sadness of the village that was bombed in retribution. Do you remember? It was thought by The Protector's men that the villagers had stayed aloof. They had not helped to destroy our men. Therefore the next day a government plane flew over that village very low and machine-gunned the people who ran out. Then the plane climbed several hundred feet and released a bomb. Villamayor felt a terrible shame, because of the bombing of that village. He was distressed by the death of our own men. He thought some of them were innocents who understood nothing. There was a young mechanic who came with the seaplane, a very late arrival. Until minutes before the landing he understood it was Nicaragua we were invading. He had been astonished by the duration of the flight. And our two men who destroyed each other in the first confusion, each supposing that he grappled with an enemy! Such accidents distressed Villamayor. And yet these he thought less evil than the death of innocent villagers. Still, he regarded all death as evil."

"It is a personal failing," Reynosa broke in. "This concern for human life does not make for strength. Villamayor was a man who hesitates. A literary man."

"You didn't know him," Peralda said. "Villamayor did not believe in executions or in useless deaths. Nevertheless, I can affirm he was a man of courage."

There was, yes, courage. And I thought of the Villamayor who had appeared in Mexico City eight years after the fiasco of Puerto Limón, at the door of Alonso Moreno: the victim of political process who loved his life enough to survive a beating in which many bones were broken.

"Why are you so sure he's dead?"

"But of course he is dead. Otherwise, we would have heard something. It has been nearly three years. After all, he could never have kept silent so long. No—Villamayor has entered into history. I repeat: *De mortui nihil nisi bonum.* . . . It will be for posterity to judge."

Peralda had been truly surprised by my question. I asked him again what he knew of Villamayor's last days.

"I know nothing of the last days in Mexico. But he was in New York in the fall of that year, just before the final disappearance. He attended one of the political meetings. If you permit me, I have here a photograph. . . ."

He led me to an enlarged snapshot on a wall devoted to commemorative pictures and documents. It must have been taken on the roof of a smallish building on the West

Side. There was a water tank on stilts and beyond it
blurred skyscrapers. A group of men in shirt sleeves
stood crowded together, heads craning with the flushed
covetous pride of *aficionados* at a bullfighter's deathbed.
Near the center, aloof and unsmiling, were the twisted
features of Villamayor. The small Peralda, at one end,
was almost out of the picture. At the other end a woman
looked out shyly from beneath a cloche hat many years
outmoded; she was wearing black stockings. She had
come with Villamayor. This was the secretary and fanatic
disciple who disappeared from Mexico City the day after
Villamayor did, and two months after this photograph
was taken: Julieta Aparicio. She too, this pale timid creature, could have been the victim of assassins.

I remarked that Villamayor didn't look very enthusi-
astic.

"It was a meeting called for the reconciliation of the
various Committees of Liberation. The reconciliation
failed."

"Did he say then what he was writing?"

Peralda closed his eyes and threw his head back theat-
rically.

"How could he? We were talking of other things.
Did I say 'talking'? Shouting rather, shrieking! Consider
such a group of men united only in their hatred of The
Protector, divided by their jealousies, all talking at once.
One had his theories of direct action, another spoke of
historical cycles. Villamayor himself—as onetime Minister of Education—gave the principal address. It was a
most discouraging discourse, the speech of a man who
had lost faith in radical measures. He spoke of the inertia
of the peasants and of the iron discipline of The Protector's army. We had hoped for a great unifying call

to action. Instead he reminded us of our disagreements, and of the dangers of premature insurrection. It was a sad and debilitating performance for a man whose words might have stirred us all."

"Do you think he stopped caring?"

Peralda paced up and down. Some very old resentment lay beneath his admiration for Villamayor, yet he was determined to be fair.

"No, we cannot say that. I am sure Villamayor is dedicated to the end—to the principles of political freedom and land reform. But he is not dedicated with his whole spirit and flesh. He is divided between his pleasures, his travels, and his writings. How can such a man be a true revolutionist?" Peralda had fallen again into the manner of the lecturer before young ladies of limited intelligence. Then abruptly he stopped. The right sleeve rose as he pointed passionately to his chest with the wrinkled cone. "No—it is only such as I can be a true revolutionist! A man whose whole being and energy and life are given undivided to the cause of liberating principles and to hatred of The Protector. Do you understand I spend not a cent on myself? The desk and bed I purchased for five dollars, all the rest was donated. Yes, even the suit I wear. For twenty years of exile . . ."

I nodded in response to his gesture which was almost an embrace. Across the room the dull faithful eyes of Sánchez had begun to glow.

"Yes," I said. "Anyone can see that. You haven't given up. But it's Villamayor the writer I'm interested in for my article, not just the man who went into politics. Do you think your friends in New York have any of the things he's written? Unpublished things. I had the idea he might have been writing an attack on The Protector."

"Villamayor the writer? He was truly a great writer, though politically disappointing. I too was intended to be a writer."

Peralda took down a small manuscript volume, and turned the pages slowly. I broke in hurriedly; I wanted to be spared a reading.

"Could you give me the names of your friends in New York? I want to find out everything I can about his last days in New York, and the last days in Mexico. And there must be manuscripts somewhere. . . ."

But now Peralda, assistant professor of languages, was very far away. He sat down at the end of that small bed vanishing as into the mouth of a grave.

"To tell the truth, I have given Villamayor little thought of late. My task is with the living. . . . But you bring back so much! You bring back the past! As I said, I did not really know Villamayor until the lamentable affair of Puerto Limón. But that was not the first time I saw him. You realize of course that I am several years older than Justo de Villamayor? Three to be exact. The first time I saw him was in my last year at the Colegio. He had come to us from another school, from France in fact, at the age of fourteen. Even then he was so vibrant of personality! So handsome, in spite of the deformation of the face, such intense and commanding eyes."

Time collapsed for Peralda in this darkening Boston room emplaced above a yellow desolation of brick and rubble.

"I can remember the very afternoon, the sunlight on

the courtyard as I looked down at these younger boys milling by the classroom door. He had just come from a school in Paris, and was entering the Colegio late and for the first time. So he was really a 'new boy,' and consequently to be distrusted by all. But no! This boy of fourteen who came to us from the great outside world was already surrounded by admirers and future disciples. I see him now in his Paris suit and with his jaunty little beret, encircled by slightly taller boys in drab uniforms. They were dullards all, staring at this superior creature who made himself taller by standing on tiptoes. And already he was talking, already they listened. A thin but strong boy with a fine shock of hair and gesticulating hands, and of course that face twisted and inquiring. Already he talked! Already he had made friends! You could see in him even then a man destined for leadership . . . if only he were willing to accept it. In a small backward country like Santa Isabella, where so much has been lost, where so many spirits have been dulled—yes, one can detect even in adolescence the few who will some day be leaders."

Peralda turned up his good left hand apologetically.

"But all these ancient memories—of what interest can they be to you?"

"Everything about Villamayor interests me," I said. "Though it's especially the last months I want to know about, of course. And the last things he wrote."

"Who knows?" Peralda said sadly. "Perhaps he even gave up writing."

"I could go to New York tonight. If you'll only give me a few names, people to look up . . ."

"No," he said decisively. "I shall write them myself. You see it is really a question for our committee to debate, and for other committees—what attitude should be taken by your article, toward the last days of Villamayor. He had his great failings. Yet he was a man many of us loved."

He promised to keep me informed. I gave him my address and telephone number. I did not, of course, mention the existence of Manuel Andrada.

IN the days that followed, my odd relationship with Andrada became much closer, while we waited for Peralda to hear from his New York friends. I did no more research into the life of Villamayor, whom I still believed to be alive. Wasn't there the crowning evidence of Julieta Aparicio's disappearance, the day after Villamayor's? I awaited more startling revelations than a library could provide. And the next days seemed to me a period of idleness and marking time; I thought nothing was happening. But in this I was wrong. For all the while Andrada was invading my life, prodding and encroaching, and he would not be beaten off. At the time I thought I was resisting him, but I must not have resisted very hard. For by the end of the week he was ready to appear at my door (bag, baggage, arsenal, magazines, framed poster larger than life) with his outrageous offer to share my apartment at a price, or perhaps even free of charge since we were engaged in the same "cultural quest."

He began by coming every afternoon to ask for my "report." It did no good to say I had not yet heard from Peralda, and to ask him to telephone instead. There he would stand in the hallway, immovable and unsmiling, looking past me into the room. So I would end by asking him in for a drink. He very quickly came to know my hours. My apartment had become his small island of security in this foreign city whose appearances were all misleading. I was his connection with Reality, and with the capital city of the splendid seaside avenue, where no deceptive temptations existed. I had been there and knew. There, for instance, the prostitutes resembled prostitutes, and there was little likelihood of misjudgment and sudden arrest. Moreover one always knew on what days certain patriotic ceremonies would occur, and at what hour The Protector's reassuring immersion in the sea. The orderly silence of the city was comforting to remember amid the chaos of this northern metropolis.

For he was homesick already, little Andrada, and he put up with a good deal of my ironic resistance for the sake of an audience. He could have talked for hours about the city of palms and obelisks and its "fine aristocratic homes." He knew well, for instance, the luxurious confiscated mansion of Villamayor, now assigned to a foreign legation. He even spoke with pride of the waterfront military installations, the warehouses and cranes guarded by miles of barbed wire. And there was so much he missed from his own poorer part of the town, which had been totally rebuilt after the earthquake and tidal waves. On Sundays "the mothers rested" and looked down from their ironwork balconies, and a rich odor of coffee filled the air. He would not accept my memory of the city as a burning solitude and of balconies as empty as the streets. Or that significant odor of pollution from the sea.

"You are unfair, Nicholas Clive, you are prejudiced. You will not allow yourself to remember."

He insisted on leaving with me a large album of photographs prepared by a government bureau. From nearly every page (against the background of whatever public

ceremony or building) the lumpy face of The Protector
stared out, or the black jowls, protruding eyes and prom-
inent teeth of the Nephew, President of the Republic.
The various steps of the national Reinvigoration were recorded in sickly green gravure, and the slow aging of The
Protector himself. High officials in evening clothes or
uniforms formed wide semicircles around him, with all
faces turned nervously to the center in attitudes of approval. I remarked on the fact that the official poses
scarcely changed at all from decade to decade. But to
Andrada this "saving stability" was a matter of pride.

I did not, I repeat, believe Villamayor was dead; I was
sure we would come face to face. This seemed reason
enough not to say anything to Andrada about Villamayor's part in the Puerto Limón invasion; or about
Peralda's, for that matter. I did not want even the small
risk of blood on my hands. But I did ask Andrada what
he thought of the invaders. He stiffened perceptibly:

"They were scum, Nicholas Clive."

"Scum?"

"Rabble, atheistic communists, filthy riffraff, and betrayers of the obligation. Minds worm-eaten by ingratitude! Also there were sordid mercenaries who would do
anything for money."

"Anything for money? That might go for some of the
Miami pilots. But not the others. You have to admit the
others were patriots."

"They were scum."

"Did you know any of them?"

"Of course not! You ask if I know rapists and mutila-
tors? These were degenerates extracted from the gutters
of Havana and the sewers of Caracas. They wanted only
to destroy, but The Protector creates. It would have been

better had all the planes arrived, and all that rabble been killed."

"Perhaps that's what the invasion was about? The rabble doesn't like to be killed. It doesn't believe in The Protector's methods."

Manuel Andrada walked to my wall of glass overlooking the river. He stared down with contempt on the pleasant spring scene.

"Severity is necessary for the National Reinvigoration."

"What's being reinvigorated?"

He turned back to me angrily.

"You have been there, Nicholas Clive. Why do you show such ill will? Such ingratitude for the benefits? You have seen the fine paved streets and the parks, you have seen the new cigar factory and the luxury hotels. Is there a cleaner or more orderly city anywhere?"

"It's orderly enough."

"Very well, Nicholas Clive. Now consider the city in the first hours after the catastrophe. I know, I was a child there! The houses were crushed and broken open. From some houses all the possessions simply floated away. I found my own pallet in the center of the street, I had to extricate it from the mud. South of the Cathedral a few walls remained standing, but the doors and the windows were gone. Many thousands were dead. And all that night there were looters at their work, filthy jackals and thieves. I heard screams, I could hear shots in the dark. And you could see the shadows of the thieves. Before morning The Protector on horseback appeared by the great fire in the Cathedral square."

"Yes, I know. The Protector restored order."

"You agree severity was necessary?"

"Yes, I do agree. But that was over twenty years ago. The severity has never let up."

"The people are corrupt and weak. Many are lazy, especially the Negroes. Many more are thieves without heartfelt religion. Only The Protector in alliance with the Church can control the base instincts and laziness. He is the protector of the Faith."

"The great Christian gentleman?"

"It was the will of God. The catastrophe was needed. From the chaos came our need for a great leader who would defend the people from their own weaknesses and also rebuild the city."

"Then God caused the earthquake and the tidal waves so The Protector could consolidate his power?"

He brushed my question aside.

"Have you not experienced catastrophe, Nicholas Clive? In a few minutes or a few hours, everything is changed. All your possessions are gone. You must begin your life again, only the blue sky is the same. It is then people like you are helpless, or a man like Justo de Villamayor, with his disbelief in God. For you perhaps there is only the sky. You cannot act, you cannot make a decision."

He would come back to that question later: to my ignorance of catastrophe. But now his mind was diverted onto Villamayor. He stalked to the window and back, then sat down facing me. The writings, he admitted, were "distinguished." He was willing to concede Villamayor and his eminent memory a great deal: intelligence, talent, even experience and wisdom . . . everything but faith. But that was lacking—the faith that "fortifies the will" and "concentrates the energy of the Nation." Andrada had perhaps not read the collected works of Villamayor, but he knew well enough the Church's judgments on them, and the clichés of the *Diario del Caribe*. He believed them with all his soul.

I faced, for the first time, the essential question directly. "So you think he ought to be punished?"

"Justo de Villamayor is dead," he said quietly. "Reward and punishment are not in our hands."

"But if he turns out to be alive?"

"Then I would like to see him rectify his political mistakes. Have we not all memorized his verses in our schools? I would rejoice to see them erased . . . the stains on his name."

THAT conversation occurred on a Wednesday, the Wednesday after my first call on Peralda. On Friday I returned from a fruitless visit to the "headquarters" (there were now two bottles of milk by the door, the place looked deserted) to find Andrada sitting at my desk. He said nothing, but continued to stare past me. I had the odd sense he was impersonating me, even to the habit I had developed in these last days of sitting at an empty desk. He was a dark unreal figure in the stillness of the yellow afternoon. Then he moved.

That afternoon strikes me, now, as an important moment in the progress of our intimacy. For Andrada had no excuses to make. He said the cleaning woman had let him in, as though that justified everything. He had even brought the whiskey and ice bucket and glasses from the pantry (since it was after all time for "our drink") and had drawn up two chairs. He might have said in so many words that the time had come for more personal revelations. And in fact he asked me at once about my "mistresses" in Santa Isabella—those lithe black silent creatures, unrequested but welcome enough, procured by a houseboy who reported my every action to certain guardians of national security.

" 'Mistresses' isn't exactly the word. I never saw any of those girls more than twice. I suppose Jorge had a long list of cousins and poor relations to run through. Or maybe they were all working for the government. Maybe each one had to have her crack at finding out what I would say."

"You are prejudiced, Nicholas Clive. Why should they have done that? You have never written anything against The Protector. And you were the son of a man who had come to the aid of the homeland in the dark time of the rebuilding. Moreover, you owned shares in the Azucarera San Tomás. There was no reason for the government to mistrust you."

"They mistrust everyone. Don't you think they mistrust you?"

"They would be right to mistrust me. I cannot control the passions. And what have I accomplished in the States, after more than two weeks? Nothing! Moreover, I have been arrested twice. I have disgraced my employers."

"Then you've heard from Eufemio Rodriguez?"

He shook his head.

"Nothing. I am troubled, Nicholas Clive. He did not even answer my letter." But then he shook off his depression, and turned to me with his queer grin, the great gold tooth reappearing. "But let us speak of pleasanter things, my friend. I have a surprise for you. This is the birthday of The Protector's nephew, the President of the Republic.

It is a time for rejoicing. I invite you to join me in this celebration. Yes, we will have dinner in a Spanish restaurant. We will share a bottle of champagne!"

I think back with amusement and almost pity on that evening which would end, as most evenings ended for Andrada, in humiliation and defeat. In the transforming light of our later journey it is tempting to see only the small diabolic presence (red of flesh, with all but horns and hoofs) whose "soul" suddenly changed. Those were his own words, and I would not smile when I heard them. But in the first weeks it was hard to take Andrada seriously at all. His desires were so transparent! I saw at once why he took me to that small walkup café in the North End, between a *pasticceria* and an Italian restaurant. He wanted the habitués there to know—the cook, the one waiter with his *Diario de Nueva York,* the table of men with their dominoes, the solitary in the corner—that he too, Manuel Andrada, had an American friend of respectable appearance. And I in turn would be shown that he had his foothold, however modest, in the teeming world of Boston: a place where he was known. He made a great show of shaking hands with the cook, and exchanged pleasantries with the waiter in rapid Spanish.

Not all of the habitués, it appears, were friendly to The Protector. For after dessert, and with the opening of the bottle of warm champagne he had brought in a paper bag, Andrada's voice dropped to a whisper as he raised his glass.

"And now, Nicholas Clive! A toast to the honor of the Nephew!"

"And to his improved health and intelligence," I added.

Andrada withdrew his glass.

"His intelligence?"

"Isn't it commonly said that he lacks it? Not all men are equally endowed. I've even heard he doesn't understand very clearly what is happening in the Cabinet meetings."

"That is nonsense," Andrada blurted out. "Who else decides what will be discussed? Who else pilots the ship of state?"

"His uncle, of course. The Protector."

Andrada nodded.

"Yes, that is true. But you must not divide too far those linked by common blood. The entire family embraces one faith and possesses one will, directed by The Protector's insights. The ancient mother and the President of the Republic, the other nephews and the many sisters, even the saintly young woman Margarita, to whom all youth in the homeland looks up for guidance. . . . Do they not all derive their wisdom and their charity from the one great fountain? They are flesh of his flesh. And to think the parents once lived in a small peasant village not far from Santiago, their aristocratic blood unsuspected!"

We finished the bottle, while the conversation slid off onto certain pleasures from which Andrada had been, these last two weeks, bereft. Later, at the immense barn of a nightclub he took me to, it was amusing to observe the fierce desires he thought he was concealing. He talked on and on about the capital city, the manly virtues of the Nephew, the relocated airport—and all the while his scarred face stared past me at the cigarette girls in their mesh stockings, and the platinum silk creatures of nearby tables, and the tall showgirls on the dance floor that was also a stage. There was a belly dance that lasted many minutes while Andrada kept up his patriotic chatter, staring more and more intently at the writhing girl. Large droplets of sweat descended his cheeks and vanished under his collar.

When the show was over he danced with one of the hostesses, after gravely consulting me: a listless creature who had been hovering nearby. He marched her rapidly across the stage and back, across and back, never pausing or giving ground. It was the other dancers who gave way. Andrada was inches shorter than the girl, and held her just above the hips. His eyes showed, peering intently, just above her shoulder; the scar was milky white in the smoky haze. They soon had a small straight open channel to themselves, between two groups of alarmed dancers. Andrada came back to the table alone; the girl had refused to accompany him.

I did feel sorry for him. So later I took him to an after-hours club for which I had a card. Here, if anywhere, he would find a "suitable companion" for the night. It was a smoky upstairs club, much frequented by earnest men with Miami coats and sick leathery tans. Tall girls moved through the haze, their porcelain faces riding high above the men at the tables. I waited by the door only long enough to see Andrada installed at the bar. His small squat figure was turned belligerently toward the crowd at the tables, with one leg not reaching the floor. The last I saw was the calm friendly approach of one of the penciled and platinum girls. She took her place at the bar beside him, long-limbed and tall. Her whole elaborate hair-do showed above Andrada's dark and dedicated head.

I still do not know exactly what happened this time. For Andrada was much too angry to make himself clear, when he telephoned. Later he refused to speak of this "unfortunate episode" at all. Had he once again blatantly begun a circular stroking of the girl's back, in the well known expedient for arousing sexual attention, while talking to her at the bar? Or had some local hoodlum, distrusting the two bulges at the armpits, drunkenly proposed a quarrel? All I know is that less than an hour later Andrada was stammering angrily over the telephone. This time he had not been arrested. But he had been evicted in the most humiliating way, the two bouncers hustling him to the stairs while his legs kicked the air.

"You must have known it was such a place, Nicholas Clive. It was you who took me there. And after our comradely dinner together! It was not a friendly act. Those people would not accept my presence, they would not even look at my documents. I found myself in the street, I blame you for everything. . . ."

He blamed me for everything. But by late the next morning I was forgiven, and he was even ashamed, I think, because he had spoken so sharply. So he had bounced back once more. He was ready to resume our "partnership" and "collaboration" in the search for traces of the vanished Villamayor and whatever manuscripts had been left behind. And only twenty-four hours after that came the most preposterous appearance of all: the small eternally hopeful dark figure at my door, surrounded by his baggage and belongings, the suitcase and large box which doubtless represented his arsenal, the fifty or sixty magazines neatly stacked and tied. And propped against the opposite wall the much larger than life poster of The Protector, with his pasty malevolent stare.

"So what happened? You were thrown out of the hotel?"

"I chose to leave, Nicholas Clive, I have come to you."

He went on to explain the absurdity of his investing, in an expensive room, money which could well be saved for "our mission." He would pay a share of the rent, if I insisted. But he wanted no more than a corner of the living room, and it would be only a matter of days before we heard from Peralda.

My recollection is that I listened to all this without laughing.

"I see. So you decided this sounded like a reasonable arrangement, and you just packed and came over. Couldn't you at least have telephoned?"

Andrada answered me honestly enough.

"I was afraid you might refuse."

so he did indeed move in, and spent four days and nights in my apartment. He slept on the couch without taking off his clothes. On the afternoon of the fourth day Peralda phoned with news that did not surprise me at all. My guess that Villamayor was alive had turned out to be correct. And if we went immediately to New York we could converse with no less a personage than María Teresa Aparicio. This was the sister of the secretary who had vanished from Mexico City, one day after Villamayor. It appears there had been, very recently, some correspondence between the two sisters.

IN New York we had connecting rooms. This was a "squandering of resources," in Andrada's opinion, but he took advantage of it to hang the portrait of The Protector above his bed, in the place of a frivolous Utrillo print. Of course he would not travel without it! This left my room for "the consultation." Andrada had procured rum, soda and ice, and a small bouquet of carnations; also he had treated himself to an hour's ministrations in a barbershop. His black hair, freshly cut, was slicked down with a sweet pomade. And now, awaiting María Teresa Aparicio, he reminded me again that his own role was "unpolitical." He would keep quite silent; I was to ask the questions. There was even no need for "our informant" (who might be prejudiced) to know he came from Santa Isabella at all. He represented a library, archives, the world of letters—that was all that mattered. He had bought a small volume of Spanish poetry, which protruded convincingly from one hairy pocket.

María Teresa Aparicio . . . a promising and romantic name. For all I know Andrada had dreamed of a "gratifying episode" with her, an evening of entertainment and dalliance, at the conclusion of our business. But the woman who came to the room, and who astonished us both by her talking, might have been Julieta herself, the secretary of the Reconciliation dinner photograph. María Teresa too had black stockings, sensible low-cut shoes, and straight severe hair. Two such women as must scorn life's frivolities. . . . Actually, the two sisters were only a year apart in age, and had lived together until Villamayor "cut them asunder." They had dressed and thought alike as they moved through the convent and through adolescence. They both attended the university in Mexico City and studied history. It was there the bemused sister Julieta had "sat at the feet" of Alonso Moreno, the historian of socialism and an old friend of Villamayor.

Some of this we learned later. María Teresa was already talking rapidly as she came through the door, angrily tearing at her gloves. She embarked on the story of her life, of their entwined sisterly lives, after the most perfunctory nod. "Listen to me, sirs, listen to what I have suffered." In her view Alonso Moreno was the first villain of the story, since he had turned Julieta over to the fugitive Villamayor, when the latter needed a secretary and well trained assistant. All this poured out at once.

"Moreno turned her over to the Corrupter as one would never turn over a faithful cat or dog or servant! And he did this, believe me, scarcely a month after Villamayor the intruder arrived at our door, still horribly bandaged. Yes, Alonso Moreno offered her up to him not long after we moved to Cuernavaca for the summer. Then it was Villamayor's own sorcery and tongue. Before the summer was over she was lost. He had violated her soul."

Andrada listened dumbfounded. The corner of his upper lip curled up as in disbelief to reveal the gleaming tooth. He looked to me for help, then went to the bottle of rum.

"Please sit down, I beg you. Permit me to offer refreshments. Is it not a very hot day?"

María Teresa measured him quickly.

"And who are you? Señor Peralda only mentioned this gentleman. Are you both writing articles about the Seducer?"

"An unpolitical man," Andrada murmured. "A purchaser of manuscripts."

"You must rescue her, sirs," she stormed on. "It is a Christian obligation. Moreover, if it is manuscripts you are after . . ."

"Rescue her from what?"

"From Villamayor, of course."

"Then you're quite sure he isn't dead?"

"Assuredly he is no more dead than you."

Andrada stared at her stolidly.

"Many things are rumored falsely," he said.

"Rumored? I tell you he was not dead two months ago, when I saw him on Barbara Swenson's ranch in California. Saw him in the flesh. And consider what this unbeliever has done to the most pious of girls, destroying even her reason. My sister thinks he, the seducer Justo de Villamayor, is destined to be revered as a saint! And she turned her back on me! In the two months I have received only one postcard, addressed from Port-au-Prince, and with no return address. During the earlier captivity she was at least permitted to write me once a week. But this time only a card with the one sentence, 'I am happy and well.' "

She showed me the card with its picture of the Port-au-Prince market beneath an iron arch: the Negro women with their white dresses and soft accusing faces. And the one neatly written sentence. I passed the card to Andrada. He too, I could see, was busily revolving a journey to Haiti and Port-au-Prince. Boston had been only a diversion.

I asked what she meant by the "earlier captivity."

"The two years and two months he held her in bondage in some lost provincial village or town, pretending to have vanished from the face of the earth for a second time. I was to tell no one but Alonso Moreno of the letters. And now from Haiti she does not even write me. Yes, of course I am sure he is alive. If Villamayor were dead, she would have rushed back to me at once, restored to her right mind."

I measured the enraged face, neglected hair and shining aristocratic nose. The shoes that buttoned might have been inherited from an aunt long deceased. I persuaded her at last to sit down.

"Why don't you go down to Port-au-Prince yourself?"

"But it is you who must go, sirs! Señor Peralda said you wished to write an essay on Villamayor. And this man who looks for manuscripts. . . . If Villamayor is alive you can speak to him yourselves. And if he is dead —who will know more about him and his manuscripts than my sister Julieta, for almost three years his assistant, secretary and slave?"

"You can't afford to go?"

She shook her head.

"We quarreled at Barbara Swenson's ranch, Villamayor and I. He had sent me the money to go out there, and for one week we were together constantly, Julieta and I, after my two years and two months of anguish. Then Villamayor told me in his corrupt manner that we had 'again reached the parting of the ways.' He offered me five hundred dollars. A bribe. . . . The very next night they vanished from the ranch without a word of farewell, leaving only a note."

Barbara Swenson, she explained, was a very rich and very old woman who had financed the activities of Latin-American exiles from many countries. At any moment a dozen "conspirators" and "theorists" would be at the ranch, boarding at her expense. She was a "true lover of liberty." And yet it was an eccentric old woman's whim, this financing of revolutionaries, and her bounties were divided among so many exile groups that little remained for any one. Also at the ranch was her companion Edward Murphree, an aging soldier of fortune, veteran of many wars and revolutions.

I reached the conclusion that Villamayor was conspiring again, these many years after the fiasco of Puerto Limón, and only three years after the Twenty-Six Days. But of this I said nothing. Andrada, however—and though he knew nothing of Villamayor's part in the Puerto Limón "invasion"—could not suppress his fears.

"I have heard of this old woman. She has many dishonorable millions."

"Why dishonorable? She is a lover of liberty, after all."

Andrada went to the bucket of ice. He once more offered María Teresa Aparicio a drink, and when she refused poured himself half a tumbler of rum. He held a lump of ice to his forehead, just above the scar. He seemed very excited.

"You speak of Villamayor as 'the Corrupter.' Why is that? Please tell me—I hesitate to ask—had Villamayor come to this Barbara Swenson for help in political conspiracies? I ask as an innocent who knows nothing of the political world."

Maria Teresa shrugged her ascetic shoulders.

"No, it was Barbara Swenson who sent for him. She brought him up there. She wanted him to join a Committee, and to confer with Eduardo Gonzales the theorist, who is preparing a constitution for Santa Isabella."

"Santa Isabella has a constitution," the astonished Andrada broke in. "Everyone knows that. There are thirteen articles and a preamble of moral principles."

María Teresa Aparicio laughed.

"What constitution is worth the paper it is printed on, when the Devil's own lineage administers it? But all that does not matter. Isn't one pious soul of more consequence than all the vain committees and constitutions? It is my sister's soul you must save. She was too innocent to resist

Alonso Moreno. Then the bandaged Villamayor came to us, like one risen from the dead."

And now she did go back—behind the "earlier captivity"—to the first coming three years ago of Villamayor to Mexico City, after his abduction from the Ministry of Education. No one had seen him come. He was simply there at the door, leaning over the cane, unable to walk.

She crossed herself hastily.

"Even as they helped him to a bed his dark brooding eyes peered out restlessly from the bandages, searching for the vulnerable soul. And soon enough he discerned her: my sister."

"Did he tell you how he escaped?" I asked. "Why didn't they kill him?"

"About that he would say almost nothing. Instead he spoke facetiously of a 'slight realignment of the bones.' Also he said these things had happened as to a man who slept and dreamed."

"Wasn't he afraid they would come to Mexico to finish the job?"

Andrada was annoyed by my question; he walked stiffly to the window and looked out. María Teresa ignored him.

"No, it was Alonso Moreno who was afraid for him, and I who was afraid, and my sister Julieta. Alonso Moreno urged Villamayor to go away and to take another name. The Corrupter's reply was that he had to discover a new personality before he would deserve a new name. But of course he did at last disappear in just that way, drawing the innocent and pure one after him. But let me tell you how, in the very first days after his arrival, Julieta was ready to become his victim."

The ensuing narrative was a little unclear. And much

of it that puzzled María Teresa—the inhumanly rapid recovery, the "diabolic mending of the bones"—does not matter very much now. From the first, it appears, Villamayor talked of discovering new selves and new emotions to correspond to his changed body and "realigned bones." After they moved to the summer house in Cuernavaca Villamayor began to write poems evoking an olive countryside and the evanescent white tops of the volcanoes. He claimed these poems sprang from strange new depths of spirit: an altered personality.

It was this irresponsible talk, María Teresa thought, that encouraged "poor Julieta" in her delusions—her fantasy of resurrection, and her belief that the agnostic Villamayor was not only a potential convert but would one day rise high in the church, would even achieve sainthood. Villamayor could speak ironically of the "miracle" of his escape, but Julieta took the word very literally.

"And he still wouldn't talk about what had happened to him?"

"Not at the first. It was as though he selfishly attended only to the mending of his body, and to the writing of his verses."

For a few weeks, she said, Villamayor would not speak of politics at all. But this could not go on forever. There were times in his talks with Alonso Moreno when theories of history crept in. One day they found themselves arguing about the tactics of the Commune in Paris. And now, it appeared, Villamayor thought back on his own story, and on his futile pleas for moderate reform. One afternoon by the pool in Cuernavaca he even spoke of these matters in her presence. Could any course of honorable action have "obviated his kidnapping" after the Twenty-Six Days. Villamayor had already discovered that he could not divorce himself from his past. He began to study his own acts and words during his brief tenure as Minister, and the motives behind them. He wanted to write, with a professional detachment, the history of his failure.

Andrada looked away from María Teresa at a blank wall, where no portrait hung to help him. Then he again offered her a drink. He helped himself generously. He was staggering slightly, as he returned to his chair.

"Did he write a political attack on The Protector? Is that what you mean?"

"I don't know. But I do know he was not merely writing an angry little essay of protest. It was to be a long work. He spoke of his need of a great library, and of his desire to consult various men who had been driven into exile. Yes: Villamayor needed facts and statistics for the writing of his book. That is one reason they went to New York, taking me with them. There was also in New York a meeting intended to effect a reconciliation among the various exile groups. Villamayor attended that meeting, with Julieta at his side. But he was disgusted with the vanity of the exiles and their perpetual squabblings. He very quickly gave up all hope. . . ."

"They are wool-gatherers," Andrada put in, speaking as to himself, "He was right to be disgusted. A great poet should not frequent dreamers dedicated to destruction. He should confine himself to the writing of verses."

María Teresa looked at Andrada more closely; she scrutinized the odd scar.

"You say you want to purchase the manuscripts of poems? You do not look like a literary man or a dealer. . . ."

"Poems, essays, anything from his pen. I will pay a fair price."

"Well, I know nothing of his manuscripts." She went back to those dark New York days and her memories of deprivation. "We had our dinners together but that was all. Even in the late evening and by night Julieta was with him in spirit. I had to read silently while she knelt in her endless prayers."

"Then when you say 'seducer' you don't literally mean, for that period. . . ."

My voice trailed off in the presence of her maidenly shock.

"He had seduced her in mind and in spirit. What more do you want? He had begun to separate two sisters who had been together since earliest childhood. Then he separated us completely. In November we all went back to Alonso Moreno's villa in Mexico City. And then they truly vanished as into a black hole. One day Villamayor was gone, the next day she. Then the twenty-four months, during which I kept their abominable secret from all but Alonso Moreno. Twenty-four months, and only one letter a week."

This second disappearance seemed to me much darker than that first and involuntary one, from which Villamayor had emerged mildly crippled. I asked what happened in November to cause the return to Mexico, and the plunge into the black hole. He had taken, in his place of hiding, the name of "Luis Hernández." Was it, this time, fear of The Protector's agents?

"Perhaps. And yet it was less fear than disgust. Villamayor left New York because he was sickened by the quarreling of the exile leaders. And after that I think it was less fear than a perverse and monstrous vanity. But I do not know. There is nothing of all this I can explain, certainly not the next reappearance. For two months ago they emerged from their hiding, quite without warning to me, at the call of that madwoman Barbara Swenson. How had she penetrated their secret? Again I cannot tell, though money can purchase anything, even the soul. Somehow she had found them and had them brought to her ranch in California. And then they sent for me."

She told us about the ranch buried in brown hills and dusty oak trees somewhere north of San Francisco. There were various people whose roles she never understood: Mexicans, Cubans, Guatemalans. There were newcomers every day who made a point of arriving before the buffet lunch, served beside the pool. And of course there was the scholarly and lean Eduardo Gonzales, framing his new constitution. Every afternoon at five he emerged from his room to join the others for cocktails. In the evenings he conferred privately with Villamayor.

As she talked about Barbara Swenson and her entourage I could detect, in Manuel Andrada, a mounting patriotic irritation. He had begun to help himself to the rum more frequently, and no longer bothered to offer any to María Teresa or to me. Almost half of the bottle was gone, and with it much of his discretion. He paced the small room heavily. It obviously disturbed him to contemplate those evening confabulations of Gonzales and Villamayor.

"Wool-gatherers," he muttered. "The victims of illusion, ignorant of political realities and the saving principle of authority. Dreamers, advocates of disorder. What business has a great poet to consort with such a man? I repeat, he should confine himself to the writing of verses."

María Teresa for the first time regarded him with real suspicion.

"You sound like an emissary of The Protector."

"I am a literary man," Andrada replied roughly. "How many times must I tell you? Did Villamayor agree to help him with his mad schemes?"

"Obviously he did not. Have I not told you he vanished from the ranch in the company of my sister? I think he had lost the last of his political will to resistance. After all, anyone who like Villamayor has lived for years without rebelling, in his youth, under the fetid evil shadow of The Protector . . ."

Andrada sat back as though slapped.

"The evil shadow!"

"Under The Protector's stinking breath, in the vicinity of the cruel one. The poisoner of the intellect, the stupefier . . ."

Andrada leaped from his chair and rushed to the end of the small room. He returned wringing his hands.

"You make a foolish and female mistake," he babbled. "You confuse The Protector with someone else. Or perhaps you are blinded by false reports? It is notoriously the weakness of women to listen to ridiculous rumors. The stupefier! Did you not know he is the patron and honorary rector of the university, learned in all the arts and sciences? I do not speak of politics; all that is not my affair. But I cannot listen without protest to female rantings. How can you call him the stupefier who each year is honored in the university's ceremonies? His portrait hangs in every schoolroom of the land. He has the true visage of one sunk in thought on the problems of the homeland."

María Teresa blanched under her full realization of Andrada's loyalties. But she faced him courageously enough.

"The Devil too is everywhere. Between the Adversary and The Protector, the soul of Villamayor has been torn to shreds."

"You blaspheme," Andrada shouted. "You have no idea what you are saying. The Protector is a pillar of the Church! Who but he erected in honor of his saintly mother the new chapel of San Ysidro? In the Cathedral there are candles which will burn to eternity at The Protector's expense. Moreover, it is known his name is mentioned in every prayer uttered in every church and every home throughout the land."

María Teresa stared on at Andrada without flinching.

"I understand everything," she said. "You are a political agent of the Evil One. It is to destroy Villamayor you have come."

Andrada, outraged and nonplussed, backed away slowly; he gulped down more rum.

"I am an emissary of the National Library of Santa Isabella, also of the Archives. I have come to purchase Villamayor's manuscripts. I have come to recover certain writings that belong to the national heritage. Do you think I am ashamed to acknowledge my love of The Protector? However, that has nothing to do with the manuscripts. It is no business of yours . . ."

"The National Library! I simply do not believe you."

"Do you wish to see my documents?"

In reply she turned her back on him and appealed to me.

"It is only you, sir, only you who must help me. It is you who must go to Port-au-Prince, where you will have a chance to write your article. For there you will find my sister Julieta, who can help you as no one else could. Not to mention the Corrupter himself . . ."

"And you haven't any address. Only Port-au-Prince?"

"I am sure you will find them. But can you understand my grief at receiving in the two months only this one card? Do you not see? It is as if Julieta wanted to draw a line between all the past in which we loved each other, and this . . . this present into which she has vanished. Why else only one card? That is why you must go down there, sir, a Christian obligation. Because in finding the corrupter Justo de Villamayor you will also find my poor lost sister with him, mumbling her prayers, doubtless on her knees."

And with that she turned and left us. One moment she was talking, the next moment she was in the corridor, rushing away.

AND should I too have turned my back on Manuel Andrada, and gone down to Port-au-Prince alone? Well, I can honestly say I tried to. I did not really think of this poor fool as a menace to Villamayor: this "representative of a Library," this secret agent given to patriotic tirades, and who traveled with a large framed portrait of his hated employer. No, I thought, Andrada was simply one of those farcical errors that can occur in even the most orderly regime: a bureaucratic accident it might be, a misplaced name on a sheet of assignments, a secretary's blunder, the single loose screw or crazily spinning flywheel in a well oiled machine. It had been efficient enough, over the years, the machine: the intelligence service of Santa Isabella. . . . But perhaps only the Andradas were left for such delicate missions abroad. Perhaps Santa Isabella, in the austere task of keeping track of all her children, both at home and abroad, had used up all its human resources. Maybe this *was* the bottom of the barrel.

In any event I found it hard to conceive of Andrada finding Villamayor, let alone destroying him.

Nevertheless, I didn't relish Andrada as a traveling companion, and I wanted to reach Villamayor before he did. I had my article to write. I wanted to have at least one or two long interviews with this slippery and enigmatic exile before Andrada's blundering caused him to shut his door in our faces, or perhaps even disappear again. So I decided—how many times have I not decided this? —to give little Andrada the slip. And that night I did so, not many hours after María Teresa Aparicio had left us. For several hours after dinner I tried to read in bed, and I listened as Andrada watched the television next door. He had bought another bottle of rum. Then I heard him moving about in the dark, stumbling drunkenly against the furniture, and at last I heard his snores. I got up at once, went out to La Guardia, and took a half-empty plane for Miami. I did not want to wait for morning and a through plane to Port-au-Prince; that is, I did not want to wait for Andrada. I was in Miami by six o'clock, in the hot still Florida dawn, with seven hours to wait.

So I went to a hotel, lay down in the now blazing morning—and almost overslept my plane. I had to rush to the airport without shaving. The small waiting room for the Port-au-Prince flight was already filled when I arrived. There were a number of Haitian Negroes dressed in white, also a few tourists.

And there by the gate, the first in line of course, was Manuel Andrada, still wearing his hairy brown suit. He had checked some of his baggage. But he was going to take a good deal onto the plane. In one hand he carried a large

fresh stack of dubious magazines and with the other held
what could only have been the great framed portrait of
The Protector, carefully wrapped in heavy brown paper.

He looked at me accusingly, but did not seem particularly surprised.

"You were wrong to leave that way, Nicholas Clive,
and in the middle of the night. It was an unfriendly act.
Did we not agree to collaborate?"

3

PORT-AU-PRINCE. From my balcony, that evening, the dusty ruined city was a bowl of darkening green. The white National Palace was half-submerged in the bowl, or as though resting on a thick bed of leaves. Beyond it the long crouching body of the Cathedral seemed poised as for sudden flight. I could not see from here the yawning holes in the streets and sidewalks, or the exposed broken drains where the poor do their washing. My hotel was one of several spidery gingerbread villas clustered on the first slopes of a steep hillside some two hundred feet above the city. This was an area of green elegance: the spoils of the unsubtle and savage corruption of the first decade of the century. The climbing streets were lined with almond and flamboyant trees and tall palms, and the villas buried in camellia and hibiscus were set well back from the street.

I looked down from my balcony on the hotel's pool, and beyond it on the public road through a break in the garden wall. Long lines of Negro women walked up toward the hills in search of water. Their robes and turbans were white blurs in the dusk, indistinct as moths. Once this hotel had been a famous statesman's summer mansion, at the very end of the era of barbarism, and the highest villa in the town. From it, with his *placée* of a legendary loveliness, he could remain aloof from the

squalor below—though in the end this did not protect
him from an enraged mob that, on discovering the Treas-
ury empty, tore him to small pieces at the foot of his long
curving classical stairway at the top of the garden. He
must have expired within a few feet of where the metal
chaise longues now rested, bordering the pool.

I stared out at the darkening city. Beyond it was the
great curving bay, almost black now, with the listing
freighter beyond the derelicts and the jetty, also the sleek
white yacht we had seen from the plane. The yacht glowed
in the dusk a few hundred yards offshore. Far beyond that
and over it all, like a thick tongue inserted in the bay's
mouth, or the clapper of a bell, was the island of Gonave,
a parched and savage place a dozen miles offshore. Sometimes it could be seen clearly, sometimes not at all. Now
in the dusk it was a huge indistinct blue gloom floating in
the sky, a thunderhead over the vanished horizon. The
hot still evening darkened perceptibly as I watched, and
a few first lights came on. I felt tired and drugged by
heat. There was a rich odor of coffee from the kitchen
below, and an odor of burning charcoal from the street,
stupefying in the hot evening. There would be much
cooking done on the sidewalks, out there in the shadowy
city, the pots resting on stones, the braziers glowing and
the black faces glowing above them.

And somewhere out there in the disappearing city was
Manuel Andrada, from whom I had separated myself
once again; and easily enough. As always he had brought
the mishap on himself, and his altercation with the Haitian
custom officials; he should have left that immense framed
poster of The Protector at home. He was still angrily
rewrapping it under the eyes of the hostile Negroes when
I stepped into my taxi. But even on the plane from Miami

he was amusing enough with his transparent patriotism. With the first sight of Haiti he pointed out the range of spiny mountains that separates it from Santa Isabella. Two such different countries—the one debauched, the other progressive—to share a single island! Andrada looked down at the shoreline of Haiti and the first small fishing villages with contempt.

"You will see, Nicholas Clive. There is nothing to be hoped for from a country governed by Negroes. They are a shiftless and lazy lot. Black dogs, who like to sleep in the dust. One of their rulers had to be roused from a hammock to appear at his own ceremonies of induction! Can you imagine that happening in Santa Isabella?" He leaned across me and pointed to the vicious line of mountains twenty-five and thirty miles to the east, as the plane began to descend. "There, Nicholas Clive! Behind those mountains lies the homeland! At this hour The Protector will be preparing for his daily bath in the sea. There will also be cocktails served by the swimming pools of the two luxury hotels. Soon the workers will leave for their dwellings. . . ."

He was trembling with excitement. I found I had to devil him again.

"Why don't you stay on the plane, then? It's going on to Santa Isabella and San Juan. You could be home in time for dinner."

"No," he said. "I cannot go back with empty hands."

Then we were landing. A coral reef was directly beneath us and with the banking of the plane we caught one more glimpse of the freighter and the white yacht before coming into the small airport. Twenty minutes later I was through the customs while Andrada still argued with the gesticulating authorities. They had threatened to confiscate the poster as intended for some obscure political purpose. Did Monsieur Andrada want to open old wounds? Was this not the hated image of one who had murdered many thousands of Haitian peasants? How could Monsieur Andrada justify his claim (in view of the inexplicable poster) that he had come to Haiti for tourism and pleasure? I watched from a distance and did not, of course, intervene. I was not going to wait to see what happened, since I was determined to reach Villamayor before he did. Andrada's hands were trembling as he tried to rewrap the portrait; that was the last I saw. Would he spend the night in the headquarters of the police, to await further questioning? Or would he be allowed to go to a hotel under surveillance? In any event I was astonished and glad that I had been able to break away from him so easily.

Somewhere out in that darkness, then, was my queer patriotic companion, with his exceptional talent for failure. I intended to take a walk, on that first evening, but suddenly felt so tired I could hardly undress. I turned on the fan and lay naked on the bed. Moths and mosquitoes and beetles whirred and beat against the screen. I must have fallen asleep at once.

I was awakened several times that night: the first time by someone moving in the darkness of the room, then across a thin crack of light from the bathroom. It was one of the servants come to spray the room. He seemed unabashed by my nakedness and crept about in the darkness, spraying all the corners and under the furniture and even the bed on which I lay. He was so quiet I thought I could hear, between sprayings, the tiny flicks of falling beetles.

Then an hour later I was brought sharply awake again, this time by the drunken enraged stammering of an American who wanted the bar reopened for himself and three companions. He offered large sums of money to the watchman, who insisted he had no key. I could hear every word. There was also a woman's voice, speaking in harsh drunken French with a Portuguese accent. Why didn't the watchman wake the proprietor, she wanted to know? Didn't he realize they were certainly the richest clients who had ever come to that little hotel . . . could even, if they wished, buy the hotel and its staff the next morning? Didn't he understand they belonged with the party in the yacht that had been there in the harbor for almost a week? That had also, at a rent of one thousand dollars a month, taken over the Sarcey villa?

But still the watchman refused. There was more angry bickering, then a slamming of doors. The car rushed out into the night, skidding violently as it reached the end of the drive. For some time I could hear the roaring and braking of the car moving down into the stillness of the city.

The next morning I learned who the drunken intruder was, and the woman of the villainous French, spoken with a Portuguese accent. Bernard, the French proprietor of the hotel, who knew everything that happened in Port-au-Prince, understood at once, though he had slept through the commotion. This had been the nephew of the "ancient millionairess" Barbara Swenson, an old woman " of great eccentricity." *Une vieille folle.* . . . It was her white yacht we could see riding in the bay. And it was she who had rented, at a thousand dollars a month, the large villa of the Sarcey's, high on the hillside behind us.

so I found in Port-au-Prince not Villamayor but Barbara
Swenson and her absurd political ménage, transported
from California. Bernard, fat and loquacious, hovered
over me during breakfast on the terrace and at last sat
down. He did not know where Villamayor had gone,
when he "vanished" into the interior two weeks before.
It was the whimsical act of a rich man noted for his unpredictable behavior. *Et puis il y avaient deux femmes,
également folles.* Perhaps Villamayor had fled, apprehensive of The Protector's police. Who knows?

Of Barbara Swenson, on the other hand, he could tell
me a good deal. She was a woman of great antiquity who
refused to grow old, and who had outlived all the doctors
appointed to treat her infirmities. There had been a great
Swiss psychologist and experimenter with drugs who for
years flew the Atlantic with treatments to keep her young.
But at last he was too feeble to travel, so she had to go
to him. She was a living tribute, Bernard said, to the
success of quacks and charlatans. Hormones had been
injected from the testicles of innumerable beasts, hands
had been laid upon her. And all drugs exhilarated, everything succeeded, she was a miracle of energy. *Un phé-
nomène de la nature.* . . . She had been in Port-au-Prince
only a week, yet had already exhausted both official callers
and native guides. Even the head of the secret police, Auguste Bataille, had dined both on her yacht and at the villa,
so too the Minister of Foreign Affairs. A significant gesture toward one noted for her hobby of subversion. . . .
Her "party" had become a national asset, moreover, since
it lost thousands of dollars each night at the Casino. Even
the brutal nephew and his Portuguese *putain* were welcome, and the motley group of exiles who engaged in un-

ceasing political argument while gambling. The companion Edward Murphree? He too was a "phenomenon of nature," though no doubt much younger than Barbara Swenson: a man who had been in all the wars. Abd-el-Krim, Sandino, certainly the war in Spain. . . .

Bernard nodded toward the bay. The green city was beneath us, and the white Palace; the indistinct water burned in the hot morning. The yacht seemed small and far-off, and the island of Gonave had disappeared.

"And what do you suppose she is doing up there with her old soldier and her house party of exiles? There are also two American pilots, disagreeable men. And that innocent yacht out there? No doubt it is full of explosives. *Vous comprenez?* A little mistake, *pouf,* and all of Port-au-Prince will blow up! No doubt she plots a revolution. . . ."

"But if she sees the chief of police?"

Bernard laughed.

"Don't take me too seriously, my friend. And yet, who knows? In Port-au-Prince anything is possible, there is no end in Haiti to revolutions. So perhaps Auguste Bataille will be our next president, if not the old woman herself."

The telephone, as usual, was not functioning. So I went up to the Sarcey villa, on Bernard's advice, a little after twelve. I would certainly be invited for lunch, he said, and I could see the whole absurd caravansary. The "villa" turned out to be a cluster of low stucco buildings built around a pool, and resembled a small resort hotel. A wide terrace thrust out from the hillside and ran off into space. Two men were lounging in deck chairs by the pool and a young woman lay face down on the diving board, naked to the waist. The men wore bathing trunks and

dark glasses and had sandy flattop haircuts. These would
be the two American pilots. Neither said a word when I
asked for Barbara Swenson, but the girl told me to go into
the house and "yell." I went in. At the end of the hall
was another terrace, and a twelve-hundred-foot drop to
the green outskirts of Port-au-Prince. The city was flat
and low, about to be invaded by the sea, and far out the
mountains of Gonave Island appeared in faint gray waves.
But the spiny mountains at the Santa Isabella border were
sharp, brown against blue. Each ridge and summit and
large angry fault was visible.

Then Barbara Swenson was with me, small and incredi-
bly old until she began to speak, the repaired and taut
flesh still hinting at every ravage. The smoothed furrows
were like penciled lines. She was rouged, pomaded,
greased, powdered. The lashes were blackened, the eyes
preternaturally alert and moving, but of a soft cornflower
blue. Her red hair had the texture of straw.

Then she began to speak, and her age dropped away. I
told her at once, without subterfuge, that I was looking
for Villamayor.

"Villamayor? Yes, why do you want him? What makes
you ask? I suppose you come to me as a friend of that
extraordinary man. I have known Justo for twenty-five
years, since to visit him was surely the only possible reason
for ever stopping in Santa Isabella. I first knew Justo as
a very young man. Can anyone deny his greatness?"

"I'm not going to. I want to write an article about
him."

"Ah? Well, it is high time the States discovered Villamayor, the great poet if unreadable historian. The human-
ist, the man of so many gifts. . . . I trust you realize
he does not have a high opinion of journalists?"

"Let's say I'm a free-lance writer. Where can I find him?"

The eyes of cornflower blue, sunk in that parchment visage, scrutinized me suspiciously.

"What makes you come to me? What have I to do with Villamayor?"

"He was at your ranch in California."

"Yes," she continued to measure me. "But then he left most suddenly. He has always had a tendency to vanish so. *C'est un homme fuyant.* He does not like to be followed, he cherishes his freedom. At least he pretends to want only his freedom and a solitude for reflection. But I know better. Those born to leadership fret when their energies lie unused. Villamayor is in this like my own Ted Murphree and like Eduardo Gonzales. Such men are born to act, they must enter the arena."

"I understood he was in Port-au-Prince."

"I don't know where he is," she said briskly. "But come, we will have a cocktail, and talk about your article."

She clapped her hands sharply, and a servant appeared at once. She insisted I try a rum drink in which certain peppers and herbs had been ground: a new concoction guaranteed to "heighten the perceptions." It had an odd licorice taste. We sat on the terrace with the city and the vast bay beneath us, and she watched me with her blue restless eyes. I told her how much I admired Villamayor's work.

"You are much too white," she interrupted. "You have brought the North with you. You must be exposed to the sunlight, you will bathe in my pool. As for dear Justo's poetry, yes! It is in keeping with his temperament, there is a richness and a subtlety."

"There's also a Miss Aparicio—do you know where I could find her?"

"Julieta? Oh she's with him. Justo Villamayor could pack off and leave me and Ted at the ranch. But you don't suppose he could get rid of Julieta?"

"I met her sister in New York. It was she who told me about your ranch. She says Julieta is Villamayor's 'victim.' His slave."

"María Teresa!" She laughed, the thin lips parting over yellow teeth. "María Teresa is as obsessed as Julieta, though her fantasies are not the same. It's a wonder Villamayor put up with her as long as he did."

"And he still puts up with Julieta?"

She laid a carmined bony hand on mine, as though to reprove me. Her toenails were painted too. Her dress was crisply gay and outrageous, an odd invention of the *haute couture* for tropical comfort, conceived under gray Paris skies. Yet such was her mobile and ravaged face, I noticed it only now.

"Why do you come to me with such questions? And how do I know what your purpose is? Yes: tell me what your attitude is toward the cause of freedom in the Caribbean. So many journalists are cynical, they have no feelings or attitudes."

"I sympathize with Villamayor, more or less, if I understand his position. As for The Protector . . ."

"We all hate The Protector in this house," she broke in. "It is the one thing on which we seem to agree. But I give you my word—I haven't seen Justo de Villamayor and Julieta Aparicio since they left the ranch two months ago."

"But didn't you follow them down?"

The restless eyes fixed me for a moment and moved on.

"You are an impertinent young man, I think, though I daresay we shall become good friends. Well, I can only tell you that Justo and I had our little quarrel. We both of us can be very stubborn, and he is jealous of his privacy. However, you must talk to Ted about Villamayor, you will join him for lunch. Poor Ted is bored. A man accustomed to action begins to rust. . . ."

We had another drink, and for the moment it seemed wise not to press any further questions. By now, too, the guests were beginning to emerge from their rooms or to arrive by taxi from the yacht. Buffet tables had appeared. We stood by the door facing the pool, and Barbara Swenson would interrupt her chatter to identify the guests. There was a light mulatto physician who also served as Minister of Foreign Affairs. And Auguste Bataille, the chief of the secret police, almost coal-black. A white man with the face of a rat was a special assistant to the President of the Republic. And there were those who had come from California, including a pale and bloodless couple named Miró, Nicaraguan exiles. Punctually at one (as Barbara Swenson had forewarned me) Eduardo Gonzales emerged blinking from a room that gave directly onto the pool; his lips were still moving, framing a few last sentences. For three years he had been perfecting the new constitution. Even the drunken nephew who had awakened me the night before turned up at last, in dark glasses, with one hand on his wife's shoulder as if to stake out his possession of her. It was she who had been sunbathing at the pool.

I had lunch with Ted: the faithful Edward Murphree. Barbara Swenson brought us together and left, after giving him an affectionate squeeze. It was her role in life

to keep "poor Ted" amused, and today she had turned up
me, who was curious concerning Villamayor. She must
have dreaded the day of boredom when Murphree would
pick up bag and baggage and wander off to the ends of
the earth, incorrigible at seventy. He was tall and firm in
a crumpled sack suit, and his rosy skin was still taut. He
had false teeth and his lips moved over them incessantly:
a faint trembling as of a man bursting to speak.

He too was a talker, given to shameless recollections.
Unlike Barbara Swenson he chose his words slowly, dreaming over the fleshpots and adventures of his life. He let
me know at once that he was a "military man." He had
been in the Legion even before the first war and partici-
pated in the defense of Fez under Lyautey. Thirteen years
later he returned to fight Abd-el-Krim, this time under
Lyautey's military successor Pétain. There had been other
wars, including two great ones, but it was to Morocco
his affections returned—to the great red spahis and the
chiefs of the tribes in their purple burnooses, and to
Lyautey himself in ceremonial dress of white breeches
and high boots, and splendid white plumes. And to nighttime flutes under silvered palms, and great banquets, and
the Ouled-Naïl girls.

All this poured out as he attacked his lunch: a creole
chicken with plantains and rice, and a marvelous chilled
wine.

Suddenly he turned to me.

"Have you been to Africa?"

"No."

"You must go, even though so much has been lost.
The Ouled-Naïl girls were the best dancers in the world.
And one slept with them of course." He stared at me with

innocent eyes unchanging. "You know, I could finish this African mess in two months, if they'd only give me the chance."

"If they gave you the chance?"

"I know the terrain, I know the French soldier, I know the Arab mentality. Listen: do you know what Lyautey did after every precaution had been taken, and every avenue was sealed and still it seemed certain the tribesmen would overrun us in Fez? Not soldiers or patriots, only a rabble coming into the city for loot. Well, he had a young officer on his staff, a man named Drouin, something of a poet. *'Let us have one of your poems,'* Lyautey said, *'And then a poem of Vigny.'* By Jove, that was a gesture! That was my generation of soldiering."

And so it went on: Edward Murphree was very amusing. But I did not know what my relations with the Swenson household would be. For all I knew they might vanish overnight, yacht and pilots and all. So I cut off this flood of recollection, and asked about Villamayor.

"Villamayor? Wonderful man, I am told he was once a great swordsman. But subtle! It's hard to follow what he's saying."

"Is his talk so abstract? Does he talk the way he writes?"

"It's not only that. He's slippery, you know, you can't pin him down. He won't let you agree with him."

"That sounds very French."

"In a way. Yes, Villamayor does have his French side. His skepticism, his irony. But tell me this—why should a man with all that money and all that charm spend his time scribbling? I stopped writing long ago so I'd have time to live."

I explained that I hoped to "do" an article that would

sum up both Villamayor and his work. And there was this succession of disappearances. . . .

"So you want to talk to Villamayor?" He shook his head. The smooth face was very pink in the half-shade of the terrace overlooking a burning sea. "Well, Mr. Clive, I can only wish you luck."

"You mean he'll be so hard to find?"

"I mean he won't talk to journalists. He's a bit nutty about his privacy."

"But you know where he is?"

"I have an idea, all right. He's somewhere on the south coast. But why he cut off and left the road before Anse de Corail, and what happened to the car. . . ."

He took a letter from his pocket and quickly sketched a map of Haiti on the back of it: the wide open skeletal jaws enclosing a gulf. He drew a jagged line from Port-au-Prince to Anse de Corail on the south coast. A "road," though often enough only a riverbed. He dotted in a few coastal villages, and ran a finger along the main stretch of southern coast: a wavy line covering seventy or eighty miles.

"He'll be somewhere in here," Murphree went on. "And somewhere near a beach. Of course you can find him, though it won't be as easy as it looks. There are dozens of villages on that coast but no roads between them. You can fly over them, but there's no place to land. The only road is this one, from Port-au-Prince to Anse de Corail. And they broke away from it sometime before reaching Anse."

"Who are 'they'? At the hotel they mentioned two women."

"The good Lord knows. . . . All this happened before

we got down here, and no one tells you the same story. Julieta Aparicio, of course, his ball and chain for life. But there was also a mad girl of sixteen or so called 'La Atrevida.' You know what that means? The 'daring girl.' . . . Villamayor simply picked her up, or she picked up him. And then there was the driver of the car. Ask his wife whether there was anyone else along! She even came screaming to us. We know Villamayor rented this car to take them to Anse de Corail and the car never got there and the driver never came back. But he sent back a message word-of-mouth. He had gone to work for 'Monsieur de Villamayor.' Imagine that, even a black driver following him, abandoning his car I guess and abandoning his wife in Port-au-Prince. It's just the kind of thing Villamayor likes to do. Pick up and vanish, with a few disciples trailing him."

I thought of Julieta's message to María Teresa: the hermetic single sentence.

"He has to have disciples?"

"He thinks he's trying to get rid of them. But there's something about the man that attracts drifters and fanatics. This little orphan 'La Atrevida' thinks God gave her a gift of tongues for the purpose of political rabble-rousing. And poor Villamayor—who's got at least these two gals with him and also this black driver. What Villamayor said he wanted, up at the ranch, was 'solitude'!"

Far beneath us Barbara Swenson's yacht was a white speck on the crescent bay. And here at the Villa Sarcey were the foolish and the corrupt a rich woman could collect by merely raising a finger. It occurred to me that Villamayor had vanished into his new solitude chiefly to escape her . . . and all the others with their visions of political upheaval. He must have known she would follow him. Perhaps he felt a sharp spasm of disgust, then the whimsical notion to beat off into a wilderness where no Barbara Swensons could follow him, no yachts or planes.

"Don't you think it's Miss Swenson he's running away from? She said something about a disagreement."

"There was a certain amount of tension at the ranch. They were talking politics all the time up there, especially Gonzales. Barbara has great plans for Santa Isabella, you know. But I'm not sure what she had in mind for Villa-mayor. I'm not one for politics, Mr. Clive. I'm a military man."

My interpretation of the affair struck me as more and more plausible: the reluctant Villamayor, who had had his fill of conspiracy and dissent, after almost losing his life . . . and the mad Barbara Swenson in pursuit, volunteering to finance an invasion.

"Is this young girl his mistress?"

" 'La Atrevida'? Oh I don't think so. Not that Villa-mayor won't always have a harem, whether he wants one or not! Some people say she thrust herself on him because she wanted to stir him up. This child has spent her life among political exiles planning revolutions; it's all she can talk about. They say one of her speeches will curl your hair."

"So why did Villamayor take her? If he's sick of politics. . . ."

Edward Murphree shrugged his shoulders.

"I've never even seen her. All this happened before we got here. But I imagine he felt she needed him."

"I see. She had the necessary screws loose, so he couldn't turn her away. Now tell me—how am I going to find him?"

Murphree looked at me with the disgust of the military man.

"Oh ask around. You might try the wife of that driver. The natives have ways of communicating."

"You're not interested yourself?"

"In Villamayor? Oh, by all means. I like him very much. And if you want to get up a party to track him down. . . . Yes, why not? But not today or tomorrow. I want to see the cockfights."

THE next morning he did, though, take me for a flight over that wild hinterland and southern coast, in a small rented plane. It would be amusing, he thought, to discover the place of retreat from the air. And not too difficult, since Villamayor and his female companions would certainly settle near one of the good beaches, and since livable houses were so few. The tiny plane climbed away from Port-au-Prince, coughing and rocking, and followed the Anse de Corail road. Beneath us long lines of women toiled inland with their baskets high overhead. The road cut through a divide in the first baked mountains, then disappeared into a pebbly stream bordered by palms. A camionette was immobilized in the water with a swarm of pygmy figures around it. After that came an orchidean jungle, the area of the great rainfalls. Wild fruit glowed through the green. We looked for paths branching east and west, and in vain for the glitter of an abandoned car.

Then we were over Anse de Corail and the sea. The town was even further declined than Port-au-Prince from the old prosperous times. A wide main street ran down to the banana wharf and coffee warehouse; collapsed power lines formed a center strip. There was a desultory native market where tiny vendors dozed over their wares. The shore, next to the wharf and half-dismantled bandstand, served as a garbage dump, with a sinkhole for sewers long since extinguished. The open conduits were bleached in the sun. Antediluvian, a small tramp steamer lay against the wharf, a ship of not more than three hundred tons, as though forgotten from the great days of coffee. There were many Negroes and a few white men lounging on the deck, the only white men we saw.

It was a fine ride, though on it we discovered nothing. At a lower price than fifty dollars an hour I would have been glad to push on to the frontier of Santa Isabella. As it was, we cruised some sixty miles of that coast at two and three hundred feet. The pilot banked and circled over each village until the one street or clearing was filled with black faces looking anxiously up. Once we came upon a group of women bathing in a shallow stream. Their black bodies shone, and at Edward Murphree's command the pilot circled lower and lower until they ran for cover.

There were a few plantation houses too, empty shells of their ancient elegance, with the formal gardens and orchards run to wilderness. Out of one dark window a tree grew and curved upward to follow the wall. Then we came in low over Caye Thomonde: a ghost city sinking into the sea. Its one wharf had already crumpled into the water and its houses were built out of ruins. They emerged from the shells of larger houses like rickety weeds. This was the "little Trianon" of the Colonial days, sacked and burned in revolution after revolution, and in modern times ruined by hurricane and fire. Fantastic flowers grew from the gutted shells, frangipani and flamboyant trees over the husks of foundations, and red immortelle in wild backyards. The tiny white cathedral was deserted and all its windows gone; birds flew out from the nave at the sound of our plane. Only a few hundred people still lived in Caye Thomonde, and the half-dozen we saw looked languid and sick. There was no sign of Villamayor.

On the way back we passed over a wilderness of green running down to brackish shores. Then we went up over the mountains and a high inland jungle where, our pilot said, few white men had ever been. Would this, I wondered, be the last refuge of Villamayor, who liked so perversely to vanish? From one sunken clearing tiny black figures stared up at us as from a deep pool of time.

So the fifty dollars had been wasted, and the prospect of soon finding Villamayor seemed much poorer. But that same afternoon Barbara Swenson came to the hotel—and without Murphree—to tell me where they were, Villamayor and his "friends." Auguste Bataille had, at her demand, found out at once. They had rented a house near the shore, some three miles west of Caye Thomonde, and were now engaged in repairing it. A number of impoverished natives had been put to work.

"It was good of you to bother," I said.

Barbara Swenson stood before me in a pink cocktail dress shaped like a church bell. The dress swept out from her bare freckled shoulders and ancient throat. She had raced up to the hotel veranda with the ease of a girl.

"It is for my own sake," she said. "I clutch at you as at a straw. Listen: I have not told Ted of this visit. I do not want him to accompany you." She gave me a ravaged conspiratorial smile. "The way must first be prepared.

Moreover you will be, for Justo, a new face. Perhaps you can shake him out of his lethargy."

"His lethargy?"

"It is a disgrace for such a man to sink into retirement. And not fifty years old! You say you want to write an article about him. Well—tell me why the great world of public affairs should be deprived of a man with his capacity to elicit unswerving and fanatic loyalties? Justo de Villamayor is a man of great humanity."

A white parchment hand and carmined nails flew out; I suddenly felt myself being propelled toward the end of the long empty veranda, where we could not be overheard.

"Listen carefully," she whispered. "Villamayor is the only possible leader of a free and regenerated Santa Isabella. In any event, he is the only one Eduardo Gonzales will trust. Two pure spirits; all the rest are corrupt."

"Do you want me to say that in my article?"

"I want you to like Justo de Villamayor. I want you to help rescue him from debilitation and collapsed will. What an opportunity for you both! You are writing for an American magazine whose words will reach millions. That would be, for Villamayor, an extreme challenge to collect his energies. I speak to you frankly. My one desire is to have Villamayor ready to step in, when the great day comes."

I felt a strong impulse to laugh.

"So you think a total stranger can walk in and urge Villamayor to give up his precious solitude so as to lead a revolution or invasion or whatever it is you have in mind. Remember he's not supposed to like journalists."

She did not answer at once. She lit a cigarette which at once gave off a sweet medicinal odor.

"I said nothing about an invasion. But if there were an invasion, well prepared and well financed—what do you think of the chances for success?"

"Not very much. Why don't you try something easier? Say pick on a smaller country?"

She turned from me angrily, smoking her queer cigarette.

"You are flippant? You've been listening to stories about me? Well, I am not a meddler for my own amusement. How better could a rich woman of democratic sentiments spend her money? The people of Santa Isabella cry out for liberation. For twenty years they have been deprived of the barest liberties. They have waited. And for once there exist two exile figures neither venal nor corrupt: Eduardo Gonzales, Justo de Villamayor."

She fell easily, sank as it were, into the Latinate rhythms of political proclamation. But her tone brought out all my skepticism:

"Do you think they remember them—the liberties? Twenty years is a long time."

"They will remember Villamayor." She stared past me entranced by her vision. "You say you want to write an article about that great man. Do you write only for money? Are you too cynical to want to help? You could be one of those chosen to prepare public opinion for the great day, especially in the States. Of course I don't want you to say anything about military operations, *ça va sans dire*. Besides, none have been planned. We are still in the realm of ideas, we still grope for unity."

I found myself, under the blue fanatic gaze, backed against the railing at the end of the veranda.

"Why don't you want Edward Murphree to go with me?"

III

"Because I do not want them to quarrel, Justo and Ted. There must be nothing premature. Justo de Villamayor becomes irritated by premature specific proposals. The time isn't ripe."

"Ripe?"

Barbara Swenson studied me with her ageless eyes, from which all discretion had fled.

"For action, of course. Because they must come at last: the military operations. There will be no fiasco this time, there will be good DC-3's, I have the necessary funds. And when that time for action comes . . . I want my Ted to have his share. Yes, he must be allowed to take his place, I shall insist upon it. I can tell you in confidence that very few men know as much as Edward Murphree about guerrilla operations and the use of rough terrain. He too has his abilities. . . . And don't you see the tragedy of these men languishing with their capacities unused? Here is Ted wasting his days, and here too is the pure spirit Eduardo Gonzales. And over there is Justo de Villamayor. Surely deep in his heart Villamayor must feel ashamed to withdraw. What is a man of that intelligence and power doing sunk off on a plantation with two such women? It is a tragic waste of the political intellect."

She broke off suddenly, and gripped my arm. The blue eyes darted.

"But you'll see when you talk to Villamayor! You too will want to bring him out."

so I would go to him the following day. I arranged with Bernard for a car and driver, who would take me more than halfway to Caye Thomonde. The driver in turn could find horses and a guide for the remainder of the trip. I was more curious than ever to see Villamayor and his queer household, and anxious to be on my way. I felt I could overcome his distrust of journalists. I was not, after all, the average prying newspaperman, and I had more than glanced through his books. I even hoped to be his guest for a few days, and come to know him fairly well.

But meanwhile I could not help feeling uneasy, guilty even, about poor Manuel Andrada; in a way I had deserted him. He had not, in his incorrigible way, turned up hopefully at my hotel . . . which could only mean that he was being detained. And after forty-eight hours in Haiti I had heard enough about the brutalities of the secret police to be apprehensive for him. In Santa Isabella the political deviant disappears or is found dead, the victim of a trumped-up accident; the methods of repression are decisive. But those of Haiti, where mild torture often accompanies questioning, are bad enough.

So I set out to find Andrada, shortly after Barbara Swenson left me, and at the airport I was referred to the Pension Beau Rêve. I found it at the end of a foul alley in the slums behind the Cathedral: a gloomy rotting villa and a small garden run wild. The proprietor consulted briefly with the taxi driver, then showed me Andrada's room, and the bed that had not been slept in. It was such a room as only he could have discovered, pervaded by an odor of cheap cigars and ancient sweat, possibly by an odor of stale excrement from the corridor. Above the bed the face of The Protector glowered in the darkening afternoon, and magazines lay in disarray on the floor. On his first night, it appears, "the tourist Manuel Andrada" had got very drunk in his room and made disturbing, inexplicable noises. Then all yesterday he had acted very confused. The proprietor had the impression that Andrada was not fleeing the police but seeking them. Time and again he had rushed out into the city—after asking directions for this or that government office or *bureau de renseignements*—only to return in an hour or so, sweating heavily and with a baffled expression. He wanted to confer with "the authorities" who were concerned with missing persons, foreigners especially. By evening on that second day, however, he was asking different questions. He had begun to speak vaguely of a need for sexual activity. *Les divertissements sexuels, le plaisir. . . .* The proprietor (when he finally understood Andrada's abominable French) referred him to the Ville des Fleurs, where an abundance of prostitutes would be found. That had been before dinner; Andrada had never returned.

This place of pleasure had been, I surmised, but a way station on the road to jail. For Andrada, already suspect because of the portrait, would have asked too many clumsy questions. Nevertheless I found another taxi—this one operated by a lean and nervous Negro with a bandaged ear—and went out to the Ville des Fleurs. The cluster of gingerbread houses and thatched wattled huts were sinking into weeds and wild grass. The outside walls were decorated with primitive drawings, but the violent red and yellow paint was peeling and flaking away. Women crouched in the doorways and made tired perfunctory appeals; others lay sprawled against the inside walls, creatures of every dark shade and race. They murmured in the gloom. Even the few white women in their silks had begun to adopt the peculiar Haitian posture, with the legs wide apart and bare to the thigh, but with the dress tucked decently between them. I could imagine what a swath little Andrada must have cut in this small city of drowsing women, with his burning purpose and his lusts.

But none of the girls would admit having seen him. I went into hut after hut, stepping from dappled sunlight into the shadowy perfumed cubicles with their odors of vice. I described, gesturing, the coarse brown suit, and I indicated with my finger that historic scar cutting down through an eyebrow. There was much giggling, and sometimes a rapid exchange of Creole between two of the girls, out of which I detected a reiterated name: *Odile*. Who, I asked at last, was Odile? Where was she? But the girls only shook their heads, and invited me to stay. My lean driver followed me from hut to hut, like a black wraith, thrusting in his brigand face with its bandaged ear, listening to my questions. I had almost reached the last hut when he volunteered his information.

"I know where he is, your friend. All the drivers know."

"You do? Why didn't you say so?"

"You did not ask me. You spoke only to the girls. Also the information is confidential. You will never find him yourself."

"How much will you take me there for?"

"I take you for four dollars."

And four dollars it was to be: for the short jolting ride back to the center of town, where I did in fact find Manuel Andrada, in a large one-room shack just off the Grande Rue, and not two hundred yards from the Pension Beau Rêve. His place of hidden joys, wedged between small shops with chalked signs, might have been the bare *atelier* and dwelling of a seamstress or cobbler, except for the soldier smoking lazily outside. He sat against the wall with a rusty rifle across his lap. And my first impression (as I looked in from the broken sidewalk) was of a dark

kennel in which small black shapes seethed. Then I detected the faint shine and tinkle of bracelets, luminous
as animal eyes. There was an odor of bodies and another
odor of coffee, emanating from that breathing dark. At
my knock, with the door already ajar and the last daylight
falling on a black outstretched leg, someone lit a gas lamp.
Then I saw Andrada. He was lying on a mattress in the
very center of the room, awake but satiate and exhausted,
his face blanched and remote. His head was propped up
on the folded winter coat that now served him as a pillow.
And the first black shapes I saw were not the one or even
several girls I had expected but a brood of small naked
infants, playing on the sawdust floor. Then I saw other,
larger shapes against the walls and in the farthest corner
a wrinkled toothless crone with a pipe, who mumbled
low protests. The room was full of Negroes sitting against
the walls.

"I knew you would come!" Andrada pulled himself up
on one elbow: grateful, trying to rise or at least turn to
face me. But he was exhausted, overwhelmed, ravaged:
sucked and drained of his lusts. "You must get me out of
here, Nicholas Clive. I have my mission to accomplish!
And The Protector waits. Moreover, I need a priest who
knows Spanish. . . ."

"What's the matter with you? Can't you get up?"

"I'm too tired. Besides, I think I'm a prisoner. Isn't that
soldier still out there? I don't understand these people at
all. And they don't understand my French. There has been
a terrible misunderstanding. I had of course expected privacy."

I went outside to speak to the policeman, who told me
Andrada was free to go where he pleased. But he would,
of necessity, be followed, since he had the aspect of one

who made trouble. Then I went back inside and consulted one of the anonymous lean black shapes lounging against the wall. He told me they all looked upon Andrada as their "patron." Later still (having listened to Andrada's own account and even to the *placée* herself, as she liked to call herself, the chosen one, tall and black and African) I could begin to see what had happened. And I could imagine the rest: beginning with Andrada's delighted discovery of the girl Odile, out at the Ville des Fleurs, and their wordless instant communication as he knelt at her feet. Then the scandalized watching of the other ones, the languid and silken girls. It had been love at first sight, a recognition by Andrada of his destined one. So without pause he had leaped upon her muttering Spanish endearments while one attendant girl feverishly cranked the phonograph and another went out for rum. His desire must have been appalling. And he was in no mood to delay the consummation of his love, after his weeks of frustration; he ripped off the precious suit.

Later, sodden wth rum and pleasure, happily indifferent to the even larger ring of girls who now watched in astonishment and envy, Andrada found himself the center of some ceremonial rite. For he had uttered, among the Spanish endearments, certain fatal words overheard during his few days in Haiti. *"Moi!"* The pleased incredulous girl, tall and black, had pointed first to herself, then to the recumbent and dazed Andrada. Now it was her turn to kneel by his feet. Meanwhile, there was more rum; the black silken shapes came and went. At last there was an old Negro in spectacles who squatted beside them lettering words on a piece of paper bordered with flowers: apparently a public scribe. Andrada happily signed this document. An hour later he found himself carried in a drunken procession of four taxis into town and to the one-room shack . . . from which brothers and sisters and parents and relatives were quickly evicted, after a hasty glance at the flowered document, carrying with them certain meager possessions. In the extremity of Andrada's drunkenness there was little opportunity for the niceties. Still, he had entered unknowingly into the most venerable of Haitian institutions, descended from the old slave days. He now had his own established mistress to be cherished and loved. He fell asleep to the low beating of a drum, consoling as a heartbeat, and to the intense gratitude of the chosen one, swarming over him in the odorous dark. In his dreams his bones seemed to crack, under the wrench and groan of her thighs.

He had not understood all this at the time, or even the next morning when he awoke to a milky light entering their dusk, and to the cries of the hawkers in the street. The girl brought him coffee. But he did understand that he had entered into some kind of arrangement with her, and was expected to remain in the shack, to live there in fact. She moved proudly around the room, pointing to the three chairs and cupboard and to the calendars and postcards on the walls. And it did seem adequate, the room, now that the family had departed. It was larger than his room at the Pension Beau Rêve, where the poster of The Protector had been left neatly hung on the wall. *Why not?* he wondered, as she came to him with coffee, cradling the cup in her hands. She knelt beside him and caressed him as he drank. Her mouth was only inches from his ear. It was the sort of thing he had awaited all his life; they made love again.

The next time he awoke, the girl was sitting upon the mattress beside him, and a tall thin Negro of perhaps thirty was rummaging in the small cupboard at their feet. He understood just enough French to make out that this was a brother, presumably returned to fetch certain articles left behind in the hasty exodus of the night before. Or was he bringing gifts? The intruder, who went on talking to the sister in a soft accusing voice, seemed to be folding carefully several shirts and placing them in a drawer. Andrada (staggering slightly, still sodden with the rum and pleasure) went to the front door, and saw the soldier lounged beside it, the rusty gun across his lap. The soldier touched the gun, and barked a command; Andrada went back inside. He was astonished to see the brother now lying against the wall: breathing heavily, already half asleep. The girl Odile (for he suddenly remembered the name forgotten during the night's holocaust) seemed untroubled by her brother's presence; she drew Andrada down beside her. The murmuring began again.

At one point during this episode of their lovemaking an old woman crept into the room, smoking a pipe. Andrada was flat on his back by now, tired and bruised and helpless, imprisoned by the girl's still raging limbs. Turning his head as for a gasping breath he noticed first the odor of tobacco rich as steaming dung, then saw the old woman moving stealthily along the wall toward a back corner, the witch's gown hanging in rags over fleshless bones, old and bent as time. She let herself down into that corner as by long habit, turning and turning like a dog before settling on her haunches. She nodded to him with a toothless grin, and resumed her muttering. Andrada was outraged. He tried in vain to summon his spent strength and throw off his chosen burden. The most he could make

of Odile's explanation was that the old woman, the grandmother, would be "glad to help."

It must have been noon at least when he awoke again.
A white blazing sunlight streamed through the open door
onto himself and the sawdust-covered floor. Friendly
passersby glanced in. The brother still slept without
stirring, but the old witch was gone. In a corner the girl
Odile was busily engaged in bathing her body from a
small pail: a beautiful crouching body, glistening in the
heat. There was also in the room, he noted, three black
infants aged perhaps two to four, also naked and impos-
sibly identical in shape and feature, playing quietly in a
corner. Still another man watched from a far corner,
grinning, the white teeth ghostly in that hot gloom. Another "brother." And there were presently three or four
more. Andrada was horribly embarrassed. *"I found myself
surrounded, Nicholas Clive. And of course I expected privacy."* The family which had moved out so precipitously
the night before had lost no time in returning. This time
when he went to the front door the soldier was still there,
but barefoot. He too intended to remain indefinitely. In
the middle of the sidewalk, huddled over a brazier resting
on three stones and stirring its doubtful contents, was the
old woman ancient and toothless, the crone, grandmother
and matriarch of the tribe. She would prepare the ceremonial banquet—the *griot* or conch stew or other deli-
cacy, purchased on the newly established credit of Andrada's future largesse—before returning to the appointed
corner of the room where she dwelt and had her being,
and mumbled her obscure complaints.

It was at about this time, he said—less than fifteen
hours after the onset of his happiness—that Andrada be-

gan to wonder when I would discover and rescue him. He knew I would not "abandon" him completely.

But back at the Pension Beau Rêve, lying exhausted under The Protector's portrait, he was terribly ashamed.

"This is the third day, Nicholas Clive, and I have accomplished nothing at all. The police officials would not speak to me. The black dogs. . . . Again and again I sat in anterooms, only to be refused admittance. And now I am too ashamed to confront those in the Consulate of Santa Isabella who might easily help me. I have squandered monies that belong to the nation. I deserve to be punished."

"Well, if this is what 'gratification' does for you . . ."

"I know, Nicholas Clive, I know. But tomorrow is another day. Tell me what you have discovered."

I was not going to reveal my plans, of course, not even the presence in Port-au-Prince of Barbara Swenson and her revolutionary ménage. Let him make his own discoveries. . . . I watched him lying there under The Protector's stern paternal gaze. It was hard to conceive of this foolish creature as a menace to anyone. And yet I would have liked to know, before facing Villamayor, how far Andrada thought he was willing to go. The "representative of the Library. . . ." I went over to the one chest of drawers and pulled open the top one. It was empty except for a scatter of magazines.

"Have you bought a gun down here?"

"It was impossible. I have been followed everywhere. Furthermore, I don't need a revolver. That was more or less a formality. . . ."

I went over to the bed and sat by his feet; the room was getting very dark.

"What if we did find Villamayor?"

"He is here?"

"No. I'm asking what you'd do if we did find him. I don't want to see him carved up or strangled with a fish-line."

"You have no right to say that, Nicholas Clive. I want only to buy the manuscripts."

"And if he refuses?"

"He will not refuse, Nicholas Clive. I will appeal to his patriotism. Moreover, he will be in need of funds. Any writer would be happy to be honored by the National Library in spite of political disagreements. But first we must find him."

"Yes, that's right," I said. "First we must find him."

I LEFT Port-au-Prince by nine o'clock the next morning, but the trip took all day: the slow interminable climb between the baked mountains past files of women with baskets on their heads, already returning from market; then the stream and the ruined forest, with the heat beating inhumanly, and the beginning of the long descent. We were stuck twice during the half-mile where the road was simply the bed of a shallow stream, and once for repairs, the driver toiling for an hour over a fuel pump long past its prime. So it was already early afternoon when we came to the car rented by Villamayor: not hidden in brush but at the side of the road, encircled by a large number of gesticulating Negroes. The *chef de section* (hired from his ordinary duties to guard the car) with his nickel badge and threadbare denim uniform, the seat of local authority, was sitting on the hood with a carbine across his knees.

Here I had to wait almost two hours for a horse and

guide, in the dense hot shade, while small groups of children watched me from a distance. Brilliant insects and dragonflies whirred in the thick screen of branches; birds clamored in the trees. Then the promised guide had come, and we descended through the orchidean jungle and the steaming rain forests into a deepening stillness. We passed through two villages which seemed almost deserted: abandoned to skeletal invalids and a few infants in the doorways of the huts, their bellies tight as drums. They watched us with the listlessness of the starving and the sick. The guide walked malevolently ahead. Perhaps he was persuaded I would contrive, somehow, to cheat him of his fee? He walked evenly, never looking back, not responding to my questions. His head seemed very high and narrow above the body clothed in rags. Now and then, without forewarning, he squatted at the side of the path to rest, and grunted commands to my horse.

Then at the turn of a hillside the sea lay far beneath us and we began to descend through once-cultivated land, now gone into wilderness. It was just possible to see the ruined plantings of coffee overgrown and the canebrakes run wild beside the gutted remains of a house. The sun had vanished over the whole western mountain range. We were pushing deeper and deeper into a great green crescent of shadow broken by stretches of brown eroded land. And once miles ahead we saw Caye Thomonde, its small white cathedral and cluster of houses, from this distance looking unruined.

The last mile was again through a wilderness of olive green. The wood that remained was too poor and too tangled to cut. It was a holocaust of tropical overgrowth glittering with fruit. In the growing darkness the jungle on each side of us was steaming and pestilential.

And then we had arrived. We came suddenly into a clearing to find fifteen or twenty Negroes swarming over what had once been a formal French garden, hacking away at the creepers and weeds. Ahead of us the evenly-spaced stumps of what had been a fine alley of trees led to the house, high and gloomy in the dusk. A balcony ran the length of the second floor above the veranda. A fine front stairway had been chopped away or ruined by termites or flood, some time in the dim past, but the house remained miraculously intact.

In the wide door a man in white trousers and shirt awaited me, obviously Villamayor. Even from a hundred feet away I could detect the alert intelligence of his face, together with its odd wrenched distortion.

4

"*SI HUYENDO de la cruz vas, otra peor encontrarás.*"
Thus Julieta Aparicio would remark more than once, of
the tall man who stood on the darkening porch, at the end
of that ruined alley. *You are sure to find a heavier cross,
if you flee the one you bear!* The lined alert face was that
of a man who persuaded himself to escape responsibilities,
yet always found himself thrust upon new ones. Justo
Vicente de Villamayor. He awaited me gravely, with the
public man's weary courtesy, no doubt amused by my
awkward progress on that small horse, still preceded by
the threadbare guide. "*So,*" he must have thought, "*one
more invasion of privacy*"—who had greeted enough
intruding strangers in his time, and nervous disciples
seeking autographs or advice. Villamayor stood there
straight and watchful, then came down from the porch.
He kept a slight formality in spite of the white trousers
and sport shirt open at the neck, and the worn white
tennis shoes. The twisted face, with the head faintly
cocked and the left cheek bulging, gave an impression of
quizzical humor, also of power. And at once I thought
of that small statue in the city of browning palms, which
I had seen only in photographs. There was no resemblance
between that remote scornful scholar and the intense man
before me, with his black, black eyes.

He addressed me in English:

"I have been expecting you for more than an hour. Welcome!"

"Expecting me?"

"Inevitably. Half the population of the district preceded you down the trail to announce your coming. Doubtless they are alarmed by this invasion of so many *blancs*. You are the fourth. At the present rate they will find themselves outnumbered."

The voice was sinuous and playfully ironic.

"I saw hardly anyone."

"They are polite and discreet, it is the best way to resist an invasion. They do not know what to make of you."

Villamayor said this with a faint smile. Yet his forehead was drawn up in intense and precise lines: lines of extraordinary definiteness. He was watching me, I thought, very closely. Then I realized that there were other watchers behind him: a huge troubled Negro presence in the shadowy hall, and, at a dark window just to the left of the door, two porcelain female faces, bodiless and of an identical anxiety. Theirs might have been the same scrutinizing face imprisoned in a mirror discolored by age. They caught my eyes and moved away. Then I saw they could have been mother and daughter, say thirty-six and sixteen: the poor captive Julieta, of course, and the fabled Consuela, who called herself "La Atrevida." The Negro still looking out at us would be the chauffeur Belesprit, who had left his wife at Villamayor's beck and call.

My intrusion seemed horribly gauche. I announced, awkwardly, my name. Villamayor bowed.

"I assume you know mine. You are identical with the journalist who has asked questions in Port-au-Prince?"

"Journalist?" I abandoned then and there all notions

of subterfuge: Villamayor's dark gaze would see through anyone. I was appalled, too, by the speed with which news traveled in a land without telephones. "I'm not a journalist, really. But I do want to write an article. An essay."

"About Villamayor?" He raised both hands in the French manner. "But you come much too late! *Il est mort, ce Villamayor-là.* However, you must come in, you will need refreshment after your long ride."

He ushered me into the long dusky room where those ghostly female faces had been. The floorboards were rotten, and all the paneling had been removed from one wall. There was another blank and darkened place where a mirror or great painting must have hung. In the center of the room two kitchen tables had been placed together. This is where we sat.

"I will tell you about this house, an incredible and historic *trouvaille!*"—and clapping his hands once Villamayor called for drinks with the pleasant bantering voice one might use with a lifelong servant or indulged child, flinging the soft command into the darkness. "I will offer you also a remarkable concoction, invented by my friend Belesprit. Then you can write about this house, rather than about me." And without pause he gave me a conjectural history of the house: for some reason not burned by the last outraged slaves, resistant to forest fire and hurricane and unravaged by the many insurrections. It was a house to which several wealthy merchant families of Port-au-Prince had retired half-a-century since, at the onslaught of plague. The very longevity of the house, stretching back into bloody and prehistoric times, had aroused, in the natives of the region, a superstitious respect.

The Negro Belesprit shuffled out of the gloom, and put

down a tray with two tall glasses: a punch richly gar-
landed with fruit. He lit a candle, and bending over revealed magnificent eyes and skin drawn glossily over the
cheekbones. Villamayor introduced us, then spoke to him
very rapidly in Franch. It was an invitation to join us.
Belesprit nodded gravely and sat down. I caught the word
maître, spoken not as servant to kindly patron but as
disciple to master, even as neophyte poet to great one.

In the thin candlelight Villamayor's twisted face was
alert and amused.

"So! You have made this long and hot journey in vain?
You wished to interview Villamayor, who is already in a
manner of speaking dead. I am even ready once again to
abandon the name, which has carried me through so many
weary times. And the personality too is all but extinguished. So you see there would be nothing to write
about."

I remarked that I had heard, in New York, of a rechris-
tened "Luis Hernández." Villamayor frowned.

"I must find a better name than that, a stronger name
corresponding to new desires. What would you suggest?"

"Why not a French name? I've been told you are very
French."

"And go back to France? I often wonder why I do not.
And why not the rest of us—who could be so comfortable
in Paris or Rome? We hover near the decaying recumbent
body of the homeland, boring everybody with our squab-
bles and our indignations. Everyone would be happier if
we emigrated *en masse* to Paris! Why do we remain so
near?"

"The Protector won't live forever."

"Are you quite sure?" Villamayor sat back in his chair.
A dark energy vanished from his eyes, as though drawn

up into the brooding mind for secret consultation. *"Voyons,* I do not want to be discourteous. Furthermore it is much too late for you to return to Port-au-Prince or to find a room in Caye Thomonde. So you must stay here tonight. Yes, it will be a pleasure to have you with us. But you must believe me: the late Villamayor is no longer of public interest, and is unworthy of an article. I have utterly withdrawn from politics."

I was dismally aware, watching him, of the inequalities of the combat, as I had not been when "Villamayor" was only a name. How indeed could this refined and subtle man, this evasive intellectual, confront The Protector's coarse violence? It was even hard to believe the historic and recorded energies: the unexpected intrusion of a critical voice, attacking a government decree; the twisted face at the Cabinet table, and the voice talking a little desperately. . . . And the rest of the Twenty-Six Days.

"I'll respect your wishes. Of course. But if I don't write an article, someone else will."

Villamayor shrugged his shoulders.

"I have already risen twice from the grave. Surely that is enough. A third time would be found annoying to the public. They would say, *'He exaggerates, this imperishable Villamayor.'* "

I found myself both irritated and drawn by these playful ironies. I remarked that the disappearances could be annoying too.

"People want to know whether you're being persecuted or not. Committees publish letters of protest. Wasn't there even a Committee formed in your name, to investigate the second disappearance? You are, after all, a symbol."

"*A qui le dîtes vous?* But believe me I am sick to death of committees, as I am surfeited with the discourse of visionaries. I want to leave all that behind. In fact, I have left it behind already. Must I be goaded the rest of my life for twenty-six days of indiscretion? I did what I could and I failed. So be it. I am not a Minister of Education by birthright, nor even a revolutionary. Now I want my freedom."

"Your freedom to write?"

"Simply my freedom. If I choose to write, very well. And if I choose only to live? That also is worthwhile!" He turned up his hands apologetically. "You must forgive me my perversities. For the moment I write only for myself, I do not want to talk about my work. It is so strange not to have to think of censorship, nor even of a public! I am not ashamed of what I have written in the past, but now it is done and dead. It was written by another man. Ashes. Let me confess I am possessed by the dream of freedom, the old old dream. I want to climb out of the past."

Into the stillness that followed this declaration Belesprit unexpectedly broke in.

"It is impossible. Many people try every day. One's feet catch in the rungs."

Villamayor looked at him attentively: at the black melancholy face and fine remote eyes. He had been summoned from his personal musings by this authentic voice with its accent of need. I think Villamayor must have always discovered his disciples thus: by drawing out the telling word or cry, and by responding to it in the right tone.

For the moment he made no reply. Instead he remarked in a distracted way that I would need a room for the night. Then suddenly he leaned forward and put a hand on Belesprit's wrist:

"You spoke as one weary or ashamed. What is it, my friend, that catches at your feet? Guilt? The memory of irreversible events? Listen to me as one who knows. There is no reason to be ashamed, there is no obligation to punish oneself. The past is past, the future is not yet here. It is in this moment of freedom we must choose to be."

Belesprit watched him intently.

"That's easy enough to say."

"Of course. But I think it can also be done. I have done it myself. So too can you!" He stood up abruptly and limped across the room. Half a dozen tin masks hung on the wall in a row: demons and gods almost invisible in the dusk. Villamayor lit a match and held it above one of the masks, then above another. The first showed a grimace of savage joy; the second an extreme placidity, the occult stillness of trance.

"I made these yesterday and the day before. It is the crude work any poor artisan could do. And yet for me they were a new experience and discovery. I could hardly recognize the personality they revealed. And now I ask myself: *Am I that happy monster? What will he do?* I await these revelations with an indecent curiosity. And all the new pleasures that await any man willing to receive them! Yes, my friend: your life in Port-au-Prince is behind you, and all your degradations. It is time to begin again."

And that was my meeting with Villamayor: corrupter and *homme fuyant,* devil or predestined saint . . . and appointed quarry of Manuel Andrada. Villamayor the

antagonist, the too-human adversary, the collector of ec-
centrics against his will. The slippery and reasonable man,
attracting to himself the violently irrational. . . . Should
I say "quarry"—of a man who more than once in the
past had embraced his would-be destroyers? Which indeed had been the unexpected pursuer in those enigmatic
incidents of flight or disappearance, and which the astonished pursued? Villamayor was the kind of man to meditate sympathetically on the motives of his kidnapper in
the very midst of the abduction; his detachment was almost a disease. Anything seemed possible of this man, for
him . . . whose poems learned by heart had been an
important moment in the education of so many Santa
Isabella schoolboys, and even of Manuel Andrada.

That was our first meeting, only a few months ago.
Now across this intervening time I still see the tall figure
in white, moving through the shadows of the house, and
the dark sympathetic face askew. And I see too that sudden gesture of encouragement to Belesprit: the hand on
the wrist. In their short time together Villamayor had
already led Belesprit some distance from the despair of his
life in Port-au-Prince, and from his snarling vicious wife.
Belesprit later told me he had been sinking back into the
abyss, a few more steps each day; before long he would
have been begging from tourists. Then Villamayor had
come, who claimed to want only his own freedom and
selfish independence. He had come, spoken, tempted.
And so I suspect it had been for the others in that strange
household, who had been touched by the corrupting
hand: for the fiery Consuela (*dit* La Atrevida) and for
the fiery Julieta, certainly for the bland and dreaming
Ezile, whom I had not yet seen. She too had left home

and at least parents at the mere sight and hearing of Villamayor; and had refused to go back: an acquisition of these last weeks, a native of the district.

We met them all at dinner that evening in the long bare room. The women who had looked out on us with such pale anxiety came in together, no longer ghostly mother and child but opponents rather, in the quiet fury of their missions—the one seeing Villamayor's destiny in revolution, the other in conversion and rapid elevation within the church. Julieta I already knew by sight, since I knew her sister María Teresa. She had the same angry patrician nose and dedicated gaze and the same black hair in spinsterish and shining coils. Only a slender golden chain, vanishing beneath her blouse, broke the dark severity of her clothing. She passed Villamayor with the slightest genuflection and shook hands with us gravely: serene, knowing whatever blasphemies she had typed that afternoon were but steps on his roundabout road to salvation.

But Consuela didn't look her part. "Consuela": for it was only in moments of seizure and gnomic utterance she called herself "La Atrevida." She wore a flowered cotton skirt and peasant blouse, many cheap bracelets and rings. Her fingernails and toes were carefully painted, and her wild eyes were darkened. The restless pupils moved constantly, mindless and alert. She might have been any pretty girl of her age striking out from her parents, and employed as waitress in a small *bodega*. Or perhaps she thought this was the way to dress for a political "mission"—who scarcely turned fifteen had become the inspired mistress of an astonished Nicaraguan conspirator said to be losing his revolutionary ardors. (She had forced herself upon him; one evening burst into his room. She saw it as her appointed role to rally him with democratic slogans and arguments in the "dark hours of their intimacy.") And yet she really looked like a normal adolescent girl, staring and abstracted, dreamily conscious of her sexual attractions. She had hardly a glance for me. I was a cold unfeeling *Yanqui*, repudiated from the start.

Villamayor later told me her story, and of how she presented herself to him in Port-au-Prince, dedicated and penniless. She had been hoping for over a year to meet him: the "revolutionary of the Twenty-Six Days." For her whole childhood had been spent in atmospheres of idealistic subversion. She was an exile at birth and an orphan at five. She learned to walk near the barracks housing the fabulous Legió del Caribe in Costa Rica and learned to read from *Acción Democratica* literature. Her father was killed in a duel provoked by supporters of the Somozas. Thereafter she was passed from hand to hand: a child of the liberal "cause" rather than of any particular family or even country. Talk of Cayo Cumana and Puerto Limón and the hated Protector must have been among her earliest memories.

This was the girl who slouched bored and silent between Villamayor and Julieta Aparicio, idly rolling her bread into pellets. There were times she stared at Belesprit across the table as at a wall. And she must have spent much of her childhood so, apathetic, not even seeming to listen. It appears there had been no real forewarning of inspiration. She had just turned twelve when it suddenly descended upon her: the prophesying power and gift of tongues. This occurred during a riotous meeting of Cuban exiles at the Flagler Theater in Miami. At least three enraged orators were speaking at once. The audience was on its feet, fists were shaking—when higher and louder than any a girl's shrill voice was heard, madly reiterant, demanding moral redemption through the nationalization of all ranches exceeding a hundred acres, and through the expropriation of foreign mineral holdings. The voices of the male orators gradually subsided; a circle was formed around the pocket of disturbance. At last the girl was carried gesticulating onto the stage, a typical olive-skinned and bony junior high school girl of that time and place, with the monogrammed blouse and carefully rolled socks of her caste. From the stage she talked lucidly and without pause for thirty-five minutes . . . only to confess afterward she had had no idea what she was saying. She knew nothing of agrarian reform or foreign interventions. But God did, and He had spoken through her.

And that was the beginning of her new life, which rapidly became legendary; a restless movement from one exile capital to another, invited to speak but often remaining stubbornly silent, welcomed and housed and fed with patience until the gift returned, and the moment for inflaming prophecy. She herself thought of the name "La Atrevida." But there were months on end when she was "only Consuela": an ordinary, rather pious girl who in time grew taller and more wayward, pretty in a gypsy way. And even at sixteen she could still spend hours curled on her bed reading movie magazines and comic books. There would be nothing about her, then, of the possessed child who could quickly turn any meeting into patriotic bedlam.

She was quiet enough, except for one outburst, through our first dinner with Villamayor: demure and calm between him and the lank lean Julieta. And yet she too was part of the evening's strangeness—through much of which Villamayor sat silent, tolerant and at times exasperated, the half-reluctant head of household.

We sat at the two kitchen tables in the center of the room long since stripped of its damask and crystal elegance: making do with tin forks. The great room was very dark around our island of light, the kerosene lamp and candles. We were already at table when the unannounced Ezile slipped into the room and took her place at Villamayor's right: just touching his shoulder in a ritual gesture as another might give a wifely kiss: tall and immaculate but barefoot and in a peasant's white frock. She might have been twenty. Was she, I wondered, cook or mistress or disciple? (A solemn and shy younger girl waited on table.) And what was Belesprit, to whom Ezile began talking at once in a gently undulant Creole? I understood very little. I thought I could detect a physical connection between the two Negroes, a shared sympathy and perhaps sexual contentment. Yet also in the strangest way this flow of feeling had Villamayor himself as its center and source, as though he had drawn the two together by sacramental *droit de seigneur*. He quietly dominated them all. Their dependence drew them together, though Consuela knew little French or Creole and the two Negroes knew little Spanish. The table had grouped itself thus: an ambiguous "family" of a few weeks' standing that might have been together all their lives. Villamayor's twisted face was at its center, ageless and benignant and calm. Later, to be sure, I came to know what exasperation could lie behind that expression of calm; with what despair, almost, Villamayor saw new disciples settle at his feet.

During dinner, while Villamayor talked about the

house, and about the economic problems of the region, my mind reverted repeatedly to those words of encouragement spoken to Belesprit. *The past is past, the future is not yet here.* . . . And suddenly I wanted to ask Villamayor how much they applied to his own case. A little too abruptly I asked him—who wanted to climb out of his past—whether he hadn't in a way welcomed his kidnappers, and the sudden change they had wrought in his life. He had been hustled violently out of one life, and into another.

Julieta Aparicio nodded eagerly.

"That is true. You said your personality changed with your beating. I remember your very words: '. . . *that subtle realignment of my bones.*' "

"Yes," Belesprit put in, "Those were your exact words."

"Very well," Villamayor said. "However, I did not inflict that historic and unpleasant beating upon myself. I cannot deny the obscure benefits of great physical shock, if one happens to survive. But I will not acknowledge that I invited my destruction. No: I did not seek that beating. I was, simply, the surprised beneficiary of obscure political process. I emerged a changed if bleeding man."

I did not know what to make of these enigmatic and bantering remarks. But I seized upon the reference to the bloody emergence from the "hut near Tuxpan":

"Why were your torturers so inefficient?"

"Inefficient? To me they seemed remarkably expert."

"I mean why didn't they kill you?"

Villamayor turned up his hands skeptically.

"That is what we historians call an 'incomprehensible event.' Also, a most fortunate one."

"It was destined," Julieta said serenely. "In the parabola of his life that first martyrdom, which without realizing it Justo de Villamayor sought out. . . ."

She spoke with assurance, and with the master's own flowing tones; she might have been quoting from a book. Villamayor interrupted her quietly,

"Julieta, dear one: Please suppress these fantasies."

"But you mislead our visitor! Why 'incomprehensible'? You told me yourself, even from the abyss of unfaith, that this meant a total change of your life. Is it not a premonition of the saving change to come?"

"I must ask you to remain silent!" It was the first time I had seen real firmness in Villamayor. But he apologized almost immediately, to Julieta and to us. "It is but one of the small irritations common to those who live in close proximity. I must ask you to forgive me."

In the silence that ensued I suspected, dismally, that my opportunity might be vanishing. I was an outsider to an extreme degree. For all I knew Villamayor would send me on my way tomorrow, and refuse to see me again. So I decided to blunder ahead. I told him I had seen his friends Barbara Swenson and Edward Murphree in Port-au-Prince.

Villamayor smiled.

"But of course you did! How could one fail to meet them? Dear Barbara is the most public and most gregarious of revolutionaries. She should be decorated as a stabilizing influence in Caribbean affairs: she brings all conspiracy into the open."

"Then you don't mind her?"

"I like her very much, and I like Murphree too. They are amusing and incorrigible and steadfast. And they recognize their own absurdity: that is already a great deal!"

"But didn't you come down here to get away from them?"

Villamayor frowned: the precise ridged lines returned, and the public man's mask.

"How can I be sure? That may have been, yes, one of my unrecognized motives. I do like Barbara and Edward Murphree. But I did not want to engage in further debates concerning Santa Isabella. The subject has become intolerably monotonous."

At these words the girl Consuela sat forward, as though prodded from a half sleep.

"The Protector must go," she muttered. "He has destroyed all the personal freedoms. . . ."

Villamayor silenced her with a gentle pat.

"I am tired of useless discussions. My mind and spirit are clogged by thirty years of slogan and political cliché."

"Then you think they're harmless?"

"Barbara and Edward Murphree? Let us hope they are harmless. I trust they are not engaged in recruiting poor Negroes for invasions."

"How can she help doing harm, with as much money as that?" Belesprit asked. "She seems to think everyone has his price."

Villamayor shook his head.

"Oh, she knows better than that! She's been cheated more than once, after paying the stipulated price. On the other hand, it is perfectly true that so much money corrupts. Let me give you an example—an example and tale that begins in Miami, as so many of our poor adventures do."

The little story completed, as it were, my first impression of Villamayor: of his ironic and compassionate awareness of failure, and of his quick eye for the spirit's twists and turns. I could tell the poor victim of unsuspected cupidity—one José Cabral—had long since found his place in Villamayor's tolerant affections. Cabral had been dispatched from Miami to collect funds for one of the several rival committees for the liberation of Santa Isabella, with a modest goal of fifteen thousand dollars. "That was more than enough," Villamayor remarked, "for the publication of a monthly journal and a decent number of tracts." But Cabral had scarcely arrived in New York when sums of wholly unexpected size fell, so to speak, at his feet. Three thousand from a man thought to be permanently withdrawn to Europe, two thousand from another who had inherited from an unknown relative. . . . It was not until he had passed the fifteen-thousand-dollar goal that Cabral became aware of any temptation to appropriate a token and trifling share. And it was precisely then, as ill luck would have it, he intercepted news that Barbara Swenson would spend two nights in New York, on her way to the California ranch.

"He was the first of the exiles to reach her," Villamayor went on. "Who can say what torment in poor Cabral's face at once caught Barbara's sympathy—torment because he knew he would abscond with the entire fund? It was such a seriousness and anguish as could not be feigned. But Barbara Swenson took that expression to be patriotic. She gave him a check for fifty thousand dollars. The next morning he was at the bank before it had opened. By nightfall he was installed in a luxurious apartment on Central Park and had hired a Cuban bodyguard. He contemplated taking up various expensive vices. Even he, poor *descamisado,* might now possess women in rich furs!"

"Such a man should have been shot," Consuela remarked.

"Perhaps. However, his mistake was that he didn't know when to stop. After only a week he flew to Las Vegas, our José Cabral, where he lost all the money in eighteen hours of play. That took determination and skill and even a certain circumspection. A man who loses his money too quickly is open to the gravest suspicions. However, José Cabral succeeded. He kept out only enough money for bus fare to Miami. So still, you see, he didn't know when to stop. I see him move from Miami back to Miami in less than a month, unswerving in his ferocious course, a dedicated man, concentrating in those few weeks the *psychomachia* of a lifetime. In Miami he quickly found employment as a waiter in the one restaurant where all exiles of Santa Isabella go. And he was there the last time I went through. He was pointed out to me: an immobile figure by the door to the kitchen, except when actually serving, ready to receive the stares of those he had betrayed. Everyone dimly realized he was a special case, and that there would be no point in shooting him."

I remarked to Villamayor that he was very inconsistent. Only an hour ago he had said one should forget the past. And now he seemed to admire this man who accepted his guilt and insisted on paying a price.

"Of course I am inconsistent, it is the commonest of my failings. You are right in detecting a secret sympathy for one so steadfast in his purpose of self-ruin. I sympathize with all intensity of living and conviction. Yes, even with such misguided intensity as his. But is it really possible to conclude that Barbara Swenson's money corrupted him? Perhaps we must say instead that the money and the temptation 'created' José Cabral . . . since before the crime he was nothing. Now, at least, he is a man with a job. He knows where to stand . . . under those scornful stares."

The room at once seemed darker, when Villamayor's voice ceased. We were left in a shadowy uncertainty. I at least was not used to his subtleties, and felt rather oppressed by these brooding ironies. I wondered how a man so cut off from the ordinary simplicities of feeling, the everyday crudities of discourse, had been able to act at all. And how could such a man possibly stand up to the wild blundering patriotism, the ferocious childlike zeal, of a Manuel Andrada? On this first evening I found it very hard to visualize (behind this delicate and evasive ironist and head of a most suspect household) the Villamayor who had insisted on joining the Puerto Limón invaders, or the Villamayor who had "spoken up" at a cabinet meeting, or even the Villamayor who had had enough firmness to want to go on living. And who had therefore turned up (after whatever mysterious Golgotha in "the hut near Tuxpan") at Alonso Moreno's door in Mexico City, bandaged and leaning on a cane.

I WENT to bed very early, as I was exhausted after the long hot day, and that horseback descent through the jungle; I was almost too tired to undress. And yet I lay sleepless for what must have been hours, unmoving and naked in the heat: listening at first to the thin plaintive notes of a flute-player practicing (it was Villamayor), then to the tropical silence broken by sudden furtive sounds. A thin moonlight glowed dully behind my window covered with gauze. The broken netting was flecked with beetles and moths. Now and then I heard the crackle of fire under the great tureen of water boiled to supply all needs, and sudden rustlings in the trees. Also, directly beneath my window for a time, indistinguishable Creole voices in the soft accusing accents of affection.

I lay there under the still hot movement of time. I am sure I had not slept at all when I was startled by a low urgent knocking; I threw on my trousers. It was Julieta Aparicio, wrapped in a dressing gown from which all color had faded years before. Her shining undone hair and frightened eyes, behind the long candle held high, were worthy of the legendary furies attendant upon the souls of saintly men.

"I found it impossible to sleep! I had to see you, I must know what you want of him."

"Do come in!" I lit the kerosene lamp and drew chairs up to my small table. Poor Julieta's meager chest panted as she glared at me. She still held the burning candle high overhead as for a better scrutiny of my motives. "Won't you sit down? I only want what I'm sure you would want: to make him better known. To honor him."

"Honor? Are you sure you do not mean destroy? What right had you to come here?"

Now she did sit down, still holding the candle.

"I want to write an article that does him justice."

"No article could do him justice, since everything of importance lies ahead."

"I'm sure that's true. All the same, people want to know about what's already happened. An important man can't simply vanish from the face of the earth."

"A great man," she corrected me quietly. "What distresses me is that you come to us from Barbara Swenson, a woman of lawless and violent purpose. Were you sent to enlist him in an invasion of Santa Isabella? I beg you tell me the truth."

"I wasn't sent at all. I didn't even know she was in Port-au-Prince when I came down."

"Justo de Villamayor must not shed blood," Julieta intoned. "Years ago Divine intervention prevented his participation in the Puerto Limón invasion, and his purity was maintained. Today, perhaps, the Devil would prove more powerful. Moreover, the possessed girl Consuela is determined to arouse him."

"Well, I'm not. I only want to write my article. But I'm a little surprised you're such a defender of The Protector."

"Of course I'm not a defender! But Justo de Villamayor's role is to destroy him by the pen, not the sword. He must not participate in invasions. There must be no blood on his hands."

"Exactly: the pen not the sword. Can you tell me what he's writing?"

She shook her unkempt head; the black coils moved angrily.

"I am not at liberty to say. Moreover, what he writes now is surely provisional. It is but one more restless turning in the long road to be taken by his spirit. It is impossible to predict what Justo de Villamayor will write— once he has fallen to his knees. Perhaps his freed spirit will rise above political matters entirely. There is certain to be a change, once he drops the mask."

"What mask?"

The bony shoulders shrugged; she crossed herself rapidly.

"The mask of a dry and corrosive skepticism. In reality it is paper-thin, one day very soon he will drop it."

We might have been, in that strange yellow light, two conspirators debating a soul in the hot midnight stillness; the odor of insect repellent hung between us. I felt a stirring of compassion for this wizened creature.

"That's what your sister told me, in a way. She said all the crimes of The Protector are less important than a single soul."

"You know my sister!"

"It was she who told me where to come. I saw her in New York. But she's very worried about you. Why didn't you write her more than once?"

Julieta was puzzled and remote.

"I couldn't write her, in time it became impossible. I can only tell you I had entered into a new existence." She looked down at her enlaced hands as at objects inherited from that earlier life: irrelevant and obsolete flesh. "Believe me, I tried to write her but it was like sitting down to write to another planet. There was no way to explain the nature of my new understanding. And María Teresa could not see Justo's beauty of character, she was blind to the secrets of his spirit. So you see any word of explanation would only have enraged her."

"I could write to her. Wouldn't you at least like me to tell her you're well? Even say you're happy?"

"Yes, why not?" She drew in her breath as for a long prayer committed to memory. "Of course I am happy. Listen: in the slowly curving destiny of any great man are humble ones intended to assist quietly at the several rebirths of the spirit. I am such a one. I knew it from the moment Alonso Moreno presented me to him, I knew it before I could see the dear face still swathed in bandages. And isn't it significant Villamayor accepted me almost at a glance?"

She waited, intent, for my confirmation.

"Yes," I said. "I'm sure that means something."

"All his life he has been restlessly seeking. He has stumbled forward following the parabola of his spirit, while all the time he thought he was drawing back. I watch with fascination as one might watch a drunken man wander crazily all night over the village to collapse at last at his own door. So it will be with Villamayor, in his movement toward the cross. One day he will accept his destiny."

I felt myself excluded from this mystical and female discourse. I plunged in almost roughly:

"Do you say all this to him?"

"I try not to; I find it irritates him. You saw how he bridled at dinner and told me to be silent. The closer he comes to salvation, the more stubbornly he resists. But already there have been the miracles, already he has sought martyrdom and survived it. So I think he is now entering into the crucial phase and period of solitude. He has cut himself off from a world that sought to praise him. We moved here through a wilderness."

"I don't quite see the solitude. He seems to have collected a sizeable household in the last few weeks."

The lean tired face went back, exposing a fragile neck. Julieta closed her eyes in exasperated agreement.

"Was ever anyone so tried? He promised, when we left California, we would be absolutely alone. He spoke of a 'transforming solitude.' There were certain ideas he wanted to 'push to their dark conclusion.' . . . Those were his own words. And what happens? Twelve hours after our arrival in Port-au-Prince the girl Consuela knocks at his door, claiming to be penniless and helpless. A subterfuge, of course! By the end of our first evening she is delivering lectures on the crimes of The Protector.

Then Belesprit, whom he hires for a sightseeing drive into the country—and who by nightfall tells Justo he has known 'peace of spirit' for the first time in years. What did Justo do but speak to him with a certain sympathy, and ask a few questions about his education and miserable marriage?"

I wanted to ask about the black Ezile but did not. I was not yet ready to listen to mystical reasonings on the bodily needs of "great men" destined for sainthood.

"It's his great gift, isn't it—the sympathy? Or should I say it's his great failing?"

"It is a saintly acceptance. He wants to be alone and cannot be. But you will see for yourself: no man was ever more tolerant than Justo de Villamayor, tolerant even of the unworthy, tolerant of the degenerate. He will listen to anyone! And this is one reason why I predict at least a few years for him as humble confessor and priest, prior to his high elevation in the church. He is unable to turn his back, he cannot thrust people aside."

"Well, I'm glad to hear that."

We exchanged glances, both of us ironically aware of how far our conversation had taken us in a very short time. Then Julieta almost smiled.

"Yes, you too, I suppose. You too will not be thrust aside. And I dare say you won't be the last."

THE next morning I awoke hot and exhausted, and much bitten by mosquitoes. But I was no longer oppressed by that nighttime aura of subtle and pervasive ambiguity. The bright day was filled with chatter, and the deeper voice of Villamayor giving orders. I went to the window in time to see him (in bathing trunks and sandals, sturdy and bronzed) speak to Ezile. She was very tall in a fresh white peasant dress and with a large empty basket on her head. She towered above the little servant girl who accompanied her, and was almost as tall as Villamayor. Her smile was remote and bland. Was she or was she not the chosen companion of the corrupter's bed? I did not know, then. But at least I could see she was not above going to market, accompanied by the timid young girl, she too barefoot. Villamayor seemed to be urging Ezile not to let herself be swindled. Then he gave both girls a pat as they turned away, already walking in file.

The house itself was less sinister in the morning light, and it was filled with the sounds of workmen. After breakfast Villamayor showed me the work he intended to have done. There were the ravages and improvisations of half a century or more to be repaired. In one room we found three Negroes hammering rhythmically on a fresh floorboard. They grinned at us without stopping their work; their clothes hung in shreds. And in nearly every room Villamayor had left some mark of his own. He limped ahead of me, restless and amused, pointing out his "experiments." There were more tin masks, also clay models for a tall depersonalized nude of flowing and placid limbs. In one room a whole wall was covered with precise chalked murals. There were the radiating designs and minute geometries of the *vever;* also twin serpents representing the powerful Damballah-Ouedo. Two angry spitting heads rose above uncoiled vertical bodies, and eyed each other across a tall cylinder that resembled a drum. Villamayor complained with some justice that his drawings were mere bald imitation of design.

He could not have been more friendly on that first morning, as he showed me through the house. But he shook his head vigorously when I brought up my article again. "A useless and boring enterprise," he protested, "An unworthy subject!" He proposed that I write instead about this remote area of Haiti into which I had wandered, and about the dying city of Caye Thomonde. That could interest "the general educated public." As for his own political career—it was at most worth "a long footnote" in an academic journal. And he himself would write that footnote.

"I do not wish to be discourteous, and I am happy to have you as my guest. But all my old life is behind me. It is a tale without public significance, those days are engulfed and forgotten. I myself take only an antiquarian's interest in it, the interest of a philosophical historian. It is not a life I gaze back on, but certain theories of causality. As for my life here—I must beg you to leave me in this obscurity I have come to cherish."

I decided not to press him. Later in the morning, he took me to Caye Thomonde, and on the way discoursed on the causes of its decline. We rode the three miles on small *bourriques* through the overgrowth and the sticky heat. The first outlying houses were splintered ruins submerged in a tide of green. Purple and red flowering trees grew through great cracks in the walls. Then we came to houses only recently abandoned. A hideous clamor and flapping came from the darkness of one house where some small animal had withdrawn to die.

The sweet odor and stillness of decay increased as we moved onto the main street, and the faint odors of charcoal and coffee. A small trickle of sewage also indicated we had reached an inhabited area, though all the houses looked empty and black. Then the small cathedral: white and delicate and dead. High grasses sprouted from the

flagstones and the windows were long black scars. Near
the shore was a cluster of spidery balconied houses, the
town's only shops. Lovely pastel shades were still faintly
visible on the walls: a reminder of the old times of pleasure. The "little Trianon" of the rich! Languid black faces
looked out from the gloom beneath fragile balconies. A
few, recognizing Villamayor, managed sick smiles. At the
end of the street a ruined wharf rose precariously before
plunging into the water. The great timbers were splintered
and rotten.

Villamayor suggested that I write an article on the
vicissitudes of the little city, going back to the prosperity
of the slave times. I could stay for a few days as his guest
and ride into town each morning. Thus I could get my
"irreplaceable personal impressions," and I would find at
least a few natives who spoke French. But he doubted
whether any of them would have a real knowledge of the
city's past. For that, for all the historical records and
even for the bloody legends, I would need to go back to
Port-au-Prince. He could refer me to the best authorities.

I did not tell Villamayor that I was not in the least
interested in writing about Caye Thomonde. I began to
wonder, though, how much he really wanted to be rid of
me. My article on himself was a threat to retirement, yes,
an invasion of his precious privacy. Yet the proposal that
I write on Caye Thomonde would have the effect of keeping me with him for at least a few days. It had been a quite
gratuitous proposal. And I felt he enjoyed talking to me,
to someone who was not a fanatic disciple, after his weeks
of seclusion with Julieta and Consuela, with Belesprit and
Ezile. I had brought him a breath of cool air, a respite, a
touch of northern sanity and calm.

But what would he think of me if Manuel Andrada

blundered in on us unannounced, as he was very likely to do—carrying his ridiculous burden of The Protector's portrait, making his absurd claims to friendship and "collaboration"? Late that afternoon, while we were swimming at the small beach near the house, I decided that the time had come to tell Villamayor that he could expect still another intruder. The beach was a strip of sand shelving to a large cove enclosed by a white coral fringe, and I watched Villamayor swim away from me sturdily and then back, circling the cove. No houses were visible here, nor even the towers of the cathedral in Caye Thomonde. To the east the *cordillera* marking the border of Santa Isabella was distinct and blue, perhaps twenty miles away. Villamayor glanced briefly in that direction as he came out of the water toward me. It might have been a reluctant glance, a gesture of self-reproach. And I wondered again why he had chosen, of all the solitary places on earth, this one: within sight of the oppressed homeland, almost within range of its atmosphere and odor of moral ruin.

He lay down on the sand beside me, his sturdy body showing no signs of his historic beating and the shattering of the rib cage. But he drew himself up quickly when I remarked that someone else, one of his compatriots in fact, might soon arrive. He gave me a quick hostile glance. Then he listened bleakly as I told him of Andrada's abrupt arrival in my Boston room, and of his mission to purchase unpublished manuscripts by a man presumed to be dead. I did not of course go into the more absurd details—the arrests in Boston, or the obscenely bulging revolver, or the voyaging portrait of The Protector. For how then could I justify (in a bare recital of such details) the fact that I had tolerated Andrada so long? But I did say that

I had deliberately given him the slip in Port-au-Prince. And I added that this "representative of the National Library" hardly looked the part.

Villamayor shook his head weakly.

"So there is to be no end of the harassments? Well, I shall have to disappoint this man too, if he comes seeking writings to publish. I would not surrender them at any price. But what an absurdity for those wretches to pretend to think I would sell any of my work to them! Of course they know better."

"I'm not sure he's from the Library at all," I said. "He looks more like a truck driver. Or someone from the secret police."

Villamayor dug his hands into the fine sand.

"You draw distinctions that are much too fine, when applied to Santa Isabella. Who indeed is to discriminate between a librarian and a thug in my poor brutalized land? Are we not all coarsened and degraded by fear? Yes, it is entirely possible this Manuel Andrada is an employee of both suspect institutions—the Library and the secret police. Why on earth not?"

"I thought I ought to warn you. And I'm not at all sure what he really wants from you."

"Let us hope it is not my life. It would be disagreeable enough to lose the manuscripts! However, we shall see what we shall see . . ."

"You sound pretty resigned."

Villamayor looked past me with an expression of grave detachment . . . looked again toward those mountains separating us from a land shadowed by terror.

"I am neither resigned nor reconciled, let us say I am merely attentive. If The Protector has determined to destroy me—destroy me perhaps he will. However, I refuse to make pessimistic predictions. Already once I have escaped, *in extremis,* thanks to some deficiency of my captors. My four captors! I was utterly helpless in their hands yet escaped."

"You fought back?"

Villamayor turned back to me. Once again the wrenched face seemed to possess its secret of power.

"Of course I didn't fight back! No, it was my captors who did the fighting, among and within themselves. I still do not know what happened or what debates ensued while I lay unconscious following the torture. One can only speculate; this matter is very dark. But when I awoke in my world of pain only one of my assailants was left, a man whose lip twitched convulsively. This man spoke to me very angrily. But also he spared my life."

"And after that? Did he take you to Mexico? Were you able to promise him money?"

"Money!" The gravity of Villamayor's expression might have been a curtain fallen between us. "No, I did not promise him money. But this is a very personal matter, also a quite obscure one, on which I choose to say nothing. No—let us speak of pleasanter things. Perhaps too this Andrada is as great a fool as you say, and will not even be able to find me!"

"He's a fool, yes. But he's also pretty stubborn. I know it's not easy to beat him off. I tried."

"So?" Villamayor raised a cautionary finger. "Then we can only await his coming. But for the moment you must say nothing about this unwelcome visitor. Above all, please do not say he comes from Santa Isabella. You understand? I do not want to create unnecessary alarm among my excitable females. I shall say to them whatever it is necessary to say."

BUT to Consuela, at least, he must have said something very soon. For she had already heard about an "expected visitor" when she came to my room at eleven o'clock that night. She had seemed to pay no attention to me at all, during my twenty-four hours in the household. But in fact she must have been watching me rather closely, and watching for some clue to my sympathies. And now she was at my door, holding her sandals. She hoped to keep her visit secret. Her toenails were freshly painted, and she had arranged her blouse seductively, with one brown shoulder bare. My first amused response, as she came into my room, was to wonder whether I would, the following night, be favored by a visit from the black Ezile. Like Julieta she began talking at once.

"I must beg you to say nothing to Julieta Aparicio! She will misunderstand my purpose. Besides, she tells nothing but lies."

I urged her to sit down. But she stood above me, fists clenched and with her fiery prettiness, at the periphery of the small light thrown by the kerosene lamp. I promised I would say nothing of her visit. Then she made, almost haughtily, her demand. It was a large demand to have thrown at one by a half-crazed sixteen-year-old girl in the middle of the night.

"I want to know your political convictions and intentions."

"Well, you certainly come right to the point! The answer is that I don't have any. No intentions, at least."

"You ask me to believe that! Listen: I think you have come here as I have—to rouse Justo de Villamayor from his bed of lethargy and political decline. I have watched you and kept silent until now. You were sent by Barbara

Swenson. No, don't interrupt me. I know. I know by experience the visage of political disappointment. I watched your face tonight as he talked. You have been disappointed by Villamayor's lethargies and by his languid indifference. And what a disappointment for me —the lethargies! Lethargies and defeatism in the one man who had courage to resist openly within the bosom of the government councils! His anger against The Protector dwindles and vanishes like sap from the loins. Julieta Aparicio crushes his resolve, she emasculates the will."

I began to remark that Julieta had other ambitions for Villamayor, they too involving the will. But Consuela waved me to silence.

"His will is entangled as in a spider's web by Julieta's fanaticism." She crossed herself rapidly. "I too honor the Church. I too love the Virgin. But I have been given the insight that it is Villamayor's place to go back to Santa Isabella at the head of a democratic army of liberation. Now answer me: isn't that why you also are here? We should work together to stimulate his will."

I shook my head, though I was sorry to earn this girl's contempt. For a brief moment I envied those who had succumbed to her political excitations.

"I'm here to find out what Villamayor is doing and writing. That's all. I want to write an article for a magazine. The article will praise him, of course. It will make him better known."

"An article!" She cleared her throat angrily. "There is only one honorable form of writing: dramatic appeals to flagging and dormant democratic aspiration through editorials, leaflets and tracts. Do you write against The Protector?"

"I'm not writing anything—just now." This girl was making me more and more uncomfortable. I found myself in an absurd posture of self-defense. "But won't you help me with the article? All I want is the truth."

Her response was again immediate; I might have touched a spring.

"The truth? The truth is that Santa Isabella lies enervated, prostrate and dazed after more than twenty years of oppression and lies. The lungs are choked by a rancid and putrid atmosphere. The Protector must go."

"I meant the truth about Villamayor. Has he shown you what he's writing?"

"He shows it to no one but Julieta, who types what he has written. One can only pray he writes at last an angry revelation of The Protector's manipulation of government and industry. And of course the atrocities, the atrocities ought to come first. But you—is it then true you are only a writer without political conviction, not dedicated to our cause?"

She looked down on me with contempt, and with the harsh pride of one who had almost surrendered her person uselessly.

"For the moment, yes. Though of course I do sympathize . . ."

"And the man Villamayor says you expect—please tell me of him. I hope he at least is not another Norte Americano with ice in his veins. Will he at least help me rouse Justo de Villamayor from his sleep?"

I was much amused at the thought of their meeting: Andrada and Consuela: my two dedicated souls. What sparks wouldn't fly! But I only shrugged my shoulders.

"He's looking for manuscripts," I said. "He says he's looking for things of Villamayor's to publish."

"A publisher! Manuscripts!"

Consuela backed slowly away. Then she stared at me, her face now white with scorn as it had once been from fervor, before flinging out of the room.

AND of course it was all I did, for certain, know: Andrada claimed to be looking for manuscripts, for unpublished writings. What would happen to them (whether decadent poem or even historical anecdote discrediting The Protector's youth) was another matter, hard to assess. Perhaps the decadent poems would be preserved and the political writings destroyed. No doubt even Andrada didn't know what would happen to the manuscripts—who was a "little man," the humble agent of higher authorities. But meanwhile he still didn't come to us, and several hot days passed. It was hard to believe Andrada, even Andrada the born incompetent, could fail to discover Villamayor's whereabouts. I wondered what his reaction had been to his discovery that I had once again given him the slip. What dismal speculation ensued? For all I knew he might have returned in despair to the Ville des Fleurs, where a new cycle of debauchery and deception could set in: devotion and excess and guilt. He would regard himself, then, as more than ever unworthy of his high mission. Confession would prove unavailing.

Well, I was to hear very soon, and from his own lips, of his progressive discoveries of my "treachery." He was much too conscious of his failure to go to the Consulate representing Santa Isabella, where he could have learned everything he needed to know. He would not dare to face them! Instead he went to the Haitian police, learned

the name of my hotel, and went there. And of course
he did everything the hardest, the most ridiculous way.
He entered the hotel by the kitchen, flourished a handful
of *gourdes* by way of bribe, and demanded to be shown
my room. *La chambre de Monsieur Clive.* . . . The
bribed and dull-witted cook took him to the dark upstairs hall, where for over an hour he stationed himself
by what had once been my door, waiting for me to wake
up. I had not responded to his first gentle knocking. At
noon he began to knock more loudly and ten minutes
later broke into the room, thanks to the expert use of a
small pocketknife. The room was empty, there was no
baggage: I was gone. Later Andrada told me of a sudden
weight of sadness and dismay falling upon his heart, as
he took in the signs of flight and betrayal. Yes: I had
left the hotel without a word, whose very journey here
had been, in a way, conceived by himself. His friend
Nicholas Clive, who had even sheltered him for several
days in the luxurious Boston apartment! And all the
money he had spent, drawn as it were coin by burning
coin from The Protector's own pocket, now irrevocably
gone! For a few minutes Andrada stood quite still, his
mind vacant. It might have been the numbness of one
who had discerned the dead end of a road.

Then he went downstairs and found Bernard, who
confirmed that I had paid my bill and left. Where to?
The proprietor shook his great fat shoulders. *"I do not
inquire into the sanity of clients who vanish into the
interior of Haiti."* Pressing more narrowly, Andrada
learned for the first time of the material existence in
Port-au-Prince of Barbara Swenson and Edward Murphree, possessed of both yacht and villa. *"Barbara Swenson! But of course, your friend Clive knows her well!"*

Bernard pointed a stubby finger at the white yacht anchored in the harbor. *"You do not know Barbara Swenson? But everyone knows her. She is preparing a revolution!"* Andrada felt a dizziness as from too long a station in the sun; this was the second outrage of the day. So! Barbara Swenson had not only followed Villamayor to Haiti but been seen by Nicholas Clive his friend—the legendary troublemaker of the California ranch, the financier of grudge-bearers and exile malcontents! Once again Andrada felt himself beyond his depths, who since early youth had trained himself to serve The Protector, who had dreamed of this from the time his pallet had tumbled out into the middle of the street after the earthquake and tidal wave, there to become imbedded in mud.

Nevertheless, he resumed the weary trail of patriotic endeavor. He made a rapid vain trip to the dock and yacht's dinghy, from which he was referred to the hillside villa. Then another ferociously expensive taxi ride at The Protector's expense: coin after burning coin. He arrived as Barbara Swenson and her dazed guests were coming to the end of their long poolside luncheon; waiters circulated with liqueurs. It appears no one noticed at first the small man in his incongruous winter suiting, who moved embarrassed among the tables filled with what he called "the conspirators"—the slipshod Yanquis and burnished exiles in snowy *guayaveras* and even, no doubt, a few traitorous compatriots. Also the high Negro officials in immaculate white; everyone was slightly drunk. Andrada caught snatches of revolutionary conversation as he walked past the tables; there were evil women indecently clad; dresses slipped from the shoulders. As he came to the last table Andrada, truly frightened now, began to murmur my name in French: *"S'il vous plaît,*

*où est Nicholas Clive? Nicholas Clive, he is a young man
known to everyone."* Here, nearing the edge of the balcony, he encountered Edward Murphree, who welcomed
him warmly. *"Nicholas Clive, mais naturellement je le
connais!"* Andrada sat down. He found himself presented,
before he had time to make his own patriotism clear, to
a slender man of scholarly mien: the constitutionalist
Eduardo Gonzales. Yes, Murphree had from the first
moment mistaken Andrada for an antagonist of The Protector. A grudge-bearer and malcontent!

Much later—telling me about this hour that lasted
scarcely twenty minutes—Andrada refused to go into
detail. He knew only that he had stumbled in broad daylight into the very hotbed of revolutionary and irreligious
fanaticism, brash and unconcealed. He sat with Murphree
and Gonzales in anguish: watching the five tables at
which men and women sat back with half-closed conspiratorial eyes, murmuring subversive thoughts. But
he couldn't hear what they were saying because of Gonzales, who had begun to speak rapidly in wheezing tones
of the rudiments of constitutional change. *Unilateral
settling of border disputes, the greed of the church, dis-
solution of monopolies, separation of judicial power from
executive prerogative* . . . the dry voice went on unappeased. When Gonzales paused to sip his glass of soda
water, Andrada pressed his questions again. But Murphree dismissed them with a shrug. He was momentarily
disappointed to hear I had disappeared from my hotel
without leaving word. But his mind soon wandered to
other things: to the vacillations of the French, to the
fleshpots of Aruba and Trinidad. Gonzales had subsided
into an indignant silence, as Murphree went on. *"So he
left without consulting me, to search for his lost Villa-*

mayor? Tant pis!" Murphree shook his reddening face
and white delicate hair. *"Ça m'est absolument égal,
Monsieur Andrada.* Let Villamayor sulk in his tent! Let
Clive go off chasing him! I don't care. There are other
and more faithful leaders, who devote eight hours a day
to the cause. The sea is large and deep, there are other
fish in the sea!"

Such was the beginning (and temporarily the end) of
Andrada's introduction to Barbara Swenson's household.
The sea is large and deep. . . . Glancing over his shoulder,
Andrada followed the sweep of Murphree's eloquent
arm in the direction of the sea thousands of feet below.
The sky was a vast blue expanse in which the huge dim
island of Gonave floated improbably, directly before
their eyes. Closer at hand the balcony on which they sat
seemed to drop off abruptly into infinite space. *"Nicholas
Clive!"* Andrada wailed, recollecting. *"Believe me, I was
utterly discomposed by the evil atmosphere and the
hateful phrases of gross political subversion. Also by our
terrible position on that balcony. That island floating in
the sky! I was possessed of a vertigo."* He felt himself
about to be engulfed. He did not remember getting up
from the table, but it is evident that he did—overturning
a glass in his haste, leaving without a word, rushing past
the tables of conspirators and out into the blazing street.
He leaped into the nearest taxi. Moments later he was descending swiftly toward Port-au-Prince (urging greater
speed on the driver, but unable to remember the name of
his hotel) ; and toward the final outrage of the day.

Of this he spoke with shamed dark eyes on the floor,
and on his now cracked and ruined cardboard shoes: his
eyes down, but the white gash through the brow regarding me, placid and unmalevolent, his body faintly trem-

bling. He spoke of it in one of those long fumbling conversations we later had in his room in Caye Thomonde.
The third outrage and the worst! For what were his
sensations to be but those of a trapped and chained victim
walking the treadmill of his lusts? Or he was reminded of
the donkeys crushing out the cane on the older plantations, and receiving a ritual blow at each round. The
taxi driver, in any event, knew Andrada by sight, as
most of the drivers now did, and knew fragments of his
recent history. Who did not know him, since his exploits
had astonished even the bored girls of the Ville des Fleurs?
I surmise the driver must have taken one look at the
scarred burning face rushing toward him, felt in panic
the great wrench of his taxi as Andrada leaped in, heard
the first incoherent stammerings . . . and drawn his immoral conclusions. On he sped, motor shut off and brakes
recklessly screeching, down into the city's heat. The taxi
went directly to the dwelling of Odile and her relatives,
to the place of hidden joys wedged between small shops
identified by signs chalked on the walls. On the boardwalk
in front of the house the old crone was back at her pot.
The family (whose new credit with *boulangerie* and
épicerie of the district had already failed) greeted Andrada with astonishment and joy. They pulled him out of
the taxi, babbling incoherently now, his small arms waving. He was swarmed under and drawn into the gloom,
a speck carried on the black tide. It was well after dark,
he said, before he made his escape.

All this he was to tell me: somberly staring at his shoes,
seeing nothing at all humorous in his renewed "moral
defeat." "*Why do you laugh, Nicholas Clive, to contemplate the ruin of a friend? I was again snared in the coils
of lust.*" And the consequences—the consequences at least

of that visit to Barbara Swenson's—were swift and serious enough. For the next morning he received an unexpected yet overdue visit from his compatriot Miguel Rubínez, more commonly known as "The Cripple." Heretofore Andrada had feared chiefly the impatience of Eufemio Rodriguez in his dark New York office, and of various uniformed authorities behind polished desks in the capital city of the splendid sea wall lined by palms. They would watch him from afar; in time his failures would be known. But there was nothing remote about the descent of Miguel Rubínez from a taxi—which Andrada watched from the front porch of his pension, where he had just finished his coffee.

The crutches touched earth inquisitively but with confidence. Manuel Andrada had never seen Miguel Rubínez, The Cripple. But he knew at once this was he from his manner of descending from a car, which was legendary throughout the Caribbean: first the deliberate crutches probing and sliding out like pale angry claws, then the vast improbable hindquarters ballooning, they in turn preceding by long moments the thighs, the carapace of a hump, the shaved neck, the white porcine face, bloated and still averted. The descent (a backward movement) must have required some minutes, during which Andrada waited with horror, shame and an acute sense that he was being honored. For The Cripple (protector of the weak against their own backslidings) did not concern himself with unimportant men, in his endless voyages to oversee The Protector's agents, and to conclude the deserved punishment of traitors and critics.

"*Imagine my dismay, Nicholas Clive, to find myself visited by Miguel Rubínez himself. The Cripple! The guardian of purity and enemy of backsliders! I who am*

*such a little man, uneducated really, obeying orders I
hardly understand. . . . In the same moment I became
aware of unexpected honor and terrible disgrace. I knew
at last the magnitude of my failure. What else could this
mean but a merited suspicion of weakness and impure
resolve? Yes, I thought I was suspected of ingratitude
too—ingratitude!—to the savior of the national economy.
That man's face was without expression as he spoke. It
resembled a dead white fish found on the sand from
which the skin has been removed. We went to my room.
Miguel Rubínez led the way, in fact. He did not have to
ask which room was mine. For a long time we stood under
the fatherly protection of The Protector's portrait, while
I received his calm unpassionate warning. I deserved, of
course, every word of chastisement I received. Also The
Cripple gave me new instructions. And what I had to
procure from Justo de Villamayor was now so much more
than I had ever anticipated or hoped or feared. Then he
left me. And all night I wondered whether a richly merited retribution would come, in spite of his generous
commands!"*

Over the last part of his interview with The Cripple,
Andrada drew a discreet veil of generality. Nor did he
clarify why no deviant or traitor marked for punishment
had ever shot Rubínez as he descended laboriously from
a car, or awkwardly emerged from an elevator into an
apartment hallway, or into the aghast victim's room, the
crutches fluttering and probing ahead. An extraordi-
narily large and slow-moving target. Yet I had read
enough of Santa Isabella's history to know why even the
briefest interviews inspired a sweating terror—quite as
though the probing awkward crutches would mysteriously become swift whirling blades or thin expert instru-

ments for the gouging of vulnerable parts. I knew as anyone conversant with Santa Isabella would know. For the history of Miguel Rubínez ("The Cripple") went back to the strong-arm squads and bloody early days of the regime, when retribution had to be both public and mysterious, and show no fear of reprisal. Thus Rubínez rode in the famous *Carro de la Muerte* of the 1930's: the great red Pierce Arrow touring car unprotected by bulletproof or other glass, and that must have looked forty feet long to its victims. Sometimes the deviant would be shot to death by the armed occupants of the car. But this was rare. As a rule the car would stop before the victim's house, conspicuous, the driver and his passengers chatting pleasantly, Rubínez among them, though even then of bloated expressionless face. The neighbors would peer shocked from behind shutters hastily closed. Afterward, it might take days or even weeks to learn what that deliberate pause of the great Pierce Arrow meant: the fatal automobile accident in some remote ravine or "remorseful suicide" in jail, the death by drowning in a swimming pool, or (worst of all) the early morning discovery in some village sixty or seventy miles away of an unidentified and naked corpse, hanging in the public square. But all that was past; the great car now rested in a barn on one of The Protector's estates, its retributory labors done. It belonged to what Andrada called the nation's "Period of Rectification." Ever since the second war Rubínez had worked abroad, probing the loyalty of The Protector's employees and visiting punishment on the most guilty of the exiles. The slow advance of the crutches down an institutional corridor could mean death by smothering in a bed of a Havana hospital, or by strangling in a Mexican jail.

Andrada went into no such details of violence. For him, Miguel Rubínez was a moral force, and he was concerned with his own now exposed unworthiness. *"He came to me as one who for twenty-five years had weighed the merits of the patriotic ones. I wanted to prove to him my fervent loyalty to The Protector and my untarnished love of the homeland. But I didn't know how to begin!"* So in the first minute Andrada behaved as a petty thief might, when challenged by a minor police official: he took out his wallet, and showed Rubínez his documents. While the expressionless face of a white bloated fish stared on, Andrada dealt them onto his table until the top was covered: his passport and *Cédula Personal de Identidad,* his Certificate of Good Conduct and discharge from military service, his exequatur and authorization to carry a revolver, his certificate of piety, and all his other worn cards of membership and loyalty: the now yellowed badge of membership in the Youth's Prefect Corps and in the Catholic Youth Association and in the Service of Informers and Inspectors, also the stamped form from the *Comisión Depuradora de Empleados Públicos,* the driver's license and letter identifying him as Third Secretary and Envoy Extraordinary, and as emissary of the National Archives. His hands must have sweated and trembled as he shuffled and spread the cards until at last the high effeminate voice of The Cripple interrupted him:

"What, imbecile, are you doing?"

"But Señor Rubínez! These are my documents. My loyalties, my identifications . . ."

"I know who you are, fool."

Miguel Rubínez, manipulating the crutches with immense difficulty, took a turn about the room. With one crutch he jabbed thoughtfully at Andrada's small cardboard suitcase, testing the strength of the material. Then he swung himself back.

"So, inadequate, what have you to say in your defense?"

"I am a little man, a humble one." Andrada found himself trembling, and talking much too fast. "I am not to blame for my sexual irregularities, Señor Rubínez. A madness overcomes me, I have an imperfect biological inheritance from my father. Also I was overcome by the very number of those Negroes who simply snatched me out of the taxi. I didn't want to go there at all. Consider that all the time I said nothing to the driver. I was upset and possessed by a vertigo, I could not remember the name of my hotel!"

Miguel Rubínez shifted his weight to his left leg. He swung the right crutch deftly, striking Andrada just below the knee.

"What is all this gibberish about Negroes? You are entrusted for a high mission and cannot remember the name of your hotel? Tell me, Andrada—do you consider yourself adequate?"

"Certainly not."

"And how do you justify your act of dining with known enemies of The Protector? That woman Señorita Swenson has financed grudge-bearers and hotheaded opportunists throughout the Americas. She is a destroyer of established order."

"I didn't dine with her, Señor Rubínez. I left almost at once."

"And that itself was ridiculous and dangerous, your behavior was without subtlety. It was reported to us almost at once by the chief of police. Do you realize you lack dignity?"

"I felt sick, Señor Rubínez. Moreover, I was filled with

revulsion and loathing for the evil political atmosphere of subversion and chaos."

"You are a fool, Manuel Andrada." The face, white and porous as the exposed underside of a fish, was still expressionless in its service of The Protector. "Also, you are unworthy of such a high mission. How long must The Protector wait for this infamous manuscript of Justo de Villamayor? And the National Library? And the Services of Security? How long must they wait? Justo de Villamayor will not come to you with the evil manuscript in his hand. When are you going to see him?"

"At once."

"Then you know where he is?"

"Not exactly."

The Cripple took another angry cumbersome turn about the room, striking randomly at the furniture.

"Andrada, you are inadequate. My own recommendation to the homeland would be to return you at once to Santa Isabella for sentry duty on the docks. You are a catastrophic mistake. However, I must obey the orders I receive. So I will tell you where Villamayor is. Everyone in this country knows except you. I will also convey certain new instructions, related to the historic fact that The Protector can be all-forgiving. There is always a place at his table for the repentant and weary Prodigal Son. But the present situation is intolerable. What must The Protector or his nephew think of the continuing presence abroad of Justo de Villamayor, capable of writing anything and of a known weakness of character, subject to subversive temptation? So. I will give you your new instructions, and you will be on your way before noon. Is that entirely understood? If not. . . ."

In the silence Andrada found himself staring directly

and from some six inches away at the rubber-mounted end of a crutch. The other end of it lay against The Cripple's cheek, who closed one eye in the manner of a man aiming a rifle. He noticed with alarm a pinkness invade the white porous flesh, and the flatulent lips begin to tremble. Then the entire face of Miguel Rubínez was in motion, the features and flesh struggling in the semblance of a thick jelly, the pink skin now veined with purple that had once been porous and white. The ensuing laugh resembled, in some respects, a shrill female scream.

So it was "entirely understood." . . . But over the rest of that interview (following upon the alarming laugh) Manuel Andrada drew the veil. He had too much respect for Miguel Rubínez to betray such professional secrets to me. For Miguel Rubínez was, like Villamayor, already a historical figure, part of the homeland's heritage. An indispensable cog in the wheel of national reinvigoration, both moral and economic. After the interview, Andrada followed Rubínez to the taxi and respectfully watched him crawl into it, backward, the gross hind-quarters first and the now calmed and white porcine face last. He watched the taxi swing away with mingled pride and shame . . . shame that the visit had been necessary. Watching the taxi, still cognizant of the crutch's blow below his knee, Andrada felt purified and renewed. *"A fresh start, Nicholas Clive! I was returning to the true path I had left."*

Then he returned to his room to pack his things, and for the ceremonial wrapping of the portrait; by noon he had set out. I can imagine him making resolutions as his taxi moved into the suburbs of Port-au-Prince: he was leaving Odile behind, he would leave behind animality and lust. The taxi climbed slowly out of the dazing heat,

and into the brown eroded hills. By three o'clock it
reached the reposing car hired by Villamayor, and guarded
by a *chef-de-section* bearing a carbine. Its headlights,
doors, and wheels were gone. Here Andrada too, after
much bickering, rented a small horse to be preceded down
the trail by the tall and scornful guide whose clothes
hung in rags.

Thus he descended toward us through the blazing
afternoon and the jungle: he was excited by the prospect
of meeting another of his country's great men. Two in
one day, it was an honor beyond his dreams! But also he
was alarmed by the emptiness of the path. For he had
come, after his brief stay, to distrust intensely the citizens
of Haiti. He must have wondered what new evil and
snare lay in wait to weaken his resolve.

And of course he did not know how many citizens were
preceding him down that empty steaming path . . . to
report his coming to us. They straggled into the clearing,
and came toward us up the ruined alley, gesticulating,
imitating Andrada's appearance and his chattels. They
were much bemused by the spectacle of a man on horseback of such solemn expression, who had what appeared
to be a small platform strapped to his back, done up in
expensive brown paper and rising high above his head.

5

IN ALL my speculations it never occurred to me that Andrada, when confronted by Villamayor, would simply be struck dumb. But so it was. He moved toward us with head averted, silent, not waving or even nodding, ridiculously small and rigid—as though he, not the horse, were being led by that threadbare guide. Andrada was somberly intent beneath the covered portrait strapped to his back. He descended awkwardly, sliding down the horse's flank, clinging to the saddle. His short legs reached for the ground. He said not a word until he had untied the black cardboard suitcase from its place behind the saddle. Then he turned—not to Villamayor, but to me or more exactly to a point in space between us. And began to mutter rapidly in a voice strangled by embarrassment: *"Such a pleasure, Nicholas Clive. So you have found your way here? Well, I too have arrived!"* He was stricken with shyness. *I too have arrived. . . .* What else could he say, who in the last years of school had been asked to memorize and recite poems by this man he was still afraid to look at.

He told me, that night, of his "numbness of mind and heart," of a shyness that held his tongue in the "presence of greatness." For he saw not the tall man in tennis shoes and sport shirt but the cultural monument and historical name. Also the statue in academic robes gazing out to sea, already immortal. Andrada continued to stare between us even as he tumbled out the first words intended for the master's ears: *"Manuel Andrada, Excellency. A humble man, an admirer of your verses. Forgive me, I am too confused by the honor of this hour. Let me only say that I guarantee publication on the finest vellum."* He was still looking shyly away. And the patriotic burden (wrapped in expensive brown paper) still rose precipitously above his head, in the semblance of an upturned platform. *"Yes. And a special de luxe edition for distribution to chosen friends."*

Villamayor did not laugh. He did not yet know what to make of this scarred little man, with his homemade brown suit designed for northern rigors. But he was sorry for him in his shyness.

"Publication on the finest vellum? Surely that is every writer's vain and pretentious dream! However, we will speak of this matter of publication later. Meanwhile, I am sure you are in need of refreshment."

"Oh, I am a humble man, sir!"

Villamayor smiled and went inside. I became aware, at the same time, of the two porcelain and bodiless faces watching us as they had watched me; then they were gone. I helped Andrada free himself of his burden. The portrait was attached to his back by a network of knotted strings that looped under the armpits; there were various knots to untie. I took advantage of this operation to inform Andrada that only Villamayor and I knew he came from Santa Isabella. His women were still in the dark; Villamayor wanted it so.

"His women! Is he cohabiting with more than one?" He looked up at me accusingly. "Tell me, Nicholas Clive

—why did you leave me again? And on the very threshold
of accomplishment!"

"I guess I thought you needed a rest, after your skir-
mish with Odile."

"I know, I know. You are right to make fun of me.
But all that animality and weakness is at an end. I have
been admonished by a high authority. It is clear I have
disgraced the fatherland, also the National Library, but
I am now on the right path. Only you must help me,
Nicholas Clive! I find myself unable to speak! Years ago
we were made to stand beside our desks and recite the
poems of this man. Now I see him in the flesh, he even
offers me refreshment!"

And he was, through most of that first evening, quite
unable to speak. He found himself cowed and stupefied
in the presence of the "nation's most illustrious writer"
—still that, though politically misguided and in exile.
Andrada sat very straight at the edge of his chair, holding his glass with both hands. He was, I could see, paralyzed by the complexity of his feelings. He was a special
agent on a mission, after all, not only an ex-schoolboy.
Moreover, there were for him the two different Villa-
mayors. There was the onetime Minister of Education
who had foolishly criticized government decrees, and
who for twenty-six days abused great honor and privilege.
The oppositionist and ingrate. . . . Yes, there was the
Villamayor who needed to be brought back to his senses
and admonished for backslidings, the political deviate
to be scolded, who might well deserve a crutch's blow
across the knee. Or even conceivably a few months' imprisonment and reeducation in the ideals of the Reinvigoration. After all, there was hardly a great man in the
nation's history (since the earthquake and tidal wave)

who had not deserved it now and then: the swift blow
of the crutch. Who is not weak at least once—except
the Protector and his nephew the President of the Republic? Certainly the political Villamayor was weak. But
also there was this other Villamayor who had written
the poem learned by every thirteen-year-old schoolboy
the length and breath of Santa Isabella: a sixteen-line
declaration of love for the savannas of the Cibao where
the poet had wandered as a child, dreaming his first
dreams. Incontestably the greatest writer of Santa Isabella,
perhaps of all Latin-America. . . .

And now he sat facing Andrada: chatting pleasantly,
his face wrenched and cocked to the side exactly as in the
well known photographs, exactly as fixed upon that
statue gazing out to sea. A monument of the culture. It
was this second Villamayor who held for Andrada the
overwhelming, the stupefying reality. At this first meeting at least he simply could not have conceived doing
Villamayor any physical harm. He might as easily have
raised his hand against the Director of the School, or
against a superior in the Corps of Prefects.

Dinner was also, for Andrada, a disturbing experience.
For he sat at the foot of the two tables, next to me and
facing Villamayor; he was horribly exposed. He kept his
eyes as much as possible on his plate. But still he had to
wonder who these others were, clustered around his
"great man," perhaps poisoning his attitudes? He too
noticed the way Ezile touched Villamayor's shoulder
gently before sliding into her place at his right—the
frank calm gesture of possession, connection, love. And
he must have been puzzled, as I was still, by Belesprit,
that great hulking presence. The whites of the Negro's
eyes were enormous; he had the deep chanting voice of

a poet. As for Julieta Aparicio—Andrada knew her at least by name. She was the secretary, the fanatic one, the typist who would commit to paper both the great poetry and the abominable political criticisms, alike cherished by the National Library. The sister of the María Teresa who had uttered such foul rantings. Well, he would pay this Julieta back, in time, stare for black stare.

But Consuela he had not heard of at all, nor even of "La Atrevida." He had still been scarcely a month away from the homeland, where her name would not even be whispered. Her exploits beginning with that thirty-five-minute speech at the Flagler Theater in Miami would hardly have been reported in the *Diario del Caribe!* And she too, of course, had not yet taken her measure of him. But at least he was certainly not a Norte Americano "with ice in his veins." Andrada became sharply conscious of her lipstick, her eye makeup and long carmined nails. And of the way her eyes stared sullenly into his own, while her chin rested on her knuckles. He told me he felt at once a rapport between them.

For a time Villamayor, Belesprit and I talked about paintings we had seen at the Centre d'Art in Port-au-Prince. The question was whether there was really any difference in method between the few primitives who kept a half-faith in the *vaudun* rituals and the sophisticates who believed nothing. For Belesprit, all superstition was degrading and could not lead to great art. It was an inconclusive discussion, which Consuela suddenly interrupted. She broke in as any girl of her age might, but broke in with political speculation. I think she asked her question in order to test Andrada, and learn where he stood. Perhaps she hoped this soon to detect some gleam of kinship, a sympathetic revolutionary ardor. He did not look like a mere collector of manuscripts!

She interrupted us suddenly, addressing Villamayor:

"Did you know Otto Cepeda?"

"Slightly." The twisted face and black eyes moved sadly from the girl to Andrada. I think Villamayor already expected the worst of this scarred visitor—though it was another twelve hours before he asked, in his usual bantering voice—"*What do you think, Clive? Does your little friend intend to kill me?*" But on this first evening, at least, Villamayor scorned caution and evasion. "Yes, I knew him. Why do you ask?"

"He died in Port-au-Prince last month, a few days after I arrived."

"I know."

"He was killed in jail. He was found hanging in his cell: a victim of the scum. It is well known that the knot was tied after his death."

"Are you sure? Suicide for political remorse would be a much more logical conclusion to his repetitive and even monotonous life." He glanced at me. "You know the story of Otto Cepeda?"

I shook my head. I too was curious to see how Manuel Andrada would behave when exposed to the full subversive scorn of another "grudge-bearer."

"Very well, then. I will tell you the not unexemplary story of his life: a small page in the moral history of Santa Isabella. You can then decide for yourself whether Cepeda committed suicide for political remorse; or was given help by another hand. Surely the facts of his earlier life must outweigh the circumstantial evidence of an improbably knotted rope? So: this story begins two years ago, when Otto Cepeda was Secretary of Commerce Without Portfolio. A trusted servant of The Protector, a man of importance in the city. And almost rich at forty-five. He would be earning the full $35,000 a year, quite apart from hidden perquisites of office. Moreover, he was happily employed: a man who loved charts, tables, numbers. Nothing gave him more pleasure than to regularize through statistics and graphs The Protector's invasion of a new monopoly. He threw himself into such labors; his office lights would blaze through the night. Yes, Otto Cepeda's *expertise* and love of order were gratified by a closed circle of graft and corruption. The ideal, the devoted bureaucrat! So why the Protector singled him out for such wild oscillations of fortune is beyond our knowledge. Did Cepeda unwittingly release a report whose statistics implied corruption? I cannot believe he would be so careless. Or are we presented instead with a private joke on The Protector's part, ferociously prolonged over years? In that event we can imagine the great one and his cronies musing over their bottle, *'So how is it with Cepeda now? When next shall we pull the rug?'* That too is possible. But perhaps the true significance of the example lies in its absolutely arbitrary character. It is the peculiarity of The Protector's system to forgive as arbitrarily as it punishes. Even forgiveness then becomes alarming. Cepeda's is a special case only because he was resurrected so often and so high—resurrected and struck down and resurrected."

The first calamity occurred without forewarning. "In this," Villamayor remarked, "Cepeda's story was quite typical." He drove happily to his office in his shiny little black Mercedes and his spotless white suit; and was arrested on emerging from the car. He never even reached the gleaming white building over which he had presided for years. An hour later he was in confinement in the Guadalupe prison, noted for its vermin and for the seepage of foul waters from the bay. There for a month he received, together with his small loaf, the usual daily tongue-lashing with three common criminals. "But that was nothing," Villamayor went on. "What must not have been the anguish of the orderly Cepeda, unable to communicate with his office, let alone his wife? All the tables and graphs and charts left uncompleted on his desk! It is said he begged for paper and for copies of the previous year's budget."

Aloof and calm, Villamayor stared out into the darkness as he talked, while Andrada stared at his own hands.

"However, Cepeda should have known better than to hope for a return to the same polished desk in the white Secretariat. Instead he found himself, on his sudden release, appointed to a much smaller post as Assistant Director of the *Fábrica Nacional de Calzados*—a shoe monopoly benefiting by many army and government decrees, including one forbidding bare feet within the city limits. Here (employed at perhaps $600 a month) Cepeda threw himself happily into the correction of extraordinarily tangled records. He had to sell his home with small swimming pool. But he was tremblingly grateful for The Protector's reprieve after the month of vermin and oral abuse. He knew how to count his blessings."

Beside me Andrada sat very straight. But his head was nodding, almost imperceptibly. He must have been saying to himself: "*Yes, The Protector forgives.*" Consuela and Julieta watched him.

"In all this," Villamayor went on, "Cepeda is but one of hundreds who have fallen from grace unaccountably.

The chastened bureaucrat becomes aware once for all of his utter dependence on incomprehensible judgment. His desk may be rolled away at any moment, the floor beneath him may vanish. However—his life is not over, his shamed family welcomes him home. And with luck he will climb slowly back toward respectability and the possibility of retiring with a pension. But not Otto Cepeda. Our Cepeda had almost brought order into the chaotic finances of the shoe monopoly when he found himself back at Guadalupe, but this time in solitary confinement and under a regimen of light torture administered daily. The oral abuse reached him in an utterly dark cell; then came the hour of torture. Can you not imagine the further anguish too of this abnormally precise man, once again separated from his statistics? Is this in fact the secret of Cepeda's suicide —that three times within two years he was torn suddenly from unachieved tasks of mathematical ordering? The chaos left behind would haunt his dreams."

"He did not commit suicide," Consuela said. "He was killed. How can a man make a second knot in a rope around his neck after the first knot has killed him?"

"Who knows? Perhaps a cell mate tied the second knot as an act of kindness?"

"Perhaps a cell mate tied both knots. For a price."

"If you wish. Still, I find it hard to abandon my faith in suicide from actual political remorse. For how could a man so often and so gratuitously punished help experiencing the very extremes of guilt? I visualize Cepeda babbling confessions, to the astonishment of his jailers in Port-au-Prince."

Villamayor returned to the second incarceration in Guadalupe. It was here, he said, that Cepeda's story became "untypical" and therefore morally significant. For after another month of prison and light torture Cepeda actually went on trial for disloyalty, was found guilty, given a suspended sentence, and returned to the gleaming Secretariat of Commerce . . . but now as a clerk in an outer office, paid perhaps $150 a month. There he shared a small adding machine with six other clerks, all much younger than himself.

"And who can say what astonishment and alarm his former underlings in the white Secretariat must have known—to see Cepeda at such a modest desk, and with one eye bandaged? A man who in one year has aged ten, and has lost twenty kilos at least? Was it wise even to nod to a man so ruined? Yet perhaps they treated him warily. Perhaps they saw Cepeda as a government agent thrust among his former employees to overhear critical remarks. Who knows? For after six months of obscurity, Cepeda experienced the most alarming of his various translations. He was invited to a reception at The Protector's Hacienda."

Manuel Andrada gasped.

"The Protector's Hacienda!"

"Yes, he was to meet The Protector at last. Face to face. Would it be for life or death? Can we not imagine poor Cepeda investing the last of his fortune in an appropriate costume? He would even have had to rent a car to get out there. Do you not see him in his tuxedo approaching the great floodlit estate, again and again stopped for an inspection of his papers? There would be the hours of anguish as he listened to a concert, as he sat through the grand untasted dinner, as he stood in the reception line. Then at the critical moment in the magnificent ballroom he found himself embraced. That is, The Protector held him at arm's length and by the elbows for a long minute, as though examining his case. And then at last that single giggle and faint suspicion of a smile which is supposed to mean all is forgiven. Overnight Cepeda became national director of the insurance company. The *Compañía de Seguros San Cristóbal.*"

"It is true," Andrada put in, with uncontrollable relief. "Everything was forgiven."

"You knew Cepeda?"

"No, Excellency, only by name. I was merely attending to your story."

"Perhaps you are right, perhaps everything was forgiven. In that event Cepeda must have committed further mysterious crimes. For after only six months in office the first letters of complaint began to appear in the Foro Público columns of the *Diario.* There were rumors of incompetence and waste in the *Compañía de Seguros.* Premiums had been lost, death benefits had been paid more than once, there were the usual corruptions. And of course you know what such letters in the *Diario* mean? Within a week these letters—as always betraying the same bureaucratic style—were growing virulent. The Director of the *Compañía de Seguros* was a homosexual and an attacker of religion. Also he had neglected his mother. He was a smuggler, a drunk, an incompetent, a jackal and scum and liar, a prematurely born inadequate. *Sietemesino! Sietemesino,* the prematurely born. Otto Cepeda must have known (seeing the fatal word appear in the letters) that the time had come for resignation. He sent a letter to the *Diario* admitting all faults and all charges, and his resignation was accepted. He was sent immediately to Puerto Rico as a commercial attaché: a broken man, almost at the end now of his incomprehensible career, demoralized by frustration and fright. He was now

a man utterly and loyally bound to The Protector's judgment of his guilt. The assignment abroad indicated a
confidence that this man was not quite crushed. For two
months he worked faithfully copying bills of lading in
San Juan, then he disappeared. Were they surprised, I
wonder, that Cepeda had the flicker of courage to get as
far as Port-au-Prince before surrendering his life in
that act of total surrender, total admission of guilt?"

Consuela drummed the table in annoyance.

"He was killed."

"Very well, he was killed. In the long run it amounts to
much the same thing." Villamayor studied his small compatriot at our end of the table. "And what do you think
of this story, Señor Andrada?"

I glanced at the flushed and burning face; even the
scar was inflamed. At the time I thought Andrada was
struggling to subdue his rage. But the fact was that he
hadn't really taken in the story. It went too far beyond
any conception of reality he knew.

"I have heard of Otto Cepeda, Excellency. But you
neglected to name his crimes."

"There were no crimes."

"No crimes? But how can this be? For repeated forgiveness there must be something to forgive. . . . There
must have been moral backslidings."

"The only backslidings lay in the systematic falsifica-
tion of financial records out of loyalty to The Protector's
greed."

"The Protector's greed!" Manuel Andrada suddenly
wrung his hands, his body began to tremble. But he managed to remain discreet. "How can I know about an Otto
Cepeda, Excellency? I am a mere purchaser of manuscripts, only a humble man representing the National

Library and the Archives of Santa Isabella. As for politics
—I know nothing of these great affairs."

Consuela and Julieta gasped. But in the face of this
revelation—not a revelation to him, after all—Villamayor
remain very calm.

"And what else do you represent? Surely not only the
Library and the Archives. . . ."

Andrada looked to me for help, then turned toward
the wall. He could no longer face Villamayor.

"It is such an honor—to be received in your house,
Excellency! How can I speak of business at such a time?
Please forgive me if I wait. . . . Did I not as a boy in
my last year at school commit your own patriotic verses
to memory? *In the savannas of the Cibao.* . . . Yes, I
remember them after all these years. The last two lines
of the poem are the same as the first ones; it is an artistic
device." Andrada moved far forward in his seat; he began
to stand up, he was babbling. "May I be permitted to
recite? It would be such an honor. *The savannas of the
Cibao.* . . ."

Villamayor raised both hands; his twisted face was
sharp with distaste.

"In the name of God, please do not! I cannot bear to
hear that wretched poem again. It has pursued me for
twenty years. It is one of the pleasures of exile, to escape
the recitations of schoolchildren and unknown visitors."

"Wretched poem! But Your Excellency—everyone
knows it is a classic of our literature."

"Very well. However, the man who wrote that poem
is dead. He is, if you wish, a footnote in the literary history. . . . Let us leave him there. I have wholly tran-
scended the naïve nostalgia of the young man who wrote
those lines. He is dead and gone, with the waving hair

he wore that year, and the great moustache cultivated in Paris with such diligence. Why should we speak twenty years later of a homesickness suffered by that pretentious young dandy? No, let us live in the present, not the past. . . . And let us not—you are quite right, Señor Andrada —let us not speak of libraries and publishing. All that too seems to me past, and the literary vanities that drag one down."

Andrada bowed his head humbly before these words, themselves as incomprehensible as a poem read for the first time.

SUCH was the first collision, inconclusive and absurd, of my two dark men, citizens of Santa Isabella. Villamayor withdrew shortly after dinner, and Manuel Andrada at once took me aside. He wanted a "confidential consultation." So we walked to the beach, leaving both portrait and black suitcase in my room. The path cut through great stalks of bamboo, and near the beach a half-moon shone in the first thick trees. The thick whiteness lay on the sand, on the still pool, and on the surf curling over that coral fringe fifty feet from shore. Our solitude was intense under the glittering sky. I pointed to the frontier *cordillera septentrional* some miles to the east, a great inked mass beyond Caye Thomonde. Its summit would be in Santa Isabella.

"The fatherland, yes." Andrada stared patriotically into the dark. Beyond the *cordillera* he would see, in his mind's eye, isolated villages and huts. "At this hour the families will be gathered in the kitchens for an hour of reading or talk. Their labors are over for the day." Then he turned back to me. "So, Nicholas Clive, the hour for consultation. I say again—you were wrong to leave me without warning. And you did not tell me you had seen Barbara Swenson in Port-au-Prince, the rabble-rouser and plotter! Why do you not collaborate? Did you know she is planning a revolution?"

"Oh, she's always plotting a revolution. Even Villa-mayor says she's harmless."

"I pray God you are right. For she has collected about herself black pigs and scum. There was that man Eduardo Gonzales, the enthusiast who spends his life planning the overthrow of established and reinvigorating institutions. Evil women too." He lowered himself and crouched with simian ease, plunging both fists into the sand. "Now tell me, Nicholas Clive—what is Justo de Villamayor writing?"

"I don't know."

"You don't know!" He looked up angrily; the scar had a phosphorescent cast. "You have been here almost a week."

I explained that I didn't want to push things too fast. For the purposes of my article the important thing was to gain Villamayor's confidence, even his friendship. Every day his conversation had revealed new subtleties of spirit. I had enough to cope with in the man; the question of his unpublished writings could wait.

"That is all very well for you, Nicholas Clive. But I can't delay any longer, it is the National Library that waits. Tell me this—have you ever been struck across the knee for moral delinquency and repeated failure?"

I could only laugh at this latest irrelevance, since I had not yet heard of The Cripple's admonitory visit.

"Are you threatening me?"

"I speak of myself. And listen: even for Villamayor's

own sake we must not delay. This is a terrible place, he is in great moral danger. There is that black woman who sits beside him. What is her role?"

"What you call 'sexual gratification,' I suppose."

"That's what I feared. What a delinquency, to cohabit with a black peasant who doesn't even wear shoes! What a degradation!"

I had to laugh again.

"How about yourself? You've done pretty well with Odile."

"Yes, I know, I have been sunk and mired in lust. And not even to have privacy! But who am I, Nicholas Clive? A nobody! I am a mere humble agent, an underling, and by birth a peasant myself. But Justo de Villamayor is a famous man. This ignoble relationship dishonors the literary heritage, it stains a public name. Can you conceive of him rising from such a peasant bed to write great poems and essays?"

"I hadn't given it much thought."

Andrada stood up angrily. He walked to the water and back.

"Listen to me, Nicholas Clive! This man's spirit is being corrupted and degraded. For much too long he has been listening to the loose talk of riffraff and atheistic scum. For three years now he has been exposed to evil propaganda, corroding the soul. Even his speech has become frivolous. A man surrounded by such base companions will soon be capable of anything."

I reminded him of the Catholic and even mystical saving presence of Julieta Aparicio, who conceived exalted destinies for her employer.

"She didn't say a word. And how about that beautiful young girl who stared at me so? Is she also his mistress?"

"I don't think so." I could already visualize Andrada backed into a corner, and the aroused Consuela spitting at him in her political fury, raking with her carmined nails. "I think I'll let you get to know her yourself."

He crouched in front of me, rocking on his heels.

"No, no—all that is finished: the lusts and gratifications. I have been reminded of my failure, I have been struck beneath the knee. I still feel the blow. Yes, and there is something else. In my belly I have a strange pain as of a very thin blade, inserted just beneath the skin. Have you ever experienced that?"

"No."

"Well, listen to me, Nicholas Clive. You have never understood that I am ready to honor Justo de Villamayor, greatest of our poets. And the fatherland eagerly awaits his writings. But that is not all! I dream of persuading him to return to his home. I shall be the one responsible for his honorable return. He has no business living in ruin among savages."

"He wouldn't think of going back."

"Why not? Let me tell you something in confidence. I have received new instructions, forgiveness has been offered. Immunity and perhaps even a partial restoration of the confiscated property . . ."

"Forgiveness! Like Otto Cepeda's, for instance?"

Once again Andrada rose impatiently and stalked away. But he was back almost at once.

"Who was Otto Cepeda? A whining bookkeeper, a backsliding accountant. A *sietemesino!* No poems of Otto Cepeda will ever be memorized by the schoolboys of Santa Isabella. Moreover, the story cannot be true. Of course Cepeda was guilty, of course there were moral failures. . . ."

I shrugged my shoulders.

"That may be. Still, I'd advise you not to rush in offering Villamayor forgiveness, if you want to find out what he's written."

Andrada pawed thoughtfully at the sand, still crouched before me, rocking on his heels.

"Of course. Of course you are right, Nicholas Clive. Everything in its proper time. And everything must be honorably frank. Tomorrow I will simply ask him about the manuscripts, we will go to him together. I will convey the National Library's offer. What writer would not be honored? Publication on the finest vellum! As for his return to the homeland—we will say nothing for a while."

"Don't say 'we.' I haven't anything to do with it."

Andrada looked at me oddly. He seemed to measure my impulse to withdraw.

"Oh no, Nicholas Clive. You cannot leave me again."

THE next morning I went fairly early to Villamayor's bedroom, from which the sounds of a flute floated down. I wanted to dissociate myself as firmly as possible from Andrada and his mission, before the proposals were made. It was no fault of mine if Andrada attached himself to me, and made his ridiculous claims! I was as hostile to The Protector as anyone else. This time I even alluded vaguely to the small ridiculous trail of violence Andrada had left in Boston. He was a fool, of course. And yet I was sure he represented something more aggressive than a Library and Archives.

Villamayor listened to me undismayed.

"It is a kindness to tell me," he said at last. "But it was not necessary. Surely anyone who has lived under The

Protector's wing would recognize this poor creature's role. There is a *je ne sais quoi* of manner, a fanatic and somber intensity. . . . Yes, your little friend Andrada is a dedicated man. But would any country except mine send such an ignorant man as 'representative of a National Library'?"

"Why do you suppose they do?"

Villamayor shrugged.

"A more delicate mentality would be more capable of treason. Yes, an intellectual might very wisely have remained in Boston or New York, if only to rejoice in the admirable libraries. It is one of the nation's great problems —the prompt and chronic defection of men sent on diplomatic missions. Even an editor of the *Diario* sent to a press association meeting in Washington conscientiously made his apologies for The Protector. A seventy-minute speech. The next morning he announced he was going into exile. And your friend Andrada? I am sure the authorities find him absolutely trustworthy. Moreover, I dare say his violent appearance is supposed to frighten me into surrendering my manuscript, and to frighten poor Julieta. That extraordinary suit, that apocalyptic and angry scar! Tell me, Clive—what will happen if I flatly refuse? Does your little friend intend to kill me?"

"He's not my friend. And he's even more than a representative of the Library. He's also an 'emissary' of your own Ministry."

"Of Education? Good God—even for Santa Isabella that is carrying cynicism very far!"

A few minutes later Andrada took matters out of my hands by arriving. So I was present at that interview after all. But I was only that: "present," an observer exempt

from their passions. Still, I could already ask myself
whether Villamayor had developed his ironic refinements
of spirit to an extreme that would make him welcome his
destroyer. He was cold and scornful at the start, with his
forehead drawn up in the precise ridges, ready to make
Andrada's ignorance the butt of a joke. But before many
minutes has passed I detected an incorrigible sympathy
returning. It was Villamayor's great lack: he could repu-
diate no one who cared deeply about anything.

Andrada stood in the middle of the room as he had
once stood before me in Boston, with his hands stiff in
embarrassment. He was much shorter than Villamayor.
He was at last prevailed upon to sit down.

"Very well then," Villamayor began, "Now we shall
speak of publication on the finest vellum."

Andrada was pleasantly surprised.

"You are agreeable? Let me say again that I represent
the National Library and Archives. I am not an exile
or subversive. No, there must be an honorable frankness,
no concealment at all. I come from Santa Isabella itself.
From the homeland of us all, from the nest."

"I did not need to be told that," Villamayor said. "I
would know that at a glance. Do we not all bear the mark
of Cain?"

"What do you mean, Excellency, the mark of Cain.
. . . The National Library desires to publish all of your
work. It is five years since the world has seen anything
from your pen."

Villamayor arched his fingers over his nose: a medita-
tive gesture.

"It will have to wait a bit longer. What made you
think I would want to publish . . . in 'the nest'?"

"I know, I know," Andrada said hurriedly. "There have been small political disagreements. However, literature is above the strife."

"Do you forget I was seized in my office and dragged away? That I was tortured and beaten to within an inch of my life?"

Manuel Andrada was alarmed by such a forthright glance into the past. He half rose from his chair, the gold tooth appeared.

"I know nothing about that, honorable sir. All that is political. The speculations of journalists, fantastic rumors."

"They weren't fantastic rumors to me. They were broken bones."

"But I know nothing of all that, Excellency. How could I know? I am only a purchaser of manuscripts. I say again: Literature is above the strife." He was babbling now. "Poetry is unpolitical, celebrating man and nature. . . ."

"My poetry is unpolitical, yes." Villamayor sat back in his chair, coolly amused. "So what, Señor Andrada, can you offer me—in addition to the finest vellum?"

"I am authorized to ask you to name the conditions. What will you take, Excellency, for everything new you have written?"

"How about immunity? Would that be a fair price?"

"Immunity? Yes, why not eventually immunity, and total honor at last?" Andrada's scar flamed in the warmth of his enthusiasm; he was getting on famously. "You belong back in our great capital city. And in your own house now temporarily occupied by a foreign legation. Yes, I have many times walked by your white house with its awnings and its splendid lawn. There is a pool at the side screened by trees; I have heard the happy voices.

Total honor at last in the country of one's birth! What more can a poet ask? And why not the Annual Prize of the Academy of History? That too could be arranged."

"The Academy of History!" Villamayor threw up his hands; he was still smiling faintly. "Is there any institution on earth more servile and corrupt? Listen: the next to last thing I want is immunity. The last thing I want is freedom to return to my swimming pool 'screened by trees.' And if the Academy of History were to make me an award—I would feel obliged to destroy all my work."

"Oh you can't mean that, Excellency!"

"I do indeed mean it."

"But why? Surely it is possible for a writer to rise above the petty strifes of the day. Don't you love your country?"

Villamayor looked off into the dark corner of the room above his bed; there was a white patch where the plaster had fallen away.

"My country? My corrupted, brutalized, vulgar, illiterate country, parched and enervated and ruined? My country that slumbers and sickens under a curse? Yes. Of course, I love it."

Andrada looked up hopefully.

"Just as I thought! What patriot would doubt it, who knows your poem on the savannas of the Cibao? Believe me, Excellency, your patriotism will triumph over these little difficulties. They are transient, but art is eternal."

"It won't quite overcome the small difficulty of The Protector's existence and the existence of his nephews. Your proposal—mind you, I don't blame you for it, I blame your superiors—your proposal is ridiculous. A few innocent poems, yes, published under the imprint of the National Library! I can imagine too the first articles in the *Diario*: 'The exile has begun to repent. The reinvigoration of Villamayor. . . .' No, I shall be quite categorical and thus save both your time and mine. I shall publish nothing in Santa Isabella so long as The Protector and his nephews are alive. Or so long as they remain on the native soil. Unless an attack on The Protector himself. . . ."

"You are writing such at attack?"

Villamayor glanced at me, then again into the darkness above his bed. He stood up.

"I shall not discuss with you what I have written. Or what I am writing now."

"But you misunderstand, Excellency. It is only a friendly literary question, by an admirer of your verses. As for the essay on historical fatality . . . everyone knows its greatness."

Villamayor looked down at Andrada queerly.

"You have failed in your mission," he said quietly. "I sincerely hope you will not be punished."

"But you will reconsider, Excellency! I know you will reconsider. A great writer wants to communicate his sentiments to the people of his homeland, not only to unfeeling northern strangers. A writer yearns for publication."

"For the present I shall have to do without it. Moreover, I must ask you as a matter of principle to leave my house. And, after all, there is no reason for you to stay."

Andrada turned anxiously to me:

"But I must see him again! Nicholas Clive, please explain to him the necessities. Please come to my aid!"

I shook my head.

"Don't say I didn't warn you!"

"But I can't go back with empty hands, Nicholas Clive. It would be the end of my career. My career! Oh you do not understand—you who live free from moral failure and backsliding. Perhaps you have never received a merited chastisement. No, it would be impossible to go back with empty hands."

"I am truly sorry," Villamayor said. "Believe me, I understand your plight. I too have known the extreme commitment from which there is no retreat. I too have known punishment, and those physical blows directed at the mind and will. But why go back to Santa Isabella at all? Why go back ever? I cannot receive you in this house, it is a matter of stubborn principle. But you could find a room in Caye Thomonde. Or you could go back to Port-au-Prince and stay there, take up a new life. Why Santa Isabella? There is all the wide world to receive you!"

"Oh, Excellency!" Andrada found himself retreating in dismay toward the door. He was outraged by this subversive proposal. "Of course I must go back to Santa Isabella. And you too! The fatherland awaits us all."

BUT he could not go back with "empty hands." Later in the morning I went with him to Caye Thomonde, where he found a sagging malodorous room. A rickety outside staircase led to the room built over a general store. The proprietor—a busy perspiring young Negro named Aubelin Camille—trotted ahead of us, chattering excitedly in French. Did Andrada want to go *en pension*, or only rent the room? Did he require any personal services? This was the same man who had rented the great house to Villamayor. He was, in fact, the one man of enterprise in that dying community: its grocer, pharmacist and moneylender, its one lawyer and scribe. As the town's only educated man he was also a self-appointed adviser, for a fee, to the troubled and the sick. He spoke to us rapidly of mysterious and useful connections with the police, with the voodoo priests and doctors, with the one ordained Catholic priest of the region. *Des rapports confidentiels.* . . . (And he certainly did have his talents! Within twenty-four hours he knew as much as I about Andrada's mission, and had heard of his many misfortunes. He had even taken under advisement certain most intimate matters: Andrada's sexual longings, for example, and his growing burden of guilt, also that strange pain as of a thin knife inserted in the belly, just beneath the skin.)

It was not much of a room. But Andrada seemed indifferent to the roaches and to the faint rustlings of his straw pallet on the floor. And he was pleased by the modest price. Moreover, a nail was already in place from which the portrait of The Protector could depend above the pallet: the face lower than usual, the dead eyes more admonishing. The effect would be, in the first gray moments of waking, of seeing a rather short man standing at the foot of one's bed. It was an appropriate room for solitary musings on defeat. In a few days, I surmised, it would have its familiar odors of soiled linen and crumbling bread; it would quickly become a lair.

But Andrada was not yet defeated. At first he shook his head repeatedly, thinking back on that interview. "I have lost the honor of sitting at his table, Nicholas Clive! Moreover, he did not permit me to recite. He did not seem to understand my arguments." Andrada's expression, as he quietly unpacked his cardboard suitcase (which was half-filled with magazines) was one of utter bafflement. What can one do about a great poet who perversely refuses the honors thrust upon him? who tries to deny his patriotic sentiments? who sinks into apathy among barefoot savages? Andrada turned up his coarse hands: it was the gesture of a defeated man. But only minutes later he began to recover confidence, and before I left he was already contemplating his return—his return to the forbidden house and table, his return to Villamayor. "Yes, Nicholas Clive, I have for the moment lost my footing. I advanced too rapidly. In that you were quite right. But Justo de Villamayor will reconsider, I am sure. He will consult the dictates of his heart. And he will talk to me at last."

And so indeed he would. That too I should have anticipated, if only because I had begun to understand Villamayor's limitless tolerance. And perhaps I should have also guessed what attention the two anxious females would pay Andrada during the next days: first Julieta, then the still oddly silent, still uninspired Consuela. (All this time, of course, I had hoped for something that would send her into the legendary mad incantations of La Atrevida, the wild political rhetoric calculated to inflame. And what more likely than some appalling remark by Andrada? At first I could not understand why, even after they had begun to know each other, there was no hostility in her fixed stares. Even on that first evening their eyes had met as though engaged in the communication of a mystery.)

It was the church that brought them together: all three in fact, but especially Julieta and Andrada. A miserable weathered box church in a sick village halfway to Anse de Corail. Here mass was said once on Sunday, at five o'clock in the morning, by the one ordained priest in the district. Julieta told me of this, of their pilgrimage, and of her discovery of "another Andrada." She and Consuela had set out at three o'clock in the last fading moonlight, shepherded by Belesprit and Ezile. There were still drums in the first hills where the *vaudun* ceremonies continued. A typical Saturday night in Haiti: they could hear the drums on their right and the low surf to their left; the horses snorted in the odorous dark. There was an hour of utter jungle blackness during which they plodded ahead, wild branches striking their knees, tearing at their good black dresses. They kept their mantillas folded. They had been too long deprived of the consolations of the church—what with Villamayor and his corrosive if provisional skepticism—and they were willing to endure such hardships.

But so too was Andrada. Julieta and Consuela arrived at the church in the first sickly dawn. White-robed peasants streamed in ahead of them, exhausted after the night's *vaudun* ceremonies in the hills. (The skeptical Belesprit, corrupted disciple of Villamayor, remained outside.) The church was a square room with two chapels the size of large pantries, and in one of these they recognized immediately the kneeling Andrada: his hulking shoulders and broad back in the brown suit, the bent and dedicated head. They took their stations behind him, they too on their knees. When Andrada rose and took his place for mass, his face was wet with tears. Julieta could see them in the yellow light of the candles.

Tears of shame? Or tears of honorable and baffled purpose? After mass Andrada confided to them that he had arrived at three o'clock, waiting for his opportunity to confess. He understood the priest had to leave immediately after mass. But this priest knew no Spanish or English, and his own French deserted him after the first painful words and first shameful incidents. There was so much that had to be explained to a total stranger breathing sleepily in the dark! So he was left with his guilt upon him, hard as a lump of flesh; also with the odd recurrent pain as of a knife blade slipped into the abdomen just beneath the skin, and there turned and turned. He began to ask about Villamayor, then moved away from them in despair. He had no horse and so did not accompany them on the return journey, through the now blazing day.

Julieta Aparicio, who also felt bereft of confession, found that meeting in the tiny lost church very moving, in the milky gray light: a church overrun by a wilderness of great white and scarlet flowers, and kept locked six days of seven. She decided Andrada's soul could not be utterly lost, Protector or no. Moreover, she wanted to know more specifically what he intended, staying in Caye Thomonde. In her deepest feelings she must have been very much afraid. Villamayor had told her nothing, and she was not satisfied with his "poor fool" dismissal. So on Monday morning she went to see Andrada in his room in Caye Thomonde, taking me as her guide.

We found him lying on the pallet: staring bleakly up at the portrait in the musty rank half-darkness. The coat was neatly folded beside him, and he had even loosened his tie.

He quickly put the coat back on.

"So, Nicholas Clive! So, Miss Aparicio! You have come to tell me about the manuscripts."

"Not at all!" Julieta looked up at The Protector's portrait with her spinsterish smile of scorn. "And to think I was afraid you were coming here to excite and stimulate his will, and to organize secret invasions. Instead you are a servant of The Protector!"

"Secret invasions! A great poet participate in chaos!"

Julieta sat down on the one flimsy chair, Andrada and I on the pallet. The crackling straw harbored its busy insect life.

"At least you are a man of honesty—to carry about with you a portrait of the enemy. The Cruel One."

Andrada squirmed beside me.

"You are not sincere, Miss Aparicio. I saw you in the church yesterday, in company with your beautiful young friend. I saw on both your faces the true downcast image of female contrition. You are daughters of the Faith. So how can you speak against The Protector, who is the great Christian gentleman? Once a week he dines with the Archbishop; he has visited the Vatican."

"Even within the church there are lost souls. Even confession and piety cannot save the corrupt soul dedicated to evil and mired in iniquity."

Andrada rose quickly from the pallet.

"You are speaking of me?"

"No, of course not. I speak of The Protector and of his use of torture as an instrument of political persuasion."

Andrada remained silent for some moments. His mind must have revolved busily.

"Torture can be necessary to purify the will. Also to correct the rumor-mongers and souls steeped in hatred. Even the true patriot must be chastened; I speak even of myself. Will you believe I too have been guilty of delinquencies? I have spent money belonging to the homeland on pleasure and personal adornment. Well: a tongue-lashing is not enough. Nor even a blow beneath the knee. I think I will not be free of my shame until I have spent a few months in prison. Then I will come out purified, to be welcomed by my friends."

Julieta Aparicio glanced at me, as to ask my assessment of this folly. What could I say?

"At the rate you're going, you're likely to get your wish."

"Enough of this," Julieta thrust in impatiently, "I want to know why you are here."

"But I have already told Justo de Villamayor. There is no concealment at all. I am authorized to contract for the publication of his writings."

"He refused. So why do you stay? Go back to Port-au-Prince, go back to Santa Isabella."

"Villamayor will change his mind. In the end he will be unable to forego publication with honor. And publication in the homeland, where his own people can enjoy and memorize his works. It is not the destiny of a great writer to remain sullenly silent and bearing a grudge."

Julieta laughed sharply.

"What do you know of his destiny? That is my affair."

"His destiny is to return to the nest as a part of the cultural heritage. It is my humble mission to encourage this. He will write great unpolitical poems on the natural beauties of the land. A cultural monument."

"A monument is correct," Julieta said. "Villamayor, if he went back, would be killed."

"Killed!" This time Andrada leapt from the pallet and rushed to the darkest corner. He stood there for some moments in the posture of a schoolboy shamed. Then he returned. "You have been listening to evil dreamers, Miss Aparicio. The destroyers. . . . And what do you know? You are Mexican, not even a citizen of our country. Have you, a daughter of the Faith, been listening to communist rabble and atheistic scum? Listen instead to me: I saw you in that church, accompanied by that beautiful girl. So I will not become angry. I know you are said to honor and love Villamayor, even though you probably did not memorize his verses as a child. Now tell me: Is it not true the great writer must be rescued from

this corrupt and degraded atmosphere? He is surrounded
by black peasants who debilitate and ruin the will. A
mistress who wears no shoes! Have you yourself no anguish
because Villamayor lies with a savage, chained as at the
bottom of a pit? Even his conversation has taken on an
ignoble frivolity. It is hard to understand what he is
saying."

"This is only a phase." The eyes of Julieta glowed
confidently. "One must first descend into the pit, if he is
to rise very high. The black pit of skepticism, even the
sewers of vice. . . . It is well known many of the blessed
of the first centuries were born into families of wealth
and power, demoralizingly corrupt. Rome, Alexandria,
Athens. . . ."

Manuel Andrada was alarmed by her tone. Child of
the Church though he was, brought up in the vicinity of
the Cathedral gates, he found himself moving into unknown and tenebrous regions. He tried to divert the flood
of mad discourse.

"Please tell me about his recent writings."

"They reveal the travails of an uneasy spirit blindly
resisting its destiny."

"But what is the subject?"

"The subject?" Exasperated, she raised her eyes to the
dusky ceiling. "The spirit winds and circles among sophis-
tries as in a maze of its own making. Contradiction upon
contradiction! Yet in time the subtle Villamayor will
emerge from the maze to find himself where poor simple
souls have been standing all the time. It will be for him a
moment of joyful discovery. And for me. It is then I expect to see him kneel."

"I don't understand at all. I asked you what he was
writing."

"What he writes now is irrelevant, I care about what he will become. Once he has knelt at the foot of the Cross, there need be no bound and bar to his destiny. Time and travail will have changed him into himself. What did you say? The Protector dines with the Archbishop once a week? Perhaps Justo de Villamayor will himself be Archbishop, if he does not first suffer martyrdom. I see him in the flowing robes. And why not a Cardinal? Already at least once he has sought martyrdom and by authentic miracle survived. If you had seen, as I did, the rapid mending of his twisted bones! If you had seen the dear brooding face emerge from the bandages!"

"Bandages? You have been listening to the rumors of riffraff."

"Not at all. I have myself touched the scars. Listen: I have been studying the lives of the saints, seeking clues to the future of Justo de Villamayor. The miracles, the restless wanderings of the soul. . . . And can you not see a destiny of sainthood in his troubled voyages pursued by disciples? Like St. Alexis he dreads veneration and shuns the fascinations of the world. Consider too the history of the blessed St. Hilarion, who also sought a transforming solitude, and who fled the throngs seeking his cure. Palestine, Egypt, Sicily, Dalmatia. Angrily he fled his destiny but all the time he was rushing upon it. He was rushing toward Cyprus where he died."

"So it must be for Villamayor," Andrada remarked. "He must return to the place of his birth. Santa Isabella awaits him."

Julieta Aparicio shrugged her thin shoulders.

"St. Hilarion was born near Gaza. Your remark has no relevance." But then she was staring at Andrada intently, even with alarm; she crossed herself hastily. "St.

Alexis, on the other hand. . . . You were thinking of his story?"

"His story? I asked only about the writings of Villa-mayor the poet and historian."

"But listen to me! St. Alexis did indeed return to the city and even to the house of his birth. After many years of travel and poverty and good works he took a ship for Tarsus but was cast shipwrecked upon his native shore. Like Villamayor he could not accept the stagnation of his soul. So on Divine impulse he returned to Rome and there took shelter in a shed adjoining his father's house, where disguised as a mendicant he lived and died. His identity was discovered only after his death. Yes, it is not impossible you are right. Villamayor will at last return home for the martyrdom and for sainthood."

"You speak in riddles," Manuel Andrada said angrily. "For a saint Villamayor lives remarkably at his ease."

But in the dark room Julieta was attending only to her reveries; her eyes burned into the wall. A stream of saintly names poured forth, both illustrious and obscure:

"St. Porphyrius too fled wealth and honor and became Bishop against his will. And he was bishop of Gaza, where St. Hilarion was born! Is this only a coincidence? And St. Peter Celestine who resigned the Papacy. Also St. Stanislaus killed by the very hand of the king, when his guards refused to dispatch him? Was not St. Francis Borgia converted by the appearance of a corpse? Yes, he was. And St. Jerome? Was he not attended by the noble ladies Paula and Eustachia, humble instruments in the glorious pursuit of his destiny? What can be the meaning of the fact that the name St. Alexis came to my lips?"

The incoherent babbling ceased. Andrada, alarmed, had

again stalked to the darkest corner and back. He turned to me in annoyance:

"What is all this nonsense, Nicholas Clive? Villamayor is a notorious disbeliever in the truths of the Church. Skepticism has eaten into his soul. No man was ever less a saint."

Julieta Aparicio stood up. She looked at Andrada, then at The Protector's portrait looming hugely in the shadows. Her hands faintly trembled.

"So you see yourself as a vessel and chosen instrument for the return of Villamayor to the homeland?"

"The homeland awaits him. Surely it is the secret yearning of any honorable man to return to his home. I can do no more than encourage him."

Julieta Aparicio went on very quietly, as though speaking in a trance. She was a shadow among shadows, in the sagging musty room.

"It is not impossible. Yes, it may in truth be Villamayor's destiny to return to Santa Isabella and there find martyrdom at the tyrant's hand. But I beg you to believe me, Señor Andrada: the time is not ripe. He must suffer further small transformations before the great one occurs. Meanwhile he has before him a long and distinguished life to live. Archbishop, Cardinal. . . . Yes, some day perhaps that will be your role. Twenty years from now it may indeed be your appointed role to take him back there to his death. But not now, you have come much too soon."

Andrada backed away from her toward the large sheltering portrait.

"This woman is insane, Nicholas Clive. I beg you to take her away!"

Then Julieta opened the door, and the morning sunlight blazed in: on the roomful of ambiguous shadows, on The Protector's calm dead eyes. And on the rumpled and insect-ridden pallet, plain as a hermit's. Julieta and I went out onto the rickety staircase. Then she turned to Andrada for a last time. And the mad glow was gone from her black eyes. She was really very plain. Her eyes were dull and sad in the clean morning light.

"It is not for me to blame you, Manuel Andrada, if this is indeed your appointed role. It is a known historical fact that the strangest instruments have been chosen, for the accomplishment of saintly destinies. And perhaps you will never know what hand has rested on your shoulder, what finger in your direction has pointed? So I say to you, '*Go with God.*'"

We had proceeded some fifty yards up the empty ruined street toward the Cathedral, when Andrada called me back. He beckoned earnestly from the top of that outside staircase. I went back to him alone.

"What an experience!" he whispered. "You agree this woman is insane?"

"I suppose so. Let's say she gets a little excited."

"And what if she recites these mad nightmares to Villamayor himself, who is already sufficiently suspicious of me?"

"I wouldn't worry about that. Villamayor thinks she's crazy too."

I began to move away, but he detained me again.

"That girl Consuela—why don't you bring her, Nicholas Clive? She is a person of beauty. And she too is a pious daughter of the Church, though not like this one insane. I would like to talk to her. Perhaps she at least will have remarks to make on the nature of Villamayor's writings."

It was evident poor Andrada, who had had only the one dinner in Villamayor's house, was still unaware of Consuela's "gift," or of her violent political leanings. The idea of such a meeting amused me.

"I don't know," I said. "I'll see what I can do."

THAT night at dinner Julieta urged Villamayor to take more seriously the continuing presence in Caye Thomonde of Andrada . . . whom he had already dismissed as a fool and "pathetic little man." My own view (though I said nothing) was that Andrada would continue to be paralyzed in the "historic" presence of Villamayor, and was bound to frustrate himself in some ridiculous way. But Belesprit was alarmed, and even the quiet Ezile spoke up. Until then I had no idea she understood what we were saying, as she sat there in her sleepy staring loveliness. But suddenly she began to address "the master" in the undulant Creole that makes every statement sound like a lover's complaint. She seemed to be proposing that he disappear again. He could go with her and Belesprit to one of the interior villages. And it was true, Belesprit confirmed: the history of Haiti was filled with the names of deposed statesmen and hunted generals who had survived for years in that green intricate interior with its mysterious lost valleys swarming with thatched huts.

"It is an amusing project," Villamayor said. "But there are at least two obstacles to its execution. First, my face is not black, anonymity would be rather difficult. Is not our coming here already a historical event of the region?

The second obstacle is that I am not a former president or general of Haiti, to be pursued by their unbelievable national army and police. The agents of The Protector, alas, are notoriously more efficient. Moreover, I find the idea of sudden flight distasteful. Flight should be a calculated departure from some dead or decayed state of being."

I remarked that he could hardly call the little Andrada efficient.

"No. But there are others behind him, whose efficiency I know too well. So if Andrada fails to obtain his precious manuscripts, someone else will certainly appear. From now on, I am afraid, we shall have to live with a succession of Manuel Andradas. The Services of Security find intolerable the fact that I continue to write without their permission."

"Why don't you give them something?" Julieta asked. "Perhaps a few of the short love poems you say you've repudiated and 'left behind'?"

"I have left them behind. Another man wrote them, a man intoxicated with his own nobility and *lyrisme*. All the same it would be unthinkable. I am too vain, insubordinate and arrogant to surrender even repudiated poems on demand. Moreover, a few poems would only whet their appetites. It is not poems they are after."

"What are they after?"

"Doubtless they don't know. But they must be sure I am up to no good, since I insist on remaining silent. What is more irritating than an air of resignation and withdrawal? I suspect they believe I am writing something intolerable and politically subversive . . . which ought to be suppressed. In this opinion they are quite correct."

"I do not like the manner of this Manuel Andrada,"

Julieta said. "He has the true look about him of a chosen one. Is he an instrument of God or emissary of the Devil? *Janua diaboli!* It is the moral duty of every man to resist and flee as long as possible the death that is appointed to overtake him. The curve of your own still secular destiny . . ."

"Do not speak of death overtaking me, dear Julieta. I find such discussions both unpleasant and unrealistic, especially after a good dinner. Is it not we who overtake death? Who even choose to overtake her?"

"I was thinking of the voyaging St. Alexis, who returned as a mendicant to his home."

"Please do not think of him—at least not in connection with me. I must ask you again not to discourse publicly on the 'curve' of my destiny, conversion and probable rapid ascent to the Papacy. Keep these reflections for the closet! Forgive me, dear one, such talk scrapes at my nerves. As for Manuel Andrada—his future seems more circumscribed than mine. I look on it with compassion. What will happen to this poor blundering fool when he goes back to the authorities with empty hands? Will they not chop the hands off? I cannot give him the poems. No, I must cling obstinately to at least one shred of principle. But if I were to surrender the poems . . . it would be only for his sake. For each of us has his Manuel Andrada, who cannot simply be denied."

"What do you mean?" Julieta asked. "Must a man leap to welcome his destroyer?"

Villamayor pondered this, smiling, as though the problem had no connection with himself.

"What indeed do I mean? Perhaps that every man is responsible for the fool who seeks him out, since it is something in himself that prompts the seeking. Without me Andrada would hardly exist, I am his *raison d'être*."

I reminded him that Andrada did not, after all, take this mission upon himself. But Villamayor shrugged off my distinction:

"I cannot see this little man as a 'destroyer,' I see him only as a victim. Yes, he is the humble and innocent consequence of his time and place. And this whole matter is a far graver one for him than for me: it is truly one of life and death. I ask again what will happen to him when he returns to Santa Isabella with empty hands? Yet return I think he will."

All this time Consuela had not spoken. She sat demurely between Villamayor and the restless Julieta, staring at her folded hands. And none of us realized at the time what this meant: that this was the silence of a woman with a mission. I kept wondering why we were spared the usual outbursts against The Protector and his "scum," abrupt and spasmodic as coughs. And why had she not already ticked off Andrada as one who deserved to be shot? Instead she sat there smiling and staring at her hands. Now from my later knowledge I see how irrelevant our talk must have seemed that night to Consuela, who had already made her womanly plans. They were political plans, of course . . . by which Andrada would presently be snared, encoiled, baffled. But not just political. She must have felt at once some human kinship with this man who did not have ice in his veins. There must have been, yes, an unconscious sincerity in her dark searching stares, on the night of Andrada's arrival. And tonight she must have told herself, thinking of the black eyes and burning sincerity, thinking even of the scar: *This man can be redeemed!*

I was to hear of it all from Andrada himself very soon:

of the snares and coils and bafflement, and of the ultimate outrageous proposal. And I would see some of it too. But for the present Andrada, still unaware, lay among his roaches and gross insects in the sagging room in Caye Thomonde. He lay there considering how to get back into Villamayor's graces. He was knowing all the aches and anxieties of failure, and the dull guilt of the rebuffed.

The next morning I went to see him again. What else was I to do, since Villamayor intended to spend most of the day in his study, and I felt uncomfortable under the eyes of the others? So I went back to Andrada. I found him crouched on the pallet, with the magazines scattered about him. The brown coat lay rumpled on the floor, neglected for the first time. He began at once to tell me of the now almost unceasing thin pain in the upper reaches of the abdomen: the precise sensation of a knife slid again and again under the skin. But still no outward sign of soreness.

"I must see a doctor. I suffer from an obscure ailment."

"I don't think you'll find a real doctor this side of the mountains. You'll have to go back to Port-au-Prince."

"I cannot go back there. Believe me, Nicholas Clive, I will now tell you the truth. My failure would be reported at once, if I went back with nothing to show. All my plans for a patriotic and honorable career would be lost. I would sink back into the mass. A nothing: a shiner of shoes, a sentry on the docks. And they would be right to trample me so: failure deserves punishment."

"Then you'd better do without a doctor."

"Listen, I have talked with my friend Aubelin Camille. He is an important man in this place, a man with connections. Moreover, he is a man of medical intuitions, he is the pharmacist of this town. He says I should go to one of the *vaudun* ceremonies for cure. There is to be one next Saturday. Aubelin Camille says he will present me to a native doctor, a *hungan* who knows many herbs and formulas. What do you think, Nicholas Clive? This man speaks of remarkable cures."

I pondered this seriously enough.

"Why not? For the pain of a knife in the abdomen a native doctor might be just the thing, especially since the knife doesn't exist."

"You make fun of me, Nicholas Clive. I suffer from a germ; the right herbs and ointments must be found." He glanced over his shoulder at The Protector's waxen yet attentive face. "But first I must visit Justo de Villamayor, again. I must urge him to reconsider his decision."

"I don't think he will."

"Has he shown any of his writings to you yet? Be honorable with me, Nicholas Clive! I have asked you to collaborate."

"He doesn't show them to anyone. Or to anyone but Julieta."

Andrada looked at me intently.

"This afternoon will he go for a swim?"

"Probably."

"You must not go with him. You must get into his study."

I remember stepping back as though slapped.

"Why me? Why not yourself?"

"The servants know I have been banished, I could not get near the door. And listen, Nicholas Clive: I do not ask you to steal the manuscripts. But at least we must know what this man is writing—you for your article, I for my superiors. The National Library is growing impatient! I did not tell you of the alarming visit I received in

Port-au-Prince, there is much fretting over my delay. Well then—you must glance through the papers on his desk. Only a glance. Is he writing poems? Or does he make false accusations against The Protector under the guise of a political history? The Library has a right to know."

"I wouldn't think of it," I said. "Besides, I'm sure he keeps his study locked, so I wouldn't try it if I were you. You'll simply have to be patient. Or else you might as well give the whole thing up."

"Give the whole thing up!" Andrada seemed almost amused. "I would never consider giving up. This is my first important mission, and my first one outside the fatherland. Listen, Nicholas Clive—have you ever heard of Miguel Rubínez, also known as The Cripple?"

"Yes. Vaguely."

"Well, one of these days I will tell you about him. But for the present perhaps you are right. I must teach myself patience."

THIS was on a Tuesday. By late Wednesday afternoon he had already taken a long step back toward the "bosom" of Villamayor's household. For he simply reappeared, riding a minute frail horse and with the wrapped portrait once again laced to his back. Belesprit chanced to look out a back window and saw him stalk solemnly into view, his feet trailing close to the ground, followed by the entrepreneur Aubelin Camille who had rented him his room and rented Villamayor the house. Behind him too, on the horse, were the black cardboard suitcase, the lumpy pallet of suspect crackling sounds, a box of cigars, a stained package swarming with flies, and a small assortment of pots and pans that jingled against the horse's rump. The procession moved toward the back door of the main house but did not get that far. Instead it stopped in front of one of the dependent huts a hundred feet away, and not far from the studio of Villamayor's secret labors. This *caille* (Aubelin Camille explained) had not been included in the rental of the main house; it was available to Andrada for a price. He could set up his housekeeping there.

Even Villamayor, after the first indignant moments, was much amused. Within an hour Andrada had borrowed matches, bread, coffee and sugar, and had established his right to share (he insisted on paying a pittance) in the great tub of boiling water. Then for a night and day he kept fairly aloof, lying on his pallet in the dusty room, or sitting crouched in his doorway. Twice during that time a feeble curl of smoke indicated the cooking of spartan meals derived from that fly-infested package. Apparently he did not want to talk to me. On the second evening he sat comfortably on his heels with his back against the hut's wall, smoking a long cigar. But this was only a pose to hide his dismay. Andrada later told me of his sentiments of those first twenty-four hours. Dismay, yes. For he had come to the conclusion that I was unreliable and not on his "side." Moreover, it made him almost sick with uneasiness to see Villamayor go to his studio, and to hear the distant chatter of Julieta Aparicio's typewriter. Who could tell what noble poems or corrupt essays were being committed to paper secretly?

Also during that first long day, Andrada waited eagerly for Consuela to reappear in the backyard. She had emerged once to take water from the great tub, and to bathe her long brown arms. He experienced then a familiar stir and ache of the loins quite distinct from that pain as of a knife delicately inserted just beneath the skin. The dazing sunlight lay between them, speckled by the shade of high palms; her wet arms glistened and her black hair fell free. She paid him no heed during these long exciting minutes, and she did not return all day. Still he was sure she had smiled, walking away, the eyes flashing once as she regarded him over her shoulder.

On Friday morning he was waiting for her; he had probably been waiting for hours. Still crouched by his door, he flung out his greeting even before she had reached the tub. And he commented on the weather. Was it not an appropriate morning for a walk on the beach? She refused his invitation, laughing, but did not go away. For almost an hour they stirred and fretted aimlessly, with the hundred feet of dusty yard between them; Andrada tossed small pebbles at a stump. Much of this time I watched them from my bedroom window, and I don't think they spoke fifty words. Then she came inside. But when she went to the tub of water again, shortly before noon, Andrada's tongue had been loosened. He addressed her rapidly on the beauties of the capital city with its fine seaside avenue of palms.

The situation was absurd: to have Andrada living there within sight of us, and aching to return. Early in the afternoon he appeared in the kitchen, where he conversed in sign language with the young girl who waited on table. His small coffee mill had broken. Would she grind his borrowed beans? And where, he must have wondered, was Consuela? Then through the next hour he again sulked crouching in his doorway, just out of the blazing sun. By five o'clock Villamayor had decided to invite him to take a place at our table. There is a point at which principle becomes ridiculous in the face of such a childish adversary.

But Consuela had forestalled him. For by five she was already busily at work in Andrada's hut: sweeping the dust of years, and preparing to cook his dinner. She must have gone about her work stoically, grimly indifferent to the portrait of The Protector hanging from the wall: a woman with a mission. And now a firm column of smoke rose from the hut, and an unmistakable odor of frying pork, of plantains cooked in cocoanut oil. What did they say during those first bewildering hours? What could they have talked about unless love of country and recollections of their Catholic childhoods? Manuel Andrada never told me. But after that first conjugal repast he smoked his cigar in the darkening evening, while Consuela completed her labors. Then they disappeared, talking quietly but intently, along the path that led to the beach.

And who shall scorn the miracle of young love, even when it is tinged or provoked by politics? For Manuel Andrada it was like entering into a luminous dream. "It was impossible, Nicholas Clive, that beautiful young girl! And she came to me almost unasked! I could not believe it had happened!" This was how he came to look back on that first day and night. But he said nothing to us then, and neither did Consuela. She had simply turned her back upon us, and had moved into the hut with her few flimsy possessions. Now and then she emerged from it with an odd secret smile to fetch water or provisions. The rest of the world had simply vanished for them: even Villamayor, even the rival Julieta. We were all excommunicated, while the two lovers walked about or sat by their doorway, happily enlaced. And all of us, of course, were amazed. How could she (famous veteran of the Flagler Theater seizure, and who had learned to walk near the barracks of the Caribbean Legion) share bed and board with one of The Protector's agents, under the very eye of the hated one, who hung on a nail from the wall?

From our distance of a hundred feet we watched incorrigibly for the signs of their life, and listened for the slightly rasping songs of love Consuela was teaching him. He would repeat them in a pleased high whine. It was evident Andrada was setting up, in this first "home" of his adult life, a typical ménage such as might exist in a modest suburb of the capital city noted for its seawall and slender palms. This was especially true in the evening when he and Consuela sat together outside the hut while he smoked his cigar, "after the labors of the day." In the gloom the cigar gave off its lazy contented glow. There were three days and nights of such calm.

Then on the third night it began: initially as a low and loving murmur in which for the first time certain political slogans of the left were interspersed among the words of love. *"In the very midst of gratification,"* Andrada later complained to me. *"I could hardly believe my ears!"* The whispering continued in time with the gentle pulsing of her limbs, which would presently increase to a rage: *social justice based on subdivision of the latifundias . . . free secular education for all . . . the six saving principles of socialism.* In the warm darkness it was like having a stranger's body substituted slowly and mysteriously for the one held in loving embrace: a bonier and more impatient body, nervously possessed. *The liquidation of corrupt tyrannies.* . . . The quiet incessant voice pressed close to his ear in affection gave the impression of a madwoman talking in her sleep: the gibberish of dreams.

During that first night of political intercession the unceasing voice was never loud enough to be heard from the main house. And it appears the name of The Protector was never mentioned. Nevertheless it must have been a sleepless night. For Andrada looked rather troubled when he emerged from the hut the next morning, like a man disturbed by dim fitful premonitions or who felt himself caught in a subtle, still invisible snare. Perhaps he simply didn't know what to make of all that mad discourse spoken in a lover's half-sleep. Later in the morning he came to me as though to ask my advice. But he only mumbled a few words, and turned away. And through the long day the two lovers, when we chanced to see them, stood a little apart. They watched each other warily, circling and shuffling their feet, as in preparation for a combat. Once in the afternoon, during the siesta in fact, we heard a brief astonishing flood of feminine abuse. But after dinner they seemed to have recovered their peace of the first days. Once again in the remote moonlight they sat in front of their "home" while Andrada smoked his cigar. Only now the more rapid rhythm of the glowing and darkening ash conveyed hints of increasing anxiety.

He never told me the details of that appalling night, during which the normal thrusting fury of his love was quickly met and overmatched by her political zeal and rage. At the very end he was driven naked into a corner, where he stood in horrified silence. But we did not need details. For about eleven o'clock we too began to hear the voice, floating across the moonlit yard: at first clear, rational and feminine, then rising to the metallic rasp of a cracked record played on a loudspeaker too rapidly. But still we heard every word: shrill, demonic, possessed, and with the pulsing madness of Havana newsboys: *Revolu-*

*ción . . . Revolución . . . Reforma Agraria . . . Reforma
Agraria . . . Reforma Tributaria . . . Reforma Tributaria. . . . .* The performance must have been not unlike
those public ones for which La Atrevida was noted. A dim
light as from a single candle shone in the window. I could
imagine her standing gesticulant above poor Andrada
helpless and naked, still cowering on the bed. The discourse
was impersonal and abstract at the outset: a chanted enumeration of necessary reforms, a calm catalog of abuses.
But before long the name of The Protector himself was
heard: *the destroyer of the decencies, the corrupt invader
of privacy, the torturer, the inadequate and prematurely
born maniac, the moral leper.* By now a brighter light at
the window indicated that she had lit more candles, in a
determination to press her advantage and forestall escape
into shadowed corners.

I can only guess how Andrada responded to all this, in
the very presence of The Protector's own watchful and
grieving face. Did he say anything at all? In any event,
and at the end of the first half-hour, the tongue-lashing of
Andrada himself began: the cold lucid uninterrupted
reductions of the pride, the admonitions and the insults,
the deprivations of manhood. *"No hay peor sordo que él
que no quiere oír!"* Indeed that deafness is worse of the
one who is unwilling to hear. *Guajalote, guajalote, guajalote!* Thus she lashed him in the guise of the turkey, most
ridiculous of barnyard animals. And then again as one in
the semblance of an ox. *The horns drop from heaven on
the man fated by birth to be one. . . . Would he not rise
at last, miserable sietemesino, from the dull torpor of his
soul? It was still not too late.* And now (the voice unfail-
ing, each metallic word reaching us) she screamed out
the stories of famous turncoats who had achieved the

spirit of revolution at last, after years of sycophancy and corruption. *Horacio Gómez, Bernardo Álvarez, José Espinal* . . . she rolled out the names Andrada must have learned to hate from the first day he heard them: names vilified in the *Diario del Caribe*. They had risen! They had turned against The Protector at last. They had mustered the courage to plot revolutionary coups, and had died their heroic deaths.

By now it was evident Consuela (fully possessed, her soft person wholly transformed into the bonier La Atrevida) looked beyond mere punishment and scorn of Andrada to his eventual assumption of heroism. But it was also at this time, after nearly an hour of unrelieved and impassioned rhetoric, that her voice broke and became almost inaudible. Then we could not hear it at all. The ensuing minutes, though, were the ones Andrada would remember with horror, and the whispered proposal that sent him reeling out of the hut and running toward the house; that would cause him moments later to knock madly at my door, himself screaming now: *"Nicholas Clive, Nicholas Clive, I have had gratification with a she-devil and fiend!"*

6

IT IS strange how my most vivid image of Manuel Andrada remains comic to the end, for all the somber role he at last assumed and the stubborn loyalty he showed—and in spite of the ultimate macabre event, itself still shadowed by ambiguities. For Andrada too was moving toward his "destiny," which was more complex than his simplicities seemed to warrant. But it is the comic not macabre events I remember best: the sudden arrests and frustrations in Boston, or the dismayed reception of a crutch's blow beneath the knee, or the helpless disappearance into Odile's residence borne upon a black tide. And most of all the way he rushed out of the connubial hut and fled from Consuela across the moonlit yard toward the protection of my room. Which Andrada is the true one: the guilty and helpless worshiper of Venus and comically defeated man in his brown suit . . . or the fiercely, tragically triumphant one?

For the moment, he had certainly been defeated again. He talked to me incoherently for hours. Then early in the morning he retreated to his room in Caye Thomonde. Consuela's proposal—that he, a trusted agent of the government, was in an ideal position to deliver Santa Isabella from its "inhuman burden"—simply sickened him, who for over twenty years had looked upon The Protector as his only father, ever since the earthquake and tidal wave in fact, and the long night of terror. Now in Caye Thomonde he lay stupefied on the floor. He had salvaged the slightly ripped portrait but left the pallet and kitchenware behind. And as he lay there the pain in his abdomen slowly changed. The knife recently slid beneath the skin, long and razor-thin, had turned inward to cut into the flesh, forming a hard impenetrable barrier. It seemed to him this wall blocked the passage of vital energies from the heart to the loins and from the loins to the heart. For one long day, in spite of my attempts to cheer him up, he simply lay there in his failure and loss, under the contemptuous stare of the damaged portrait, accepting the pain. Then, when Aubelin Camille again renewed his proposal that they go to the *vaudun* ceremony and consult a native doctor, Andrada accepted at once. He was in the mood of a man who, supposing all doors definitively closed, is ready to place a fingernail in any crack, in the absurd hope of widening it.

But I shall not speak, here, of that most grotesque of Andrada's ordeals, since I was not in a position to observe it. (Andrada the supplicant and patient was the only white man there.) Moreover, I found all the accounts of that prolonged and painful therapeutic assault—even the dim dazed account of Andrada himself—wildly improbable. Suffice it to say that he did not stir from his room for twenty-four hours, after returning from that castigation of body and spirit. I went to him (after hearing Belesprit's lurid report) half-expecting to see grotesque new scars. But he looked much the same, his indestructible small self, and at first waved my questions aside. The treatment had been successful and the mysterious knife was gone, also the sum of two hundred gourdes. But a more rational anxiety remained. In the face of it mere money, or such matters as food and drink, had come to seem unimportant.

"I must act, Nicholas Clive, no more shilly-shallying is permitted, no more delays. All this has been but another shameful diversion from my purpose. And listen—I did not tell you everything Miguel Rubínez said to me that morning. The Cripple made his patriotic demands."

"For the manuscripts?"

"Not only for the manuscripts. It is Justo de Villamayor himself we must save, before it is too late, before the soul is corroded and lost. This was not only my personal dream. Miguel Rubínez insisted the historic personage belongs at home, among his compatriots and admirers. At least he must be protected from temptation. Consider the temptations here! Consider he now lives with a barefoot savage, a madwoman and a traitress. A traitress who vomits political grievances, and tries to incite even the most loyal to assassination! Daily Villamayor's spirit will become further steeped in hatred and lies. Every conversation is corrupt."

I suggested that it was Villamayor himself who did most of the corrupting. Most of the talking, anyway.

"No! It is that fiend of a girl, who spouts venom as once she uttered endearments. Political subversion in the very moment of gratification! And listen again, Nicholas Clive—I must act before my own sanity is destroyed. Her voice is at first irresistible, though her statements are untrue. She made abominable accusations against the Services of Security and against The Protector himself, while she stroked my face and neck, also the back of the wrists. And I found myself believing what she said. Later she shouted, it was similar to the buffeting of a storm. And I believed. Yes, for a few terrible minutes I too

clenched my fists against The Protector. What am I saying? Her eyes were on fire as she talked; a demon enters
her. I was compelled for these moments to believe.

"And Justo de Villamayor also—whose poems I recited
as a child, while standing beside my desk. He too has a voice
that penetrates the soul. I found myself believing his
words, even when I knew him to be wrong. And what will
happen if that spitfire of a girl throws herself at Villamayor as she threw herself at me, in enticements, and in a
total abandonment of the person? For hours I was powerless, Nicholas Clive. Even from the start I knew in my
mind she belonged to the enemy. But I did not know this
in my heart. So I poured out my heart to her. Yes, and the
story of my childhood and youth. On the second evening
she listened with such wide-open eyes and such a purity of
expression, such a flowing from within! She sat there
holding my hand, and stroking the back of my wrists.
And I told her of all my experiences at school, also of the
months of hardship after the earthquake and tidal waves.
There was a softness of her body when I touched her.
But then it vanished. The bones and muscles became hard,
she stiffened angrily in my arms. Soon she was scratching
like a cat in an attempt to terrify my soul. And spitting
out her foulness, her awful propositions. . . ."

I brought him back to Miguel Rubínez and the patriotic demands. Just what did Rubínez expect?

"Success is expected, Nicholas Clive. He will tolerate
nothing else. You understand, of course, The Cripple
possesses a special role and authority? The Protector forgives, also his nephew the President of the Republic. That
is in the province of their fatherly overseeing of the weak.
But it is not in the province of Miguel Rubínez to forgive.

He brings backsliders and shilly-shalliers a warning. Words of admonition, perhaps a single blow. But on the next visit it is his obligation to punish the weak one and if necessary destroy him. It is as in the military forces, or the Period of Rectification: disobedience must be punished by death."

The calm statement left no doubt as to the power of Rubínez to carry out these obligations.

"Why don't you hide?"

His head jerked up, the scar was a curving white gash.

"Where? Can you name me a place Miguel Rubínez cannot go?" He shrugged his shoulders heavily. "Besides, I would not want to hide. It is the duty of everyone to accept the punishment he deserves."

In the ruined sagging room, and under the poster's stare of icy assurance, I found myself unequipped to cope with such patriotism.

"All right, then you don't hide. How much success does Rubínez want? Or maybe I ought to ask how little he will take."

Andrada at once began to speak very rapidly:

"If possible they want all the manuscripts, for scrutiny and publication by the National Library on the most favorable terms. If that is not possible—they yet must know what Villamayor has written and is writing. A detailed accounting. And if what Villamayor writes is vile, if there is indeed a vomiting of resentments and rumors, malicious and scornful remarks—then he must be brought back to the homeland. It would be for his own good. But how much better for all if he were to return joyfully and of his own will to a position of honor, freely offering both his writings and himself, and destroying any pages un-

worthy of the national honor! A cleansing of the con-
science, to be followed by friendships and appropriate
rewards!"

"Suppose he still refuses to show you anything? And
refuses to come?"

"I will make him come. Yes, Nicholas Clive—what
must be must be. And there can be no more delay. We
will speak to him tonight. It is too dangerous for him to
remain here, in the company of the traitress. Consider
what evil things she might lead him to write!"

I looked around at the empty room.

"Make him come? Let's say lead him on horseback over
the mountains, tied to a saddle along with the poster? It
doesn't sound very easy."

"He must come of his own free will, after thoughtful
persuasion."

"His free will? Have you got the fishline hidden somewhere? Or some more esoteric instrument to help with the
persuading?"

Andrada looked at me furiously. He began to wring his
hands.

"Why do you mention again that book I bought in
New York for entertainment and innocent instruction?
I want to persuade him by speaking to his heart. You
know my admiration lingering from childhood for the
poet Justo de Villamayor! Would I want to give him
pain?" He looked into a dark corner: forgetful of the
portrait and perhaps even of my presence. "It is indeed
strange he doesn't run away."

"You want him to?"

He looked at and beyond me.

"And why does that Julieta not help him? Why does
she not put the truth into his stubborn head? And you,

Nicholas Clive—who came here almost at my bidding—
why do you do nothing at all?"

"I give you advice," I said. "I'll keep on giving it. Villamayor isn't going to scare easily. In fact he isn't going to
scare at all. So you might as well clear out, and try to save
yourself."

At these words Andrada looked over his shoulder and
returned The Protector's quizzical downward stare.

"You do not understand, Nicholas Clive. That is the
one thing I could never do. However, I will speak to Villamayor tonight. Will you please make the arrangements?
At least you can do that."

HE came to the house after dinner, and we went together
to see Villamayor in his bedroom. The flute lay on the
table under the tall candle; there was a new painting
propped against the foot of the bed, a still life of mangoes
and guava. I sat down near Villamayor, with the small
table and the flute between us. His twisted face was compassionate in the yellow light. But Andrada stood away
from us in the shadows: rigid, his hands stiffly at his side
in that posture of schoolboy attention.

"I have come again, Excellency."

"So I observe."

"I am not one to be discouraged, even by mysterious
pains. But I can delay no longer. Yes, the time has come
for an answer. Once again I offer publication on the most
favorable terms."

"I have already given you my answer."

"It was a hasty answer, not flowing from the heart.
What is literature without publication in the homeland?
The writer in exile among cold strangers is stifled as by a

cloth in the mouth. Do you wish to be forgotten? The schoolboys impatiently await new poems for memorizing. The members of the Academy await your thoughts on history."

"They would be scandalized by my thoughts. And the printer too! He also would be scandalized, my manuscript would burn his fingers. Please believe me: no one in Santa Isabella would set the type for certain things I have written."

"But there are your poems," Andrada said. "Who could criticize poems celebrating nature? Why not publish a new volume of verses and return home to receive the honors? I imagine a public ceremony on your next birthday, with the schoolchildren presenting chaplets of flowers. There would be a procession of children to your home. There would be speeches and music."

"That all sounds most tempting. However, I find myself obliged to decline." He paused, a queer grin came and went. "On second thought I do not want the procession of children. In fact, I do not want to publish in Santa Isabella at all."

"You must come home, anyway. Why not come home joyfully, and to reap appropriate rewards?"

Villamayor glanced at me. On his forehead, the even ridges returned.

"Must?"

"It is what your heart truly desires." Andrada pointed accusingly to the broken wall and the shreds of plaster still clinging. "Why should a man of your riches live in squalor, in a house rented from savages? It is not a worthy place for the writing of poems and historical essays. You must return to your own white house with its pool and

its green lawn. Also to your *finca,* and to those wild horses
you loved. I remember well your poem on the horses."

"The wild horses were symbolic. All our horses for riding had been trained."

"Your friends would welcome you, Excellency, even if
you published no more. There would be a birthday celebration in any event. But how many praises and pleasures
await the writer who returns to publish honorable books
and patriotic poems! Forgiveness, immunity, the restoration of your estate—that would be only the beginning.
Within months of your return you would have a position
of honor at the banquets, in sight of The Protector and
his family. Also at the parades and inaugurals."

"Anything else?"

Andrada glanced at Villamayor appraisingly. He
walked to the dark window and back.

"A great poet deserves the right female companions,
Excellency, to soothe and inspire. Appropriate mistresses,
daughters of the aristocracy. Why should you not have
one companion in the city and one on the finca? It is the
privilege of great poets to lead such lives of freedom
denied to ordinary men. That was explained to us in
school: the romantic spirits of a poet overflow. However,
they should be women of good blood and manners, who
would not debilitate the will. At the least they should be
appropriately dressed, not wander about in bare feet."

Villamayor, smiling, half-covered his face with one
hand.

"And they too will be supplied by the National Library
. . . my two mistresses? Can you offer anything else?"

"You make fun of me, Excellency, but I speak the
truth. In this ruined place your mind will be enfeebled by

solitude and unworthy companions. And consider the soul granted to you by God! It decays. Here you will soon come to believe everything is permitted."

"In my opinion, everything is permitted. In theory, at least."

Andrada crossed himself quickly.

"You see? It is as I have said, you have forgotten the teachings of the Church. Skepticism eats your soul."

Villamayor turned up his hands.

"No doubt. However, I find this conversation becomes very philosophical. You have no further pleasures to offer?"

Andrada stepped forward into the light.

"I know you better than you think, Excellency, and your patriotic heart. There is the maximum pleasure of returning to the homeland. In truth what else matters? You have wandered abroad several times, and you know the pleasures of return. I am away from home for the first time. But I have read the accounts in the *Diario* of those who return—how they detect the first gleam of the white seawall at the edge of the watery horizon. Or by plane the great moment of passage over the chain of mountains dividing the nest from the savages of Haiti. Surely you can hardly wait to see the wide avenue above the seawall, and its fine collection of statues! There stands among them a statue of yourself, erected when you were thought to be dead."

"I've heard about the statue. In fact, I've even seen photographs of it."

"Of course. But do you not long to see it? Or to see the Cathedral square, with the black starlings thick in the trees? The old men sit there in the afternoons, after their lifetimes of labor. There are also the zoological gardens and the horticultural institute to be seen, and the university's new buildings. Also the two luxury hotels, each room with bath and toilet. It is said iced drinks are served by the swimming pools of the hotels. Waiters serve even those engaged in swimming."

"It is true," Villamayor said. "They are excellent pools."

"There are fine buildings throughout the city. New warehouses have been built to serve the port, the dockside facilities are among the best in the Caribbean. In the interior are 700 miles of improved road. Yes, and let us not forget nature. There are also the beauties of the forests and the cool mountain retreats. The rich plains of the Cibao . . ."

Villamayor silenced him (who seemed on the verge of recitation) by quickly raising his right hand, the palm extended outward.

"Forgive me for making fun of you. Believe me, I respect the depth of your feeling. But you must understand once and for all that I am not going back. Or not until The Protector is gone. And you too must not go back."

"Not go back!"

"Yes, I do not wish you to be punished. But punished you would certainly be. So I think you must break away and renounce. You too must go into exile."

"Exile!"

"I can give you what money you need. In fact I am indebted to you in ways I cannot explain. I could send you to Barbara Swenson, who would hide you on her yacht. She could get you to Cuba. There you could disappear, and begin a new life."

With the full comprehension of Villamayor's proposal, Andrada began to back away. His face was flushed more deeply than ever, the scar angrily flamed.

"Are you trying to purchase me, Excellency? Are you trying to corrupt my loyalties?"

"I would like to save them. And I repeat: I do not want to see you punished."

For a long minute Andrada watched us silently from the shadows near the door. Was he tempted by Villamayor's vision of an irresponsible and vagabond life, eked out among grudge-bearers and betrayers of the trust? Or was he trying to master his anger and shame? At last the voice came to us out of that darkness, oddly thin and high,

"Is it true that you do not want to see me punished?"

"It is true."

"Then you must show me the writings, so that I can make a full report on their contents. That is the least I can go home with. And surely it is a reasonable request! Surely you grant the homeland the right to know what its children are doing and what they write?"

Villamayor shook his hand.

"I can grant nothing of the kind. I must refuse to show you anything. In this matter, I am as powerless as you."

After that, there was nothing further to say.

AND even then it was hard to take little Andrada seriously, or to imagine him taking any action. There was the angry fiery patriot of the ominous scar and gunman's appearance . . . who would always be immobilized, I thought, by the depths of his appalling innocence. And by his childhood recollections of reciting Villamayor's poems. He would be deterred by his troubled image of the great

monument of the nation's culture, who inadvertently had
stumbled into error. But in these suppositions I was wrong.
Andrada did not, after leaving us, return at once to his
room in Caye Thomonde. Instead he must have remained
in the vicinity of the house (perhaps even in the cabin he
had rented) until all were asleep. I can imagine him in
solitary discourse there, hardening his resolve. Then—
quietly, expertly—he broke into Villamayor's study and
made off with an armful of papers. Chapters from the
book, notes, letters, Daybook: he scooped them up pell-
mell.

The next morning Villamayor awoke me with this news.
We went out to the study, and together contemplated the
wreckage. Papers and the few books were scattered on the
floor. One pile of typescript was rumpled where an animal
paw had descended and seized the pages on top. Andrada
must have worked very fast, perhaps holding a match for
a few seconds over each handful of pages. No doubt he
filled the pockets of his trousers and coat.

"It is an imbecile act," Villamayor said. "Is it not most
typical of their blunted mentalities—to snatch up pages
at random? They are brutalized beyond even the desire to
discriminate. Yes, these creatures have no time and no
need to read whole books or even essays in their search for
criminal intent. Any page will do. For somewhere on each
page will be a phrase punishable by death, if only one
knows how to interpret it. At the same time I surmise
Andrada thought he was ruining several manuscripts,
rather than only one, by seizing pages on all sides."

"And he wasn't?"

Villamayor pushed at the litter of papers with one foot.
It was as though his work had been soiled beyond cleansing.

"It is hard to say. Perhaps some of the statistics are lost irreplaceably. For everything she had typed, however, there exist copies in Julieta's possession. As for the rest, as for the Daybook and diary especially—perhaps the loss will prove a secret benefit. I shall now be compelled to consider anew much that I took for granted." He kicked at the papers again, then stooped to pick up a page. "But he won't like what he reads, your little Andrada! The Daybook especially will give him pause. His patriotic heart will in truth be sickened by my speculations."

"What speculations?"

"My meditations on The Protector's lust for brutality. On his madman's cruelties, on the origins of his greed. What is my task but to analyze coolly the secret formation of a monster, and the nature of an ultimate depravity? And not only my speculations. . . . Of necessity I record certain facts normally kept hidden from the young citizenry of Santa Isabella—the fact, for instance, that The Protector as a youth was engaged in the stealing of horses. That is not regularly taught in the schools, nor the gross swindles and corruptions of the later days. No, Manuel Andrada will not enjoy reading these pages. His world will be darkened and overthrown, I can almost feel sorry for him." He turned to me sadly. "And yet it is a hateful sickening act, this brutal destruction of the word. Your scarred friend is a true evil servant of The Protector, after all."

I had to acknowledge this seemed true. But I was in fact very surprised. I had come to believe the blundering, hesitating Andrada would never go beyond words.

"Words? Well, I prefer to lose the papers thus by violence, than lose them by persuasion. And yet? My vanity is such I do not think he could ever have persuaded me.

I would have hoped to persuade him instead. I would have liked to rescue him from his terrible culpable ignorance. Andrada is but one of thousands of my compatriots who act thus with childish simplicity of heart and on the worst of premises. Yes, I would have liked to save Andrada's soul while he was trying to save mine. But now the chance is gone."

We supposed, of course, that Andrada had vanished up the trail with his loot, in the direction of Port-au-Prince, sacrificing the suitcase of dubious cardboard material and even the damaged but sacred portrait. He would rush toward Miguel Rubínez and this small fulfillment of his mission: his pockets stuffed, a mass of papers in his arms. How far could he have got? I surmised there was always the chance he might have got lost on the dark trail, and by morning be huddled near some cluster of huts only a few miles away. Or he might have gone down into Anse de Corail.

However, all our reasonable conjectures were wrong. Belesprit and Ezile made a widening circle of inquiry, while I went to Caye Thomonde. And there I found Andrada in his room squatting beside the pallet, with the manuscript on the floor in front of him. He had ranged it in neat piles. When I went in, he showed no surprise. But he looked up at me with the cold dreary distaste of one who has been suddenly disabused of many illusions.

"Villamayor is not a misguided one, Nicholas Clive. He is truly a criminal. Who could have surmised the poet of 'The Savannas of the Cibao' would become the worst of traitors? He too has contemplated assassination."

"I don't believe it. A man can have theories . . ."

"I also have not wanted to believe, Nicholas Clive. For many days I have hoped he would prove innocent, in spite of his abominable talk. But no: this man's soul is lost. Understand that I have been reading since dawn. And before that I read as much as I could, until the last of my matches were gone. I felt a sick dread coursing through my veins. Then for two hours I waited in the dark for the first morning light when I would be compelled to read some more. In the darkness I lay as in the presence of Satan the Adversary, fearful for my soul. And now I have read all."

The stinking heat lay about us, and the morning light shone through cracks in thin streams of dust. Andrada squatted beneath me, rocking on his heels, talking of his long night and early morning of discovery: the unfolding, deepening nightmare. It appears he had allowed himself minutes only for ransacking the study. All he could do (afraid of course to use a candle, cupping the precious matches in his hand) was try to take sample pages from many places, together with a notebook containing handwriting of great elegance. It never occurred to him to search for the guiltiest pages; there simply wouldn't have been time. Moreover, he still naïvely hoped there would be no guilty pages at all.

Then on the way back to Caye Thomonde, safe now in the jungle night and empty trail, he did look at the Daybook, opening it in the middle, holding the steady match over a few lines in the center of the page. And the first thing he read was an obscure proposition: *All pleasures are good, though some are inopportune.* He turned a few more pages and read: *In intercourse the flesh is renewed, and returns to its burning youth. But the spirit? For precious moments it frees itself even from youth, and enters into a timeless joy.* These were the lines that would prompt Andrada's first real impression of the literary burden in his pockets and hands. Justo de Villamayor (once an honor to the pure literature of the homeland) kept his writings secret because the writings were indecent. They spoke even of gratification! And Andrada marched on steadily toward Caye Thomonde, shamefully aware now that he was actually looking forward to a corrupt pleasure in the reading.

Unfortunately this first impression of the writings did not last very long after he had returned to his room. He found with dismay that his stub of a candle would not light, and he had no more than fifty matches left. But these were enough to disclose the first terrible pages on The Protector, with their hideous suggestions of a brutal lawless youth during which the Father of the Country had even stolen horses. *"The words were there before my eyes, Nicholas Clive. I could not rub them out! And there was—I cannot say how or why—the very ring of truth in Villamayor's magician way with words. I had to ask myself what motive the writer Villamayor would have to lie, in such a private diary, not intended for other eyes?"* Then a few minutes later, with the supply of matches almost gone, he perused another of the entries that suggested disgusting activities. The words slid into his consciousness, serpentine, leaving him with a sick chill. The Protector in his Rolls Royce might indeed seek out companions for the night in aristocratic homes discreetly left dark. Was that not in all ages a historic privilege of great men? But could it be possible he would also long for foul brothel odors and the corruptions of the street corner? The proposition was so absurd that it struck him with the blow of truth. The Protector of the country, with every justice its richest man, had a sick longing to touch the sweating bills of pimp and lottery salesman! In the dark-

ness, with the matches gone, Andrada for the second time
in his life questioned the pure image of the country's savior. The first time had occurred as he cowered on the bed,
listening to Consuela's harangue. And now he hated Villamayor for having written these lines. But he hated him as
in childhood he had hated the Adversary: with a terrifying awareness of Satan's power to discover and reveal.

He waited sleepless for the first morning light, and
watched it come with a sickness of the stomach and the
heart. He lay in the blackness with his hands behind his
head, until at last the face of The Protector began to
appear above him as a lighter shadow among shadows, the
face at last gloomily distinct in the growing morning—
a betrayer or one betrayed? Andrada dragged himself
wearily to the center of the room where the papers lay
scattered on the floor, and the sinister black notebook
among them. Then he took a sheaf of pages onto the
balcony, with the tropical morning all around him now,
and read without understanding very much a discussion
of the coffee and cacao industries. But soon he returned
to the black notebook as so often he had returned to his
vices and lusts: with a wild excited beating of the heart
and a nauseating shame. Villamayor had done his plausible,
corrupting work well; he was ready to believe the worst.

"It was thus, Nicholas Clive: I felt doubt of The Protector moving through my veins like the chill of a mortal
disease. Was it true he had appropriated lands and factories
without justice, for the benefit of the nephews? The pages
of Villamayor were filled with numbers and names. I
found myself helpless before the numbers especially. And
page after page struck me like blows across the face. On
one page I am told The Protector is not a learned man, on
the next I am told he is cruel. What had I been listening

to all my life? The poor, honest and studious boy's struggle to achieve his great learning, and his care for his saintly mother, and his youthful labors for the poor and sick, and his sudden discovery of military genius, and his astonishing power to suggest remedies for baffling diseases, and his mastery of the arts and literature—was it all then a book of lies?"

"I'm afraid it was."

He leaped up and began that rapid angry stalking.

"No, you are wrong! For suddenly I turned a page and saw the black face of truth. Yes, these pages were written by a man who would stoop to anything. Listen: Villamayor reveals he was at Puerto Limón! He was with that atheistic scum and murderous riffraff, plotting the overthrow of orderly institutions. He was even—listen to me—supposed to be their political leader."

"So?"

"You shrug your shoulders, Nicholas Clive! Are you a believer in rapists?"

"My recollection of Puerto Limón is that there wasn't much opportunity for rape. Most of those men died on the beach."

"It was their plan to despoil churches and overthrow the government. Everyone knows that. And listen to me: on another page Villamayor makes remarks on the ultimate crime. He regrets it would now be difficult to assassinate The Protector. What do you think of that?"

I stared up at the portrait. One eye looked askew in the thin dusty light.

"If all these things about The Protector are true: the cruelty, the thefts, the deaths . . ."

"I know," Andrada broke in feverishly. "That was the ultimate poisonous question, twining itself about my heart. Yes, even I had such thoughts sent from the Adversary. If the noble youth who knelt at his mother's knee was in fact only a horse thief—then why not assassination? Why not disorder and chaos, and the overthrow of orderly institutions? Why not a spitting on the sacred images of the Church? Oh I tell you there was a terrible moment this morning when I was ready to renounce everything: my country, my Protector, my Church. I stood right there, at the top of the stairs, and I looked back at the empty sky. The soul of things was gone."

"But you changed your mind?"

The fanatic eyes stared at me in their triumph, then at the portrait in gratitude.

"I turned the page, Nicholas Clive. I went back to that evil book and there read villainous remarks on the conduct of The Protector at the time of the earthquake and tidal waves. And suddenly I understood that the whole book was a lie. Yes—in that one moment, in the Satan's remark that The Protector had enriched himself at the time of the catastrophe—my lost world returned to me. For I had been there and I knew the truth."

"He did get rich from the reconstruction."

"Listen to me, Nicholas Clive. You do not understand anything because you are a *Norte Americano* who has not suffered. Moreover, you were not there. But for me that night was the ending of one lifetime and the beginning of another. Without The Protector I would not have lived. None of us would have lived."

And he told me about it: standing now with the massive shoulders straight, and the torn portrait watchful behind him. He remembered in detail the terror of the child (no angry scar cutting through the eyebrow then) who shined shoes in the Cathedral square but who had never worn any. On the afternoon of the earthquake there had been no customers, and he was lazily regarding the birds in the almond tree directly above him when a faint trembling began. It might have been a trembling of his bones. The old men on an adjoining bench stopped talking; beyond them, an untended bicycle fell away from a post. The clatter of the bicycle was succeeded by a rumbling, then by an utter silence in the sultry late afternoon. A moment later the small Andrada found himself lying on his side, the contents of his shoebox scattered, and across the square a two-story building was shaken angrily from side to side then split in two. At once he saw exposed half-a-dozen rooms, their furnishings and even their inhabitants, one of whom seemed to be climbing a wall. Then the earth shook again, and one-half of the broken building slowly crumbled. He heard the first shrill screams.

On his own side of the square the Cathedral stood untouched: a great fortress of ancient stone. He found himself running toward it, then pitched off his feet by the fourth striking of the earthquake. He picked himself up again and ran inside to pray. He had no idea how long he remained on his knees in the dark Cathedral, with the murmurings of the faithful around him and the distant hysterical cries. An orange dusk blackened with particles had settled over the ruined city when he emerged from the Cathedral, just in time to hear the thunderous roar of the first seismic wave and to see the first wild rush of waters through the streets. Later he heard of this from the lips of those who had been near the snapped and twisted bridge: how the very waters of the sea had drawn back as though sucked in, leaving a stretch of the harbor dry: the smaller boats tumbled like toys, and the wreckage and abominations suddenly exposed, together with horrible fish. Then the first gigantic wave appeared, advanced and struck. Even the breakwater vanished, and the buildings still standing near the port were crushed in an instant. A few blocks inland occasional walls remained, bulging out rather than driven in. They fell before the wave. Within minutes the city was leveled, burying or half-burying thousands. A second wave struck and boiled through the ruins. The child Andrada ran back to his home past the screams of the dying, and the irrelevant protruding limbs of the dead. He found his mother dazed but unhurt in the center of their room, from which everything had vanished: walls and furniture and roof. Hours later, in the blackness, while they searched for the body of his brother, they found his own pallet buried in the mud and plaster of what had once been a street.

It was the element of preternatural malice, and not only the total loss of possessions and the many thousands dead, that left people dazed: first the malicious double blow of land earthquake and gigantic wave, the earthquake undermining the buildings, and the great waters washing them away. Then a second and a third wave and at last the descent of night, preternaturally dark. In that darkness—groping for bodies, following the groans behind mounds of rubble—they also became aware of the first looters: stealthy shadows armed with knives. The rumors crept from street to street, and from one huddle of survivors to the next. These rumors too suggested the visitation of divine or diabolic wrath. The inmates of the insane asylum were loose and running in a pack; not one had been killed. But in the maternity hospital a zinc roof torn free and descending on a row of beds had cut like a scythe, decapitating many women. Within hours some authority, doubtless The Protector himself, had taken shrewd action.

The soldiers engaged in digging for the injured were ordered to fire a single shot upon the discovery of a dead body: to summon the relatives of missing ones, also the prisoners assigned to remove bodies. Moreover, these single shots served as warnings to looters. But the shots in the great darkness were also terrifying to the innocent. In the momentary glare of a lantern following the shot one might see a prisoner dispute with a huge rat the possession of a corpse. Long before dawn the shock of despair had given way to a sleepwalking indifference. The crowds picked their way toward the Cathedral square, over which hung the glow of a huge fire.

"But he had acted, Nicholas Clive. The Protector had uttered his commands to save us from mortal disease! When I arrived the prisoners were already flinging bodies onto the fire while the priests stood by pronouncing the last rites. It was terrible to see the departure of so many unshriven souls, a man could not cross himself fast enough! I watched in fear the passage of the small bodies, looking for the body of my brother. And yet it was also consoling to know The Protector understood what to do. He was acting on behalf of the living. With each new body the groans of the crowd were as the sighing of an autumn wind in the trees of the Cathedral square. After an hour of watching I felt again despair in my heart, I saw despair in the faces around me.

"Then it was, near the last hour of the night, The Protector himself appeared and saved us. I see him now on his white horse advancing near the fire. And in that great light I could see on his face a true scorn of the catastrophe. He turned and addressed his underlings in a loud voice, while we listened breathlessly to the firm promises: *the dead would be burned and there would be no plague,*

*those still alive would be saved, the streets would be
cleared, the looters and profiteers would be shot, the city
would be rebuilt.* And with a consoling wave he was gone
. . . who many times in the next days we saw in the
streets, exhorting the workers and even working himself
as a sacred example. By morning the radio station was repaired, The Protector was making his historic appeal to
the silent outside world. *'Ciudad Santa Isabella. This city
is demolished, there are thousands of dead, we need tents,
cots and all medical supplies, we need everything, we need
immediate assistance from all neighboring republics.'* And
they listened to his voice, Nicholas Clive, they came at his
command! At first only a single small plane and a trawler
offshore, but then many planes. However, the airport was
destroyed, they could not land. By the end of four days
we were starving and without water to drink. More rats
had appeared, there were mad dogs on the streets. But on
the fifth day it was possible to land food from a ship under
the protection of the army. And The Protector insisted
it be shared. To the poor and to the rich alike! Do you
not understand now? It was he alone who saved us."

"Do I understand he acted efficiently at the time of the
catastrophe? No one ever denied it."

"Not only that. Do you not understand why I must spit
on and deny all the blackguard writings of Villamayor?
I was corrupted almost into believing him, I was en-
chanted as by an evil spell. What might I not have believed, had Villamayor said nothing of the catastrophe?
But now he has tried to stain the great heroic rebuilding
of the nation, and our salvation from the black night.
And now I know all his words are lies."

"So what are you going to do?"

He looked down, puzzled, at the offending page.

"I must take him back to Santa Isabella, where he will beg forgiveness and official clemency. There must be a purifying confession in the *Diario*, including details of Puerto Limón. Yes, he must throw himself at The Protector's feet. Those who are truly contrite, The Protector forgives."

"And how about his writings?"

"They must never be published. The National Archives must keep them under lock and key."

"He won't go."

"He must go, Nicholas Clive. Do you ask seriously what will happen if Justo de Villamayor refuses to go back? It is very simple. If he refuses to ask for forgiveness . . . there will be no forgiveness. And punishment must come to him here."

7

AND EVEN so nothing might have happened, had it not been for the first unfortunate newspaper story, and the consequent appearance of a white yacht off Caye Thomonde. The fact is that Manuel Andrada was more paralyzed than he knew by the thrust and pull of his feelings. He hated the political blasphemer, whose corrupting voice had for a few dark moments convinced him. Yet he was still drawn to the poet of schoolboy recitations, eminent enough to deserve a small statue. This Villamayor had been courteous, kind, seductive. Had the seductive voice even gone on in his sleep, in his dreams, inducing loss of will? This much I know: for two days Andrada remained evasively in his room in Caye Thomonde, with the criminal manuscripts in his hands, undecided how to act.

Villamayor was delighted when I told him of my discovery and of my talk with Andrada; he dismissed the threats of punishment with a shrug. He was more pleased over his illusions concerning the scarred emissary than that his papers were not irretrievably lost. A book can be rethought and rewritten. But here was a human being not yet lost, whom he had given up on utterly.

"So he cannot tear himself away? Excellent: his mind is still in travail. Bewildered, he cannot accept the con-

sequences of his act. Yes, he should have rushed off to
his superiors at once, with my subversive writings punishable by death. Now it is already too late."

Belesprit had sent a message to the *chef de section* in
Anse de Corail, reporting the theft. A futile gesture. He
was in favor of going at once to Andrada's room—the
three of us or himself alone—to take the manuscripts by
force.

"No," Villamayor said, "With The Protector, the
struggle must be of flesh and flesh, since there remains no
soul to be saved. But with our poor Andrada it is a struggle of the word. It is my writings that must speak to him
now. Yes, he will pore dismayed over my pages: I have put
into his mind doubts he cannot destroy. I think this little
man is crippled by our common humanity whose very
fallibility is its saving grace. Why else does he hesitate?"

I was appalled by Villamayor's confidence.

"Because he expects you to go to him. To go with him."

"And I expect him to come to me." Villamayor smiled
wearily; he turned up his hands in a gesture of acceptance.
"Do you not understand? We will have further passionate
talks, Manuel Andrada and I. More than once again I
shall hear about the warehouses of Santa Isabella and the
statues and the pools. A dreadful nuisance and burden.
. . . Nevertheless, I am glad. It is my obligation to listen
to him and deny."

But Villamayor had not heard Andrada talk of the
earthquake and tidal wave. He had not heard the scarred
dedicated man who had once been a boy without shoes
on the Cathedral square, and who had seen The Protector
on horseback, scorning the catastrophe.

"I'm sure you're wrong. I think he's quite capable of
punishing you himself. In fact, he's capable of anything."

"It is true," Julieta broke in. "Surely it is clear now he is an emissary and instrument stubbornly persevering in evil. Or persevering at least in commands he cannot understand. I know. Blindly he crouches like a dumb animal in a cage, waiting for the next command."

Villamayor smiled and touched her cheek.

"Your theology is obscure, dear one, obscure and also heretical. And would you have me run away?"

"I would have you leave this evil place."

"It is no longer possible to leave. For I too am crippled. I am held fast, yes, by my curiosity as to what he will do."

BUT we cannot know what Andrada, unprovoked, would have done. For that absurd newspaper story was written—some twelve hours, as it happened, before Andrada stole the manuscripts. And the yacht of Barbara Swenson did appear off the ruined wharf of Caye Thomonde, to be joined some hours later by a coughing Grumman seaplane of great antiquity coming in at low speed. Presently too there were further intruders who arrived by the trail, one of whom lacked a hand. Yes, even Assistant Professor Peralda turned up among the veterans of revolutionary ardor, their old hopes awakened by that convincing political dispatch. Our solitude was indeed invaded by those exiles on horseback descending the trail to Villamayor's house. But even before that, Andrada had found himself, as he thought, with no choice. Upon Barbara Swenson's arrival it became clear to him that an invasion of Santa Isabella involving Villamayor not only had been planned, but was forming before his very eyes. And so at last he acted.

How did it happen: the ridiculous story, the few inches

of irresponsible newsprint that would begin to bring
everything to a close? Bernard gave me the most lucid account of that long night of political inquiry conducted
on the veranda of his hotel, at a table covered with glasses
endlessly refilled. There was a new correspondent transferred from Brussels, a man unaccustomed to the heat and
to the excellence of the Haitian rum. This was his first
evening in Haiti, and he was in a genial inquiring mood.
Evidently the evening began with the usual talk of conspiracy and revolution: the old yarns of vast sums spent
on surplus arms and in the purchase of intelligence. And
of course the talk was richer than the correspondent from
Brussels was used to, in this city of imaginative men: the
long intricate talk of politics, corruption, revolution.
Moreover, Barbara Swenson had that very afternoon intensified the whispered speculations (these at times erupt-
ing into angry and rapid babble) by her act of going to
her friend Auguste Bataille, the chief of the secret police,
to ask for information concerning Villamayor. And why
had I not returned? she wondered. Was Villamayor up to
something after all?

So it was indeed inevitable the name of Villamayor
should be drawn into the evening's talk. And what, after
all—the Haitian informants must have asked themselves
—what could Villamayor be doing on that forsaken south
coast unless plotting revolution or invasion? No doubt
the chief of the secret police knew well enough what was
going on in our retreat near Caye Thomonde: nothing
was going on. And yet even Auguste Bataille was half-
persuaded by that story appearing in such a reputable
New York newspaper, with its specific mention of men
occupying an abandoned army barracks on the south
coast—the papers flown down from New York, and an

hour after that removed from the news racks by the alarmed head of Army intelligence.

So it is not difficult to understand how it began: with the thin, cautious, reserved young correspondent new to the country, listening on his first evening in Haiti to the wild rumors, on the veranda of Bernard's hotel. He would have been intoxicated already by the first blazing afternoon, and by the files of white-robed women walking up into the hills, and at dusk by the occult blue presence of Gonave floating hazily in a deepening sky. And there was always the rum: the first astonishing rum punches before dinner and the long lazy rum and sodas with it, as he listened to the fine old yarns of rack and garrotte and poison, and took his first lessons in the country's history. By ten o'clock (with the historic names and assassinations revolving in his brain, and the lights of the city shimmering as in a deep pool) the conversation had turned to the present day. The new correspondent explained he had been sent to write a detached and unbiased summary of the political situation in Haiti.

The local man, the "stringer" who for years had seen such dazed outsiders come and go, could not suppress a smile. He urged the newcomer not to take too many notes. At first there was chiefly Bernard to do the talking, with his complicated stories of graft. But then (perhaps eleven o'clock now) the "reliable informants" began to materialize at the head of the veranda stairs, with their burdens of rumor and counsel. They arrived in their white suits, gravely intent, disinterested, unsought and demanding no fee . . . attracted to the light on the veranda of Bernard's hotel, and by the report that a new correspondent had arrived. These were the patriotic students of politics and lovers of conspiracy; the relicts, even, of minor cabinet office. To the veteran of Brussels, unused to their talk and unused to such a flow of rum, their intelligent dark heads appeared to sway gently and continuously, above the suits of immaculate white.

I gather he was genial and expansive by midnight, and to all appearance less thin, with his shirt now unbuttoned to the waist—the new correspondent. By then he was regaling the stringer and his other new acquaintances, the circle of black faces, with stories of journalistic escapades in Brussels and Antwerp and Paris. He was also buying all the drinks in spite of faintly murmured protests. Yes: together they would write a great unbiased story of politics in Haiti. *And how about Santa Isabella?* he casually put in, while clapping for the waiter, *Were things still quiet over there? Were the exiles still plotting?* A long silence ensued. The stringer (representative of a network as well as of the great New York newspaper) remarked drily that the situation among the exiles of Santa Isabella was always very complicated.

So that was how it started. It must have been well after midnight before the frank summation of Santa Isabella affairs began, the incautious voices speaking more rapidly now, the grave compassionate voices, telling of torture and assassination and fear. Then the names: the dead Horacio Gómez and the dead Bernardo Alvarez, and the mysterious death of one Otto Cepeda in the Port-au-Prince jail. Also the recent appearance in Haiti of the elusive Justo de Villamayor. *"Justo de Villamayor,"* the correspondent interrupted, *"He sounds familiar. Who the hell is he?"* He was told that Villamayor was an exiled statesman and writer, and that he was living in secrecy on the south coast. And then, as the long dazing night wore on, there emerged the names of others, the eccentric Barbara Swenson and the eccentric Edward Murphree, the Caribbean Legion, the soldiers-of-fortune, and the outlaw fliers both past and present. So it must have been almost dawn when the correspondent (manipulating his pencil with great difficulty now) began to write that story involving an "abandoned barracks." The stringer, who to the new correspondent seemed uninformed, had long since gone to bed.

It must have been something like this, to judge by Bernard's report, and to have facts become so distorted. What matters was the story itself, filed late that morning: a plausible recounting of political conspiracy and adventure, in which the cautious words "rumor" and "unofficial informant" were used several times. The gist of the story was that the exile Justo de Villamayor was organizing a small invasion army somewhere on the south coast of Haiti. There he had some eighty soldiers-of-fortune and onetime members of the Caribbean Legion, who were housed in an abandoned army barracks. The expedition was to be financed by wealthy Venezuelan liberals and by exiles from Santa Isabella. The eighty or so men were seasoned guerrilla fighters, adequately supplied with arms. But they were now awaiting reinforcements, the arrival of other exile leaders, and the delivery of two transport planes. There was no way of confirming the rumor that several Americans were also among the combatants.

Barbara Swenson later told me of the profound outrage she felt on reading these lines. She did not know whether to be more angry with Villamayor (who had backed away from all her proposals) or with me, who had sent her no word of these secret doings. It appears she was having an apéritif by the pool, with Edward Murphree swimming lazily at her feet, when the New York paper of unimpeachable seriousness was brought. Thus she read the issue of that journalistic debauch some thirty-six hours after the debauch itself ended with the new correspondent staggering up to the telegraph company's counter in the hot Port-au-Prince morning. By long experience she knew where to look for Caribbean news. So the words on an inner page at once caught her eye, and the significant dateline: *imminent invasion rumored . . . exiled writer . . . Caribbean Legion . . . Villamayor.*

Her first reaction was one of irritation with Edward Murphree because he continued to languish in the pool, floating on his back in a position of sybaritic ease. The shoulders, it seemed to her, showed signs of flabbiness and age. And then she thought of Eduardo Gonzales in his cubicle: the theorist of purest motive, who would now have to redouble his efforts. But what an outrage—Justo de Villamayor daring to organize an army without her knowledge and after refusing almost rudely her aid: money, arms, pilots, encouragement, and the constitutionalist Gonzales! And I, known by everyone to be on that south coast with Villamayor, had not sent back a word.

She told me of going to the edge of the balcony, too enraged to talk, and looking down on her yacht resting at anchor in the glittering afternoon. It might take many hours to round up the crew, and have the ship ready for sea. Moreover, the plane, veteran of several wars fought near jungle rivers, was still undergoing repairs. She turned to Edward Murphree, brandishing the newspaper:

"Get out of the pool!"

"Why should I?"

"He has come out of retirement, you fool. There is to be an invasion of Santa Isabella, you are to have your chance at last. Yes, the men must receive proper training based on skillful use of terrain. Get out of the pool!"

Murphree pulled himself up dripping: rather lean and trim after all, in spite of the fleshpots and indulgences.

"What's up. Who has come out of retirement?"

"Villamayor. He has shaken off his pose of languid indifference, he is organizing on the south coast. But he will be helpless without a man of your military training. Why don't you get dressed? There is no time to be wasted."

Murphree gazed at the pool, tempted to go back in. The brazen afternoon had left the tiled walk on fire.

"He won't have anything to do with us. Don't you remember what he said?"

"He was demoralized, he simply wasn't himself. And he knows how much experience you have had with rough terrain."

Edward Murphree lit a cigarette carefully, squinting in the terrible descending sun.

"You might as well face it, old girl. Justo likes us all right, but he doesn't take us seriously."

"He will have to. He's going to need my money. Yes. And furthermore I want you to get dressed. We must leave as soon as possible. And please knock on Eduardo's door. He must have at least rudimentary proposals ready for Villamayor's acceptance."

Actually, they could not leave until early the next morning: the yacht newly burdened for its twenty-four-hour run around the thin western promontory of Haiti: a cruise of two hundred and fifty miles to cover thirty. And in all that time not one of the participants in the journalistic debauch openly questioned the likely truth of that story. Where there is so much smoke there must be fire! In fact I surmise the rumors must have intensified during those eighteen hours of feverish preparation, after the New York newspaper arrived and was quickly suppressed. How soon would an "imminent" invasion occur? How many men did Villamayor have at his disposal, in addition to the eighty in the barracks?

It must have irritated Barbara Swenson to have to move so swiftly, after so many months of waiting. The nephew Charles Knutson and his wife Luiza were in Jamaica for a few days, as were the two sullen pilots recruited in Miami; they would have to be left behind. A pilot of the Haitian Air Force was hired to bring the ailing Grumman seaplane. Meanwhile three unofficial observers of the Haitian government and armed forces appeared at Barbara Swenson's villa to ask questions; they were on board the yacht when it left. So too were several migratory guests (late of the California ranch) and a large supplementary Negro "crew" collected through the evening from among the unemployed by Murphree himself.

Action at last! A chance to show one's knowledge of men! For hours Murphree stalked the streets and the waterfront slums with an expert appraising eye, followed by a rented truck. He interviewed the men briefly, scrutinized their muscles and their expressions, and put the chosen ones in the truck. Yes: these wiry tattered men well equipped with machetes and knives, and bearing many scars, looked capable of learning to fight in rough terrain. The truck, filled at last, went directly to the dock; from here the future guerrilla fighters were taken by dinghy to the yacht. They were quartered on deck near the stern. Also on board, when the yacht left, was the lean cautious correspondent of the New York newspaper, together with the stringer, his new drinking companion. They had gone up to the villa to interview Barbara Swenson, and had been invited to come along. A small truck carrying a machine gun, and hardly camouflaged at all, was lashed to the deck. Even the skeptical stringer had by now begun to believe in their material existence: the abandoned barracks and Villamayor's eighty men.

Meanwhile in Boston the same unimpeachable and sober newspaper was read by Peralda, who purchased it when he went to the corner for his loaf of bread. One can imagine his reception of the news. He too by long habit knew where to look, and skimmed through quickly, standing on the broken sidewalk under the gray chill sky. *Villamayor had been found! He was organizing an invasion army! He had consented to accept leadership! He had surmounted his contradictions!* Hurriedly (perhaps thinking now of the heroic plans for Puerto Limón, under the yellow Yucatan sky, perhaps even of the lost years of the Colegio and Villamayor's swordsmanship) Peralda called a meeting of his committee. Reynosa was summoned from the roomful of linotype machines, Gutierrez from the savory odors of a hotel kitchen, Sánchez was found on the docks. The committee met to consider its strategy, or more exactly to hear the powdered Peralda discourse. Two sentences of the news story especially bemused him. One— that wealthy Venezuelans had made contributions—suggested a serious invasion was at last in the offing. The second referred to the "expected arrival of other exile leaders."

Other exile leaders! I can imagine Peralda stalking the small feminine room in the presence of his three subordinates, pointing for emphasis the wrinkled cone of flesh. *"We must be represented too,"* he would say, *"Our ideas and political concepts must be heard."* Doubtless the committee's immediate problem was how to purchase a one-way airline ticket to Haiti. An attempt to float a loan must be made; private savings must be liquidated; a new reserve fund must be created for leaflets and brochures. Yet all the while they must meditate on ultimate problems. Should their small Boston committee submerge its identity in that of the *Partido Revolucionario,* a patriotic but clumsy monolith? Should the noble but dilettantish Villa-mayor, a man of so many contradictions, be the first President of the Provisional Government? Should the Colegio and University be closed during the purification process, and pending the appointment of new professors in all fields? In any new government, Peralda assured his listeners, there would be opportunities for the humblest.

And so it must have been, wherever the exiles of Santa Isabella foregather, as the ashes of political hope flickered once again. There would be hastily called meetings in clubrooms or darkened restaurants, in New York and Miami and Caracas, in Havana and San Juan. The grave discouraged Latin faces would be there, and the mulatto doctors and lawyers with them, and of course the long black cigars. And the old words of skepticism and passion, the old anecdotes of terror, the old fears of reprisal. Dusty yellowing manifestoes would be brought out and discussed. And for some men of fifty and sixty it would perhaps take the whole long night of talk to rekindle the rage of ten years before. Those with sufficient ambition and sufficient funds hastily packed their bags.

AND all this happened unknown to us, unknown to Villa-mayor. No doubt the shrewdest of the exile leaders were rendered suspicious by that allusion to the "Caribbean Legion" (an old journalistic *canard*) and by their own impressions of the poet who had gone into politics so reluctantly. *Villamayor organizing an army? It did not make sense.* Nevertheless, one had to act on the distant possibility that the story was true; one could not risk being left behind. So by the afternoon of the third day after the lean correspondent's long night of interviewing (and with the white yacht already on its way to Caye Thomonde) the first batch of leaders arrived in Port-au-Prince. Fifteen more, including Peralda, arrived on the same flight twenty-four hours later. And that was all. Thereafter all citizens or former residents of Santa Isabella were turned back by the immigration authorities, on the shrill insistence of The Protector's consulate.

Yes: all this occurred without our knowledge, and without the knowledge of Manuel Andrada. We had existed outside time, without newspaper or radio, and with enough passionate conflicts of our own. We had our queer truce that lasted two days, after Andrada's theft of the manuscripts. I was the bearer of messages: of Andrada's blunt demands that Villamayor return voluntarily to the homeland, and of the excited pleas of Julieta and Consuela to Andrada to give up all the papers and "renounce." Villamayor himself kept an attentive silence. And even Andrada through these two days was silent much of the time, stupefied as by drugs, or as though he were slowly losing heart. He would crouch beneath the portrait, staring at the purloined pages, turning those of the Daybook almost listlessly.

Then late on Thursday night the white yacht arrived, some forty-eight hours after the theft of the manuscripts, and dropped anchor a few hundred feet from the ruined wharf. It appeared thus, mysteriously: a scatter of unaccountable lights in the moonless night, and with the sound of many voices coming over the black water.

By dawn it was plainly there for the citizens of Caye Thomonde to see, Manuel Andrada among them: the graceful white hull listing slightly to port because of the large number of persons lining one rail. Andrada recognized the yacht at once, and even the pink hair of the subversive Barbara Swenson and the white head of Edward Murphree. Also the high forehead and hopeful face of Eduardo Gonzales the constitutionalist. But he noted too the grave official black faces, and the horde of tattered Negroes at the stern. He was astonished by their number.

Evidently the captain of the yacht was highly distrustful of that ruined wharf shelving into the water over broken pilings. At first there was much shouting across the water. Then a dinghy was lowered containing Edward Murphree and the lean correspondent of the New York newspaper, as well as an officer of the yacht. It moved cautiously toward the wharf until at last the men in the dinghy were rocking at its crushed base. They looked up at the citizens of Caye Thomonde. Murphree at once recognized Andrada and waved. He saw again the somber and scarred young man suddenly taken sick at the villa, who had rushed from the table after overturning his glass. . . .

"*Bonjour, monsieur Andrada!*" he called up. "So we have come to the right place!"

"The right place?"

"Where are the barracks? Is this as near as we can come for the landing of men and materiel? What is the draught at the good side of the wharf? What is the condition of the road? Have you any transportation at all?"

Edward Murphree hurled up his practical questions with the joyful vigor of a man at last coming into his own.

His nautical cap and blazer buttoned tight gave him the appearance of wearing a uniform. Andrada understood nothing.

"What barracks do you speak of?"

"Villamayor's, of course. The barracks for his men and the training grounds."

"For his men!" Andrada found his gaze rising reluctantly to the swarm of villainous black creatures at the stern of the yacht. He crossed himself quickly. "Is Justo de Villamayor expecting these men?"

A man of tired and puffy appearance (it was the new correspondent) stared at Andrada uneasily. Perhaps this was his first view of a "guerrilla fighter" and veteran of the old Caribbean Legion. He noted with journalistic interest the odd scar . . . souvenir of some desperate democratic uprising. Probably a machete slash. He posed his first question rather timidly.

"How many soldiers do you have here, señor?"

"I have no soldiers, there is only myself."

"I mean Villamayor's men. Aren't you one of them?"

"Never mind that," Murphree interrupted. "What we want to know is where the captain can bring in the yacht. There's not just the men and supplies. We also have a small truck carrying a machine gun." He was puzzled by Andrada's expression, "Why do you just stand there? Why don't you answer me?"

But Andrada was standing there no longer. He had begun to back away, with the sky suddenly darkened, and the rotting wharf insecure underfoot. *Barracks, training grounds, soldiers, Villamayor's men, machine gun.* . . . Andrada backed away step after trembling step until the dinghy and its four intruders were out of sight beneath the pilings. Then he turned and began to walk quickly in the direction of his room, trying not to run, thinking very intently of The Protector's incriminating portrait and of the precious manuscripts he must not lose, must not be compelled to surrender. For two days Andrada had waited in his sagging room, fearing not at all the combined forces of Villamayor and his household. Even that enormous Negro of the effeminate manner he could have upended easily enough. But now, walking still more rapidly up the broken and deserted main street of Caye Thomonde, Manuel Andrada was acutely conscious that he was much outnumbered by the enemy. *Yes, by the enemy: by a boatload of mercenary scum and rapists dragged from the gutters of Port-au-Prince, by communist spoilers and Norte Americano atheists, by sietemesino theorizers on constitutions, by poets who betray the trust, oh yes* (he would be running now, the full horror of the discovery striking him like a blow on the back: his own utter simplicity and Villamayor's Satanic pretense of unpolitical withdrawal, Villamayor's sly secrecy and his own criminal inadequacy, who was certain to be punished now) . . . *yes, by the enemy: by the man whose patriotic poems he had learned by heart, a name in many books, the criminal ingrate in spite of the honor of a statue in the row of heroes above the seawall . . . who not once but now twice had collected and organized dreamers disbelieving in God for invasions of the homeland. . . .*

Then he was in his room, collecting the papers, closing the suitcase, taking the portrait hastily and lovingly from the wall. In the ruin of his world he must have longed to strike out against anyone. Instead he crept down the outside staircase, with the unwrapped portrait held awkwardly in his left hand and the black suitcase in his right. He was relieved to find the street still empty. In fact it might be many minutes before the subversive ones would land. So he walked as fast as he could with his two burdens: toward the first crumbled and overgrown suburbs, and the green wilderness beyond. He had no idea where he was going. And indeed it would be another thirty-six hours before we began to learn where he had been and what he had done and how he had survived with his thoughts; and how (using his own special training at last) he had watched us covertly and made his plans.

WE were at breakfast when the first frightened reports reached us of a great white ship off Caye Thomonde, its decks filled with Negroes of murderous appearance and city-dwelling *grands nègres* in white suits. There were also various *blancs,* including two of advanced age—a man of white hair, and a woman of hair unnaturally red. Her blue eyes were as of a soul imprisoned in the fragile flesh of the dead. A third *blanc* asked incomprehensible questions. Thus the excited reports. So we were prepared, even before the meeting itself, the absurd confrontation on the ruined main street of Caye Thomonde, to find Barbara Swenson and Edward Murphree. But that was all we knew to expect. And they in turn, especially the rum-sodden and viciously sunburned correspondent, were unprepared for our revelations. Instead we advanced upon them and upon their ignorance with what must have seemed (to the correspondent from Brussels) the determination of a guerrilla *état-major:* the twisted grave face of the limping and dedicated leader, his women assistants of fanatic intensity, an enormous Negro bodyguard. And myself, the usual ambiguous American.

They stood in a semicircle waiting: Barbara Swenson,

Edward Murphree, the correspondent and the stringer,
and the several representatives of the Republic of Haiti.
Also the theorist Eduardo Gonzales. Beyond them we
could see the yacht, its afterdeck filled with Negroes in
tatters, many naked to the waist. It was Barbara Swenson
who stepped forward to demand explanations. The eyes
of cornflower blue darted from me to Villamayor:

"We have been friends for twenty years, Justo! I did
not expect this shabbiness, I did not expect to be betrayed.
You had a right to remain silent, yes. But I did not expect
lies at my own table and in the presence of men of purest
motive devoted to the cause."

"Lies?"

"You said you would have nothing to do with an invasion of Santa Isabella."

"So? I haven't anything to do with an invasion of Santa
Isabella."

"You're quite right," Murphree broke in. "This mustn't
be shouted from the housetops."

The languid citizens of Caye Thomonde watched us:
anonymous black wraiths dumbly present at the unfolding
of history. Villamayor followed my gaze in the direction
of the yacht.

"I have nothing to hide," he said. "At least not any
more. And who are all those Negroes on your ship?"

Murphree stepped discreetly closer.

"The crew."

"It's quite a large one!"

"Reinforcements for you," Murphree whispered. "Men
who require only a short course of training in small-arms
fire and the use of terrain to be ready for anything. I
know men. I picked them myself."

"Reinforcements?" Villamayor turned now to me. "But

what madness is this? Do you know anything about this?"

I could honestly answer I did not. And now attention began to converge on the perspiring correspondent of the great newspaper, transferred recently from Brussels.

"You have eighty men here," he said. "It is understood you are training them . . ."

"I have eighty men?" Villamayor turned and nodded to Belesprit. "I have one man here who works for me, and one who is a guest in my house."

"But they told me! I had my information from unimpeachable sources, former members of the Haitian Cabinet. You have veterans of the Caribbean Legion, soldiers of fortune, exiles. . . . They are living in an abandoned army barracks."

"Are they indeed? To my knowledge there are no barracks near here."

"But there must be some mistake!" the correspondent shrieked. "Isn't there anyone here?"

There was no one; there had indeed been a mistake. But the words had been uttered on that hotel veranda, by the unimpeachable authorities, through the long hot drunken night. Now they had been scattered to the wide world, and could not be recalled. And so too the process could not at once be reversed, that had already caused secret meetings from Boston to Caracas and sent selected exiles on their way. For an hour more the correspondent questioned the citizens of Caye Thomonde, with the amused stringer in attendance. The veteran of Brussels could not accept at once such an embarrassing defeat. But meanwhile I had learned of that early morning interview between Murphree and Andrada which had sent the latter into precipitate flight; and I verified the emptiness of his room. The portrait and suitcase were gone, as well as the man-

uscripts. This meant, I surmised, that we had seen the last
of Manuel Andrada. Would he simply vanish now? Or
would he return to the higher authorities with the manuscripts, and to accept reasonable punishment . . . the
sietemesino who had been unable to detect the formation
of an invasion army before his eyes?

His inward struggles must have been ridiculous as well
as obscure. Yet now, with the events known and done, and
having listened to his babbled account . . . now it is in
part through Andrada's eyes, rather than my own, I watch
the shifting, ambiguous appearances of the next days. For
he did not immediately run away. Instead he spent the
first hours in the overgrown ruins of a house at the northern edge of the town: a place of hiding well off the path,
to be disputed with centipedes and lizards. And it was
here he saw the old seaplane circling overhead, and then
heard its coughing descent: a horrible thing, the very
instrument for bringing death to innocents in the homeland. The evil design shaped itself before his eyes, before
his scandalized thoughts. There was first the yacht for the
landing of men on some deserted beach, now the plane
to release paratroopers and supplies on a mountaintop.
Would there be further planes and men? Where would it
end? For hours Andrada crouched miserably beside the
portrait and the suitcase revolving his fears.

The indignation of Villamayor too became more intense, with the arrival of that ancient plane. It lay heavily
on the water, bearing its stains and scars of brush-fire wars,
the cumbersome obsolete patched thing which was nevertheless adequate for the transport of troops a scant fifty
miles. Villamayor was certain there would be more planes
to follow, purchased by Barbara Swenson; his privacy had
been invaded in the worst possible way. His first impulse,

in fact, was to turn his back on her and on the other "invaders" . . . leaving them to me to dispose of. But someone showed him that New York newspaper of unimpeachable reputation, and the plausible quiet circumstantial story that was really at fault. *The abandoned barracks, the hope of reinforcement, the support of Venezuelan exiles.* . . . Barbara Swenson at least, the incorrigibly hopeful one, could hardly be blamed for rushing to his aid. In the end Villamayor shrugged off the misadventure with a wry grin. There was nothing to be gained by discourtesy. At last he even offered to show Barbara and Edward Murphree and the Haitian officials his house, since they had come so far. A luncheon could be improvised, if they were willing to do without wine. Meanwhile the lean American journalist, author of that authoritative story, had quietly left in the direction of Port-au-Prince without bothering to say good-bye.

But there would of course be others: the less fortunate ones without access to a yacht. Late in the morning a contingent of native journalists from Port-au-Prince arrived: appearing on minute rented donkeys in slow indignant procession, their notebooks and cameras poised. One car had broken down yesterday. The other carload of correspondents had been diverted by false rumor to Anse de Corail, where the whole evening had been spent foraging for water and food. One by one these reporters took us aside, Belesprit and me especially, still unwilling to believe there were no barracks and no soldiers on the premises. They were enraged by Villamayor's refusal to be interviewed.

Then in midafternoon the first white-shirted prosperous exiles from Caracas and Havana and San Juan arrived, who had come to Port-au-Prince on Thursday planes.

They appeared on horseback, a round dozen in all, the wealthiest of the rebels: the lawyers and importers and even two financiers, each eying the others with embarrassment. They came by twos and threes, patriotic but exhausted and perspiring, fat, their white shirts or *guayaveras* ruined, and their expensive travel cases stained . . . they too astonished to find no soldiers drilling, and a decayed mansion instead of a barracks. They descended painfully from their beasts, the old revolutionary muscles softened by the years of taxis and air-conditioned offices. When Villamayor saw the first contingent appear (two fat grizzled veterans of Cayo Cumana who had squabbled sporadically ever since) he turned stiffly on his heel and went inside: there seemed no limit to the outraging of his privacy.

But then he decided to make the best of things; his whimsical tolerance prevailed once more. And in the end he was greeting the newcomers as he had once greeted me, with the twisted aloof smile, and with humorous references to "abortive revolution." A few he even embraced: old friends encountered on trips, and even several who went back to his university days and to clandestine political conversations in the first year of the tyranny. It seemed bitterly appropriate and amusing that their heroic adolescent dreams should end in such fiasco.

The first indignation of the newcomers also gave way to wry amusement. Doubtless some were secretly relieved to discover an invasion was not imminent. They had come prepared to endure once again the discomforts of Cayo Cumana: the weeks of bickering and stench on that burning shelf of sand, while the arms and men were collected. Instead there would be only talk: a day and a night of talk, at most two or three. Then they could return to the air-conditioned offices and the limousines to await a more propitious occasion. But there might as well be, since they had come this far, the talk: at first the anecdotes and the old remembered hardships of ten and twelve years before, and the memories of terror in Santa Isabella. And then (since so many leaders were present, and especially Villamayor himself) at least some discussion of the steps to be taken upon The Protector's death by accidental or natural causes. From a distance Consuela watched these conversations hungrily. She was deeply envious of Barbara Swenson, who knew most of the leaders, and who was getting more attention than herself.

That evening there was a party on the yacht: a political meeting of the exiles held out of earshot of the Haitian journalists and other outsiders. Barbara Swenson and Edward Murphree were there of course—who would supply the brandies and champagnes and eventually, perhaps, the necessary armaments and funds. But I was excluded and so was the rest of our household, even the furious Consuela. For a while I talked with Belesprit, then went to bed. And all the time poor Consuela stalked angrily in the vicinity of the ruined wharf, tantalized by the lights of the yacht, and by the indistinct voices coming to her over the black water, pessimistic and passionate. She was missing, she felt, the opportunity of her life.

Villamayor himself went to that meeting most reluctantly. He did not want to answer questions on the rumored theft of certain papers, and he knew from experience how circular and nebulous the debates would be. What chance would even a well financed invasion have, when the invaders could agree on nothing? The next morning, Saturday that is, he was tired and irritable, and spoke at length of the exiles' wild self-delusions. They had

talked on and on through the night, spinning their fantasies of military *junta* and purified provisional government . . . not once acknowledging their common relief
because no armed expedition was presently possible. These
rich men had come courageously enough, out of historical
and even inherited obligation, accepting the discomfort
and the dazing heat, and those plodding rented horses.
But they adjusted quickly to reality, and without ceasing
to utter slogans: to the realities of brandy and champagne,
of beds with sheets or at least well cushioned sofas on
Barbara Swenson's yacht. And to the old reality of passionate but harmless talk. It was decided they would hold
informal discussions through Saturday at the house, and
another meeting Saturday night, once again on the yacht.
Then they would return home. This time, Villamayor
made it quite clear, he would not join them on the yacht.

But meanwhile history, mad and inconsecutive, was
happening very fast. Those first outraged confrontations
had occurred on Friday morning: of Edward Murphree
looking up at Andrada on the ruined dock, of Barbara
Swenson and Villamayor. By Saturday evening the lean
correspondent, saddened, vomiting frequently as a result
of excessive exposure to the sun, had cabled his brief story
from Port-au-Prince, together with his request for a new
assignment: two stinging paragraphs dismissing the rumors of an invasion army as the fabrication of excited
local statesmen of high repute. But the disclaimer came
much too late. The second batch of exiles arrived in Port-
au-Prince on Friday afternoon. These were the more
modest ones who had needed twenty-four hours to lay
their hands on the necessary funds for airplane tickets:
the leaders of incorruptible splinter groups, the taxi drivers and waiters and teachers of languages, the two

dancing masters, the printer, even the proprietor of a small café noted as a meeting place. There were fifteen of these belated ones, who scattered themselves among the cheaper *pensions* of Port-au-Prince. Over dinner they heard the first disquieting rumors. Still they too, having come this far, could not simply turn back. So during the first hours of Saturday afternoon they in their turn appeared at the end of the ruined alley of stumps and at the house, to be greeted by Villamayor. Several of them limped in, having considered the price for horse or donkey (which had inflated several hundred percent since we came) excessive.

They too observed with dismay the absence of any sign of military preparation, but they knew by sight some of the wealthy leaders who had preceded them. In the shaded area back of the house, and near the great tureen of water, they smoked and argued through that Saturday afternoon: renewing old friendships and tentatively making new alliances. Consuela found herself more at home with these humble newcomers; some of them had heard her speak. I quickly discovered that I was universally distrusted, because of my rumored connections with Andrada, an "agent of the tyranny." So I spent most of the afternoon in my room. Villamayor (who had flatly announced his refusal to attend the meeting that night, and who looked forward to a collective departure in the morning) moved from group to group amiably enough, discounting all allusions to the vanished Andrada, and insisting on his own "unpolitical withdrawal."

I did, as it happened, witness his meeting with Peralda, though I could not hear what they said. From my window I even saw their first moment of recognition: the onetime schoolmates of the Colegio, the veterans of Puerto Limón.

Villamayor must have taken in Peralda's life at a glance: the slack sleeve and poorly refitted suit, the imperfectly rinsed hair, the countenance of passionate failure. And Peralda in his turn must have discerned at once that Villamayor still refused to accept leadership. The champion swordsman, the boy who had promised so much . . . ruined by the *wanderjahre* and European subleties! For a long moment they stared at each other in friendly yet austere disillusionment, as though to say *So this is what life has done to us, this is not what we hoped for at all!* Then they had embraced and were walking briskly toward a quiet corner of the yard. I wonder what new pleas Peralda made, to stimulate Villamayor's slackened will? I only know Villamayor listened to him patiently for half an hour, now and then shaking his head. Once he nodded to the yard of disputing exiles, and threw his hands up in skeptical despair. Didn't they have evidence enough before their eyes that a successful invasion could not yet be mounted? His gesture seemed to say that.

A few of the exiles did, prompted by Consuela, ask their questions about the departed "agent" and the manuscripts he was said to have stolen. But for the most part Andrada was forgotten; and forgotten even by us. There was too much else to take our attention. The fact is that Andrada had vanished from our lives as abruptly as he had stepped into mine less than two months before. He had simply left, taking with him the unclean burdens: the portrait and the stolen pages. Belesprit spoke of pursuit, of mobilizing the exiles, even of putting Edward Murphree's villainous platoon to good use. But Villamayor shrugged off his loss; it was already, for him, in the past. *"Let the poor creature go, even the detestable deserve to live. Yes, let us hope my miserable pages will at least pur-*

chase his life." Moreover, it seemed reasonable enough to suppose he had already reached his Consulate in Port-au-Prince. Had he, we wondered, stepped off the trail to hide as he saw that file of indignant Haitian journalists come down it, Friday noon, and later the first perspiring exiles? The portrait, at least, he would have taken precaution to hide.

We assumed, in other words, that he had looped around the house and returned to the Port-au-Prince road by the one trail we knew. But in this we were wrong. Sometime early Friday afternoon (still dazed by the discoveries of the morning, still sickened by the coughing sound of that evil plane) Andrada had left his hiding place of crumbled stone on the outskirts of Caye Thomonde. He plunged into the brackish wasteland north of the town, then climbed straight up into the hills toward the rain forests and the orchidean jungle. It was after dinner on that first night—with Villamayor on the yacht, and the rest of us in Caye Thomonde—that the first puzzled reports reached the house, relayed from hut to hut and changing slightly with each telling, at last to be told to Ezile: how a terrible little man with a flaming scar, and bearing both a great picture and a suitcase, had stamped somberly by, scarcely deigning to remain on the path. It was, they affirmed, the same man who had appeared at the recent *vaudun* ceremonies, and who had insulted the priest and his assistants. They gave him a wide berth, though some left propitiatory fruits by their doors. In the burning afternoon he stalked on, finding his way because he took only trails that climbed: a man who appeared to be entranced, a man with a mission and a burden, and who seemed to cherish the solitude created around him.

These were the first reports, and no doubt they were

accurate enough. It appeared Andrada was trying to get back to Port-au-Prince his own way, avoiding the frequented trail and the one road. The rest I would reconstruct from his own cryptic words about his "days of solitude." All Friday afternoon he climbed through what must have appeared to him a land stricken with death: the empty crisscrossing trails and abandoned huts, the strange mounds of fruit, and no human sound but a distant bamboo flute or drum or perhaps a conch shell blown high in the rain forest above. He rested for a few hours in one of these huts but did not sleep. On Saturday morning (still thinking himself in a solitude, still watched every step of the way) he continued to climb. But after only an hour, and shortly after the sun appeared, he suddenly turned east as though to challenge the *cordillera septentrional* itself, and cross over into Santa Isabella directly. By now in the minds of the frightened natives he had become an occult creature of the forest roaming as a spirit-ridden animal would: the scar larger and the suit more hairy with each report, and the soiled and ripped portrait growing to preposterous size. At the end of the morning he spent another hour in one of the abandoned huts, and fed on the mangoes he found there arranged carefully on a dish. At this point in his journey he was not more than fifteen miles from us, and he had traced two-thirds of a circle.

What made him pause on his solitary path that morning, and then turn to the east and toward the spiny mountains, after going so far north? Perhaps he realized that in Port-au-Prince, face to face with an austere Consul or with Miguel Rubínez himself, he would still be far from home. Very far indeed. . . . And now within sight lay the blue mountains, whose crests were in Santa Isabella.

So it may be he was drawn, suddenly turning his back on Port-au-Prince, by a vivid picture of himself crossing the border on foot: of touching the sacred soil; of surrendering his burden, the manuscript that is, to the border patrol or first rural policeman. Who can conjecture what his thoughts were then, or through the sleepless night to follow? The impulse, in any event, survived scarcely an hour: the impulse to go directly home. Early Saturday afternoon, and after over thirty hours of his sleepless solitude, he turned again to complete the circle . . . turned back toward us.

In a way we were forewarned by the excited narratives of Ezile's friends. And perhaps we should have been able to predict to the hour this last lap of a ridiculous journey, and the fulfillment of orders he had tried to ignore. It was Andrada's characteristic way to come painfully roundabout to the place he could not avoid; it was his way, to blunder at last onto inescapable obligation. Still, we did not hear of this final change of direction until late Saturday afternoon, when the exiles were already beginning to drift off toward the yacht and its material comforts. By then, however, Andrada had long since completed his wandering. He had, two hours before, reached the *caille* about three miles from the house, and there left both portrait and suitcase. And by then too he would have already spent that terrible hour watching us and the collected exiles from a thick screen of underbrush and bamboo just beyond his own cabin, the place of lost connubial bliss. He called this his "hour of complete and sick awakening." Why were we not told (who had been told so much) that he was in fact watching us from a hundred yards away? Looking back, I was puzzled at first because the last report to reach Ezile was so delayed and so obviously evasive. But later I understood well enough. The possessor of such information was too terrified to report it.

I know well enough, however, what happened after that. And I can imagine Andrada's horror when he first came in sight of the house and crowded backyard. He drew back at once, he said, to find a better place of hiding from which to watch. For now there were more of his compatriots than had come by the evil yacht, many more: important men smoking long cigars, and whose fierce countenance of treason he knew too well. As many as thirty stood about in groups, no doubt uttering indecencies. *There before his eyes was happening the thing he had dreaded all his life: conspiracy, the planned overthrow of established institutions.* The betrayers of the trust were clustered near the back door, arguing, while still others formed a circle near the tureen of boiling water. Some with the long cigars and scornful faces were obviously wealthy, others might have been servants. The fanatic swarm and atheistic dreamers. . . . Among them he could detect too those who had particularly betrayed him, notably the lost Consuela. Did he from that hiding place perhaps a hundred yards from the house also hear the wild discourse of that afternoon: the detailed propositions of overthrow? Did he recognize from my description the personage of Peralda: the powdered face and wrinkled cone of flesh raised to punctuate dangerous remarks? Certainly he would hardly have failed to see Villamayor at least once in converse with Eduardo Gonzales, the emaciated mad architect of disorder. Time and again I myself saw Villamayor that afternoon, walking with hands behind his back and eyes half-closed: submitting, listening in quiet despair to one radiant theorist after another, as he moved from group to group.

So we were indeed forewarned: forewarned repeatedly, even, in this wilderness where news could travel so fast. We knew Manuel Andrada was in the vicinity. We knew he had returned, after making his plodding solitary circling effort to break away. But still Villamayor refused to become alarmed. And he would not let us say anything to the intruding exiles, the "voluble outsiders" who were already leaving for supper on the yacht and for their long night of political debate. *Let them go, to leave a solitude which would make Andrada's return more propitious and more welcome!* It was Villamayor's considered opinion that poor Andrada, confused and corrupted by the manuscripts, was returning to give them back, and perhaps even to "renounce"; at least to make one more verbal plea. *"Didn't I tell you we had not seen the last of him? Yes, tonight or at least tomorrow I will be subjected again to his patriotic discourses. That is the only violence of which Andrada is still capable. Is it not violence enough?"*

Julieta and Consuela protested, all of us protested in vain. During our long subdued dinner, subdued at least after the wild voices and surprises of the day, Villamayor shrugged off our every effort to make him take due precautions. And in retrospect it strikes me that Villamayor was even determined to go out of his way—to give the hiding Andrada his chance. For he insisted, with nightfall, on going out to his cabin alone. He said he wanted to begin to make up for the two days lost from his work. He wanted to recover his "shattered solitude." But now I suspect he went out into the night to bring on precisely the confrontation that did occur, the event . . . and to welcome perversely his "antagonist." Almost angrily he pushed aside Belesprit's effort to accompany him.

And so he was quite alone, though only fifty yards from the house, when at last Andrada struck. From the back porch we had surreptitiously watched Villamayor limp toward the cabin. We had seen the white shirt and trousers become gray and then vanish in the first trees. Then we saw the lamp in the cabin go on, yellow at the one window. But we did not see Andrada "strike." We did not see the rough hand that went over Villamayor's mouth, seconds after the lamp began to burn. And we heard nothing at all. In that first, silent long-delayed act of violence, Manuel Andrada (who had failed in so many ways since setting out from the homeland) at last showed himself expert enough.

HE had only half an hour of grace, the Antagonist. But this was more than he needed. I had gone to my room and was making notes on the various exile leaders when I heard Belesprit go outside and walk toward the study. Moments later he returned running, crying *Au secours! Au secours!* in shrill feminine tones. We ran back to the cabin, with Consuela and Julieta and Ezile behind us. There were few signs of struggle. The lamp near the door burned undisturbed. The rattan chair was at the crude table Villamayor used as his desk, and all the papers seemed in place, as though untouched for days. There was no indication, in fact, that Villamayor had ever reached that desk. We knew (looking at each other as though seeking already someone onto whom we could cast the blame) that Andrada must have acted in the first moments after Villamayor went inside. And acted without sound, without permitting the slightest protest. Belesprit later told me he had been made apprehensive, after the half-hour, by the extreme stillness of the night and by the yellow unchanging glare at the cabin window. But why should the light have changed? All the same he had been sure, even before he opened the door, that something had gone wrong.

There was little enough we could do in such darkness, with the trees and the underbrush and even the gaunt house itself scarcely blacker than the sky. We could only make token gestures. So for half an hour we scoured the vicinity of the house and the first encircling wilderness, carrying our dim lanterns like children playing a game . . . and with a full knowledge of the game's futility. Then I sent Consuela to notify the people on the yacht, and to bring Edward Murphree with his "crew" of Negroes. For the moment I had quite forgotten them. I also sent Belesprit, guided by Ezile, to Anse de Corail to find the *chef de section* and demand police help. Another futile gesture, as all of us knew. . . . Still, it seemed better to act blindly than not at all. For two hours I waited with Julieta for Consuela to return with help . . . more than enough time unless she too had been abducted or was lost. We sat facing each other in the hot silence, Julieta musing desperately, I suppose, on her old predictions of martyrdom. Now and then we rushed out into the yard, pursuing imaginary sounds. Then at the end of the two hours I decided to go to Caye Thomonde myself.

I did not find Consuela there, but I did discover why she had not returned with help. The yacht had moved at least a quarter-mile farther out to sea, either to escape the stagnant sick heat of Caye Thomonde, or to be out of earshot of those enraged Haitian journalists. The yacht's lights were distinct and very small riding on the water; the scheming political voices were not even a murmur. And, I later learned, even the strident tones of Consuela had been unable to rouse anyone on the yacht. It appears the journalists (housed among the rats of Caye Thomonde) had made nothing at all of her Spanish voice shrieking in the stillness. They had gone back to sleep. And I gather Consuela herself must have returned to the house. We had missed each other on the way, taking different paths through the outlying ruins.

Then I knew there was nothing to do except wait for morning. So I went to Andrada's old room. I had neither the energy nor the desire to find another. Moreover, to return to Andrada's room (where we had had such intimate conversations) struck me as the natural thing to do, the inevitable thing. I lay down on the floor, in the exact place formerly occupied by Andrada's bulging pallet, and at once detected the familiar odors of stale food, cheap cigars and sweat. In that blackness Manuel Andrada was all around me. The rats behind the walls went on with their scurrying unafraid. I had begun, in fact, to reason as though I were Andrada. And I recognized that my one chance of finding him was to remain in precisely this place; and permit him to find me. He had come here without subterfuge after stealing the manuscripts, knowing I too would come. And where else would he go now, to whom else could he appeal . . . if the stubborn Villamayor proved more than he could cope with, or if his own act of violence suddenly became unacceptable to himself?

In retrospect all this would seem almost obvious: Andrada was driven, helpless and protesting, to his absurd obligation. He could no longer circumvent me, since he had shown himself so incapable of circumventing himself. I began to believe this even then, as I lay there on the floor. And so I lay awake in the blackness and the stinking heat, already half-expecting him, already expecting his confession. I waited in my odd waking lassitude until I saw morning growing on the wall, and the blank place where The Protector's portrait had been. I began to listen for footsteps on the outside staircase, and a thick animal breathing.

AND I heard it at last: the sound of a man running down the empty street, breaking into the great stillness. I had time to take one long breath as he ran up the stairs. Then he was crouched beside me, his hands lightly touching my shoulders and trembling. His face had the gray texture of a paste; the withdrawn eyes stared past me at the blank wall where the portrait had hung. *"Nicholas Clive! Nicholas Clive!"* His hands still held my shoulders. Then he began to shake me, gently, as though I were not already awake. *"You are my friend, Nicholas Clive. Did we not come to Haiti together, did we not once share a room? You must tell me what I have done. Is it true this man is a saint? I struck him first with my bare hands and then with a great stick. But he would not fall. Stubbornly he refused to die."*

I tried to twist away from the hands still gently holding me.

"He's all right?"

"How can I know? He breathed, yes. I think he will breathe forever. The black woman of the hut has bandaged him. And now he sleeps. Yes, he went down at last beneath the blows of that great stick even as I felt the strength depart from my arms. My will dissolved, Nicholas Clive! My soul changed while those blows descended on his head. I loved him, I saw the blood spurting. Then I could strike him no more. And he lay still breathing at my feet."

"The woman was there?"

He shook his head in the thin dusty light. He would not look at me. And I wondered which was his deepest shame: that he had tried to kill a man, or that he had failed in his mission. At this darkest hour of his life Manuel Andrada must have felt he had failed everybody.

"I do not know when the woman came. She brought cloths for bandages, the hut belonged to her, she came at sometime during the night." Suddenly he took his hands away from me, as though even that meager human touch burned. "But I pleaded with him, Nicholas Clive. Before God I submitted every patriotic argument and he answered me with blasphemies. Once again he wanted to corrupt me."

I tried in vain to bring him back to the material facts of Villamayor's wounds.

"Where is he hurt? Is his head still bleeding?"

"I do not know," he said quietly. "However, it would be well for him to die—though his death be the perdition of my soul. I think he will never see Santa Isabella again. The opportunity for redemption is lost, he does not even desire forgiveness. And I, Nicholas Clive? What am I to do who have failed in everything? I must still live and breathe."

I got up and put on my shoes. The first thing he could do, I said, was take me to Villamayor. It appeared the hut was not more than a mile from the house. He could take me to it then go for help. We went out into the bright morning. And on the way he told me what had happened: of his long hour of failure and his moment of discovery as the blows fell, and the sudden "change" of his soul. We walked quickly through the ruined overgrown suburbs, then took a path a few hundred feet north of the one that led to our house. And Andrada talked, rapid and incoherent, even gasping as though mortally short of breath, as though running short of time. The giant bamboo and wild palms enclosed us, and the dense overgrowth of green. Andrada insisted on walking behind me as he talked. He did not want me to see him.

Only in the first moments had Andrada felt himself truly in command of the evening's events: only in those long seconds during which Villamayor, having entered the cabin, advanced to the lamp and lit it. *"At this instant I silenced him. I had no decision to make, the thing had to be done."*

At this instant he silenced him. . . . He did not then say exactly how—whether by single blow to the twisted sardonic jaw, or by catching the neck in the crook of the arm to stifle outcry, with a hand over the mouth. But the first gross moments of this violent evening seemed unimportant to Andrada: the thing was done. Apparently they lay for many minutes in a corner of the cabin, the watchful Andrada and the unconscious Villamayor. Then Andrada simply slung this breathing corpse over one shoulder and walked off into the night, and to the hut near which he had left the suitcase and portrait. Sometime before that Villamayor regained consciousness, and was ordered to walk ahead. Then they had arrived. They were face to face at last in the small shadowy *caille* lit by a single thick candle.

"Can you believe he tried at once to corrupt me, Nicholas Clive? Before I could find the words to speak of his salvation, he was speaking of mine. There in the solitude and unprotected by his friends he began to spit out his old words of scorn for the principles of order and authority. I was bewildered. I stood before him speechless, a *sietemesino* do-nothing. Yes, it might have been Justo de Villamayor who had dragged me through the night, and not I him. There he stood before me with his twisted devil's face and his expression of tenderness, and he said to me, *'Manuel Andrada, you must renounce. You think you have come here to persuade me. Perhaps even to do me violence? But no! It is you who wish to be persuaded, in the depths of your soul.'* I interrupted him. *'Persuaded of what?'* I cried. *'How can you who believe in nothing persuade?'* And he replied to me with that serpent's or devil's voice, *'Andrada, I believe in you.'* Thereupon this man I had knocked senseless discoursed as calmly as might the teacher in a child's schoolroom. He walked about the hut as though nothing had happened. And I heard again the evil propositions of dreamers, twisted to seem things of good report. . . . Once again he told me everything is permitted; therefore each must judge. Also he told me a man has no master but himself. And again as when I read his corrupt writings I found myself beginning to believe. His voice is a silken net paralyzing the limbs. For a moment I forgot my God. I forgot the horrible vacancy of the blue sky from which the soul of things has fled. Yes, Justo de Villamayor was demoralizing me again, only an hour after I had captured him. He tried to possess my soul."

Andrada, walking behind me in the greenish gloom, fell silent.

"I gather he didn't succeed."

"How can I know, Nicholas Clive? I think his voice will be with me always. But then it was my turn to speak, and bring him to salvation. I did not have to tell him he must come back to Santa Isabella of his own will. I could not carry him on my back thirty miles! But I spoke to him as one man who loves his country to another of the balm of confession and punishment. I was honorable with him, Nicholas Clive, I could no longer promise immunity. But what is mere punishment of the flesh or a few years in prison? The shameful one is almost received back into the homeland at the moment of confession. And he is accepted completely at the hour of punishment. The child who experiences the ferule on his open hand or the mother's slap of the face for evildoing—is this not also the sacred moment when evil is washed away and he is taken back into her love? I spoke to Villamayor of the joy of confession, who cannot know it, having separated himself from the Church. In confession of political crime also there is communion with a higher soul. Someone listens, Nicholas Clive, a scribe takes note of your words! And I said this to Villamayor: *'You are no humble peasant without honor. Your words of confession will be published in the* Diario del Caribe. *It is even possible you will be admitted to the sacred presence of The Protector, who will hear your confession himself. You will kneel in front of him, perhaps he will forgive.'* Then an awful thing was said, Nicholas Clive. Satan spoke again through his quiet scornful words. *'I would not kneel, Manuel Andrada, I would spit in his face.'* It was at this moment I understood the terrible thing would have to be done after all. But still I gave him every chance to repent."

Suddenly Andrada stopped. The silence of the forest

surrounded us. Had we come two hundred yards or two miles?

"You've lost the way?"

"No, Nicholas Clive. I know too well the way. In the blackest night I found my way straight to the hut. But listen: have I not shown great patience with this man who refused to be saved? So now I gave him a final chance to deny his written words. I asked: *'Were you in truth among those who conspired against Puerto Limón?'* and he said *'Yes.'* And then I told him without concealment the orders given me by Miguel Rubínez, The Cripple: *'If you will not come back to the homeland for punishment and forgiveness, you must die.'* And he said with that quietness as of one aided by the Adversary, *'You must disobey your orders, Andrada. Instead you must come with me.'* "

"And you?"

"I asked him one more time *'Will you come?'* and he said again quietly *'I will not.'* Then a blindness came over me as of a child whose eyes have filled with tears. The hut was dark, he seemed very far away. I approached him and lifted my hand; the darkness was terrible. *'Then die!'* I cried out to him—*'Die, miserable one, die!'* My right arm rising to strike him might have borne a terrible weight, so hard it was to move. It came crashing down. And I struck again: blows that would have felled most men. Yet I could hardly lift my arm. And Justo de Villamayor did not move. For one moment he defended himself and reached for my neck. I struck his hand away as one might strike away a child's. Then I was trying to hit him again and I knew all the strength of my arms was leaving me, there was no force to the blows. Yes, Nicholas Clive, my soul changed while I tried to strike him down.

I wanted to embrace him. I picked up that great stick
which lay at hand as though sent by providence to aid me.
I tried to beat him with the stick. And again all the
strength went out of my blows. I was hardly hitting him
at all. But by now the blood was spurting and one eye
was closed where my fist had fallen at the first. Then at
last he lay on the floor beneath me, and his breaths were
like groans. What happened after that I do not know. I
was trying to bandage his head when the woman of the
hut came. What was I to say to her, I who had failed in
my mission? Everything was lost, I could hardly get to
my feet. So I came to find you. You must tell me what
I have done."

Then we had arrived: a hut at the end of the path, and
a small fire burning outside under a crude pot. The small
caille, hardly a shack, lay just out of the sunlight and
against the dense wilderness with a forlorn and improvised
air. It was open at both ends. But at the far end a row of
black faces, grave and compassionate and curious, formed
a wall that merged with the forest. I went inside the *caille*
and saw Villamayor lying on a bed made of underbrush
and ferns, and an old Negress with a headcloth squatted
beside him. She was chanting in a low voice, and she
rubbed his forehead with a white cloth. It must have been
the remains of a man's shirt. The bandages stained with
blood ran from the left eye and a great discolored swelling
to the top of the head. The bandages accentuated gro-
tesquely the wry twisting of the features. Except for the
region of the eye, Villamayor's face was white and calm
and withdrawn, in an attitude of death.

But he was not dead. I felt the pulse, with Andrada
leaning over me, and it was faint but regular. There was
an unsubdued flow of life. Villamayor breathed as in a

very quiet sleep. It was evident the bleeding, at least externally, had stopped.

"He will live?"

It was Andrada's voice immediately above me, disembodied from his hot animal presence: a thin voice now, distracted and afraid.

"Yes. Unless he's bleeding inside. Did you hit him anywhere else?"

"Only on the head, but with that stick of great weight."

I felt the cool hands, and tried the pulse again.

"Julieta was right," I said. "You have come too soon. Perhaps years too soon. And next time you'll need more than a stick."

I turned and saw him go back against the flimsy wall, reeling. He struck his head against the one strong timber. He was off in the darkest place of the hut.

"The next time! Listen, Nicholas Clive: I think he will breathe forever. Who is there to destroy him? You were not there. He did not look into your soul as he looked in mine, you did not hear his words."

I addressed the old Negress in French, and then the row of grave attentive faces. But no one understood me. I told Andrada to go to the house to fetch the others, and to send someone to the yacht. Also to bring rum and whatever clean cloths they could find. He remained unmoving in his shadowed place.

"Won't you go, Nicholas Clive? I want to remain."

"And scare him to death if he comes to? No, I think you've done enough. Anyway, I probably couldn't find the house."

Andrada moved out of the dense shadow and into the light at the doorway. He stared down at Villamayor's white face as though to ask a question; he did not want to leave. Then he too was kneeling beside Villamayor and as with the same motion I felt myself pushed off balance and away. He began to pray very rapidly. The Negroes at the end of the hut murmured. Then the character of his whispering changed and he was no longer praying. He began to whisper in Spanish in a curiously stilted way, as though he were reciting a poem. His voice trembled in embarrassment, and I could catch only a few words against the plaintive mourning of the Negroes standing above us. *Las sabanas del Cibao*. . . . Then he was finished. He took Villamayor's right hand in his, as with the pretext of feeling for the pulse. Then he let it drop and was gone. He sprang away from us, backward, and was outside the *caille* and running out into the bright sunlight. He was consistent to the last, with his awkward gesture of tenderness and his odd immobilities, then the sudden translation into violent motion, and his squat figure vanishing in the trees.

For it was in a way "the last," for me, though there remained one more phase of Andrada's political mission to attempt and fail at . . . and one more phase to achieve. I did not speak to him again, and I saw him only one more time. That was some twenty minutes later when he trotted back to us out of the trees, leading the rapid angry procession; Belesprit and Ezile and the little servant girl, and Julieta keeping up with them, her face flushed and twisted with anxiety, and flinging at us from a hundred yards away, "*Is he all right? Will the saintly one survive?*" In the interim Villamayor had opened his eyes once and had recognized me and smiled . . . as though to comment with irony on the fact that the rhythms of his life seemed unpleasantly repetitive. How many times was he to be beaten inconclusively? He gave me a calm confident smile, as much as to remark that all this had happened before. Then he went back to sleep. So I could call out, as they came toward us over that last hundred yards—but Andrada already hanging back, already detaching himself from the others and moving to the side:

"*Yes, he's going to be all right.*" Then they were crowded in the *caille,* Julieta kneeling and praying, and Ezile beside the old Negress who was again wiping his forehead. So we did not notice for some minutes that Andrada was gone. He had led the others to the *caille,* feeling doubtless the mark of Cain on his back not his brow. Then he had heard my words, and had left.

THIS time too the convalescence of Villamayor was remarkably quick, though his injuries (unless there was some hidden injury to the skull or brain) were mild enough. They were hardly comparable: that expert tightening of the ropes that broke and "realigned" certain bones, and Andrada's poor ineffectual blows. He did seem one of those destined by congenital inadequacy to fail in every enterprise. Villamayor himself, who had been knocked out not once but twice in the course of that absurd night, had been aware of Andrada's sudden collapse of strength. He had been stunned by the first blows, and was dimly surprised both by the taste of blood from his head and by the fact that he was still on his feet. He was also aware of the distracted scared look on Andrada's face, and that the rising and falling fist had ceased to carry much force. It was as though some perversity of will arrested the descent of the blows at the last possible moment. Even when Andrada picked up that "great stick" (in fact a thick but not heavy branch which we identified by the blood) Villamayor felt confident he would not be killed. In the last seconds of consciousness he saw Andrada staring aghast at the work of his hands, and with an expression of ultimate and baffled questioning.

There were no broken bones and the bleeding had already stopped when Julieta and the others came running toward us, guided by Andrada. So we had Villamayor back in the house and in his bed before the first contingent from the yacht arrived, with Barbara Swenson and Edward Murphree on horseback and in the forefront. But Villamayor would not speak to them, or to any of the exiles, or indeed to anyone but Julieta and Ezile, and occasionally to Belesprit and me. He lay through that hot Sunday with damp cloths over the discolored eye, breathing heavily in the heat and at times talking weakly and even incoherently. But at intervals he was his whimsical and elusive self. *"From this date,"* he once remarked, *"begins still another renewal of the flesh and spirit. And in spite of the inefficiency of my poor assailant, who expected a transformation more radical. Yet still I ask: where will it end?"* Villamayor spoke again and again of Andrada with a puzzled irony, an irony that lacked his usual assurance. The incoherence and confusion seemed in a way metaphysical: a bafflement in the presence of motives dissociated from acts. His one firm statement, reiterated through the day, was that Andrada must not be pursued. *That episode,* he insisted, *must be allowed to run its own course.* And what did it matter if the scarred and ineffective attacker still possessed his manuscripts? Villamayor remarked wryly that there would always be words to spare (if he himself were permitted to live), and manuscripts enough.

So he lay there, at times almost good-humoredly, with

the strength returning visibly to his face. The parchment whiteness was gone from beneath the discolored eye. But he became more and more irritated, as the hours passed, by the loud sounds of the exiles arguing in the courtyard under his window. On Monday morning they were back, still angrily debating. So late that morning Villamayor sent Julieta out with the firm and graceless announcement that he would speak to none of them again. *C'était fini! Il en avait assez!* He had come to this abandoned place in search of freedom and solitude . . . only to have both shattered by the inanities of a drunken journalist and by the enthusiasms of well meaning but misguided friends. *He had had, yes, enough.* On this occasion too, not a word of blame for Andrada. In fact he insisted once again that the little agent of autocracy must be allowed to go his own stumbling way. Who could say what new futilities lay in wait for him, who had already "failed in everything?" The manuscripts, Villamayor reminded them (all this again through the fierce protective agency of Julieta, speaking rapidly in Spanish) implicated only himself. Perhaps it little mattered into whose hands they fell. As for himself, he had already been condemned to death more than once, and with consolingly little effect.

Barbara Swenson, Edward Murphree and the now thoroughly irritated exiles put up with Villamayor's evasions and rudeness for another twenty-four hours. Then late Tuesday morning (and not so many hours before Manuel Andrada committed his ultimate act of stubborn loyalty) they all left together on the yacht. No one wanted to face those horses and *bourriques* again, or the slim chance of catching a camionette on the road from Anse de Corail to Port-au-Prince.

But there were still the rest of us, going in and out of

Villamayor's room. Inevitably, during these three days, we talked about the vanishing Andrada and his "change of soul." My own impulse was to see the "change" as singularly imperfect, since the converted one not only fled whatever punishment we could have brought him to but also took the suitcase of manuscripts. He had abandoned the portrait but not the manuscripts: left that portrait not fifty feet from the *caille,* to be recovered ultimately by the woman of the hut and perhaps worshiped as a household deity. Julieta meanwhile, whispering angrily, still had her crazed notions that Andrada would some day return, years or even decades hence, to complete his part in a martyrdom that had not been ripe. But Consuela, who looked back on the worst missionary failure of her life, wanted to dismiss Andrada as an ordinary coward. There had been such a fire in his eye, such a burning of desire! Now she wondered whether he would even have had the courage to report to his own superiors, in Port-au-Prince or elsewhere, with the meager spoils of the suitcase. She thought he would flee everyone.

"He will sink, if he is fortunate, into some slum of Santiago de Cuba or Havana. Will he not creep through life with his hand over that telltale scar, afraid always of us and afraid especially of The Protector and his spies? No hole will be too shameful or ignominious for him to creep in, no hole will be dark enough to hide his dishonor. The inadequate had his chance for salvation and refused it."

I remember Villamayor's puzzled frown as he listened to her, and his grimace of distaste. He was very far from accepting this simple view.

"For me who dazed and fainting yet clearly saw and knew the agony on his face—his behavior is oddly unaccountable. I am puzzled. For it is not in the character of a man whose 'soul has changed' to run away in this fashion."

I suggested that he had run, especially, from Villamayor himself, and the moment of his wakening. And yet I did not really believe this. Neither did he.

"No," he said. "It is impossible for a man of such stubbornness and desire to break off as banally as that. I cannot even be satisfied that he wanted to spare my poor bruised flesh yet go off with my papers. There is truly something lacking in this history. The further reach, as dear Julieta would have it, of the parabola. . . . No, I simply cannot imagine him running at this moment. There would be, in that, too great an ambiguity, an unacceptable incompleteness and paradox."

A CERTAIN completion was achieved, however, and it did involve an act of running . . . though hardly of running away. The world heard of it (of this one more incident of Latin-American perversity and outrage) many hours before we did, since we were without newspapers or radio. The incident was first reported on Tuesday evening from San Juan, where the astonished deplaning vacationers from New York and Miami related what they had seen and heard; Santa Isabella itself said nothing. So only a few hours after the delayed plane with its vacationers touched down in San Juan there were enigmatic stories in the New York early editions for homebound theatergoers to frown over and at last shrug off. The incomprehensible acts once again, of Latin-American fanatics; the unpronounceable names. . . . But it was two the next afternoon before we heard anything in our house near Caye Thomonde;

before we saw the dozen weary men on horseback appear out of the wilderness at the end of the formal alley of stumps: the police this time, and a representative of the Santa Isabella Consulate. They said nothing at the very first, only stared with mounting indignation at the erect figure of Villamayor waiting to greet them, his head still lightly bandaged.

Thus the story was almost fifteen hours old when we heard it. Manuel Andrada had taken the midafternoon plane from Port-au-Prince to the city of the browning palms, a flight of just under an hour. So it had taken him two nights and days to reach the airport, or at least to reach his decision. To all evidence he had done it the hard way, working his way by foot trails over the mountains and again avoiding the Anse de Corail road. Perhaps he needed a certain solitude for reflection, or perhaps he was only afraid of premature detection. In any event no one the reporters and police talked to had seen Andrada until he suddenly appeared in and then emerged from a file of Negroes going down to the market in Port-au-Prince. He stepped away from the line of black faces, still carrying the suitcase, to flag down a taxi. The driver reported that he had distrusted Andrada from the first because of his vicious scar and peculiarity of expression. But he was will-ing enough to drive him after being paid in advance. They went first to the Cathedral, where his passenger remained five or ten minutes, then directly to the airport. There Andrada had just enough time to show his permit of re-entry and passport and to buy his ticket; and, as in an afterthought, to leave the black suitcase in the baggage room. He had intended to take it with him. In fact he was already walking toward the plane when suddenly he turned, rushed back past the officials of immigration and of the airline, and flung the suitcase—flung it angrily, cursing rapidly in Spanish—onto the baggage counter. He explained that the suitcase was to remain in Port-au-Prince. At first he simply shook his head when offered the claim check, then shrugged his shoulders and accepted it. He was the last person to get on the plane, and he got on with nothing. Possessions were irrelevant for what remained to be done.

The rest of the story was filled in by those appalled vacationers, primarily female teachers of Spanish from New York; and by the stewardess and pilots. Especially by the stewardess, who had observed Andrada's clothes and stubbled face with some alarm as he came aboard, and who had the best opportunity to report on his behavior and emotions during that fifty-minute flight. He withdrew as far as possible from the other passengers in the half-empty plane, and during the first twenty minutes of preparations and flight appeared to be in a sick stupor. She had to remind him several times to fasten his seat belt and to fill in his landing card. He made no sign at all when she offered him a pillow, magazines, gum. But when she brought coffee he seized the cup so greedily that much of it spilled on his brown woolen suit, already stained with filth and of an unmentionable odor. The rest of the coffee he drank at one gulp. Then he returned to his immobile and withdrawn staring. So she was very surprised when (with the plane now at ten thousand feet and directly over the great spiny ridge of mountains and so passing from one country to the other) he suddenly pressed his face to the window and looked down with the intent fascination of a child on his first flight. He stared down at the barren blue slopes and craggy rocks and on the coral coastline with a queer expression of pride.

Gum, pillow, magazines! Andrada had indeed gone beyond such frivolities and creature comforts, as he advanced to meet his obligation. And of course it is through
his eyes not the stewardess's I imagine the last twenty
minutes of that flight, with the plane descending slowly
toward the capital. He would observe with love every mile
of that low historic shore with its coral reef broken by
coves, the first small fishing villages and the tiny clusters
of cocoanut palms, and the vast sugar plantations. In the
last miles, with the plane beginning its wide circling, he
would see a few peasant huts near the white empty roads,
then to the north and west the capital city itself: the first
low white and golden gray buildings emerging from trees
of a dusted olive green, the villas of the wealthy and near
the fair grounds the two luxury hotels securely set above
the seawall and the destroying sea. He would indeed have
become very excited: seeing now that wide empty curving
seaside drive with its orderly palms, and its statues small
as white insects, and at the very last (coming into the
airport now) the great bulk of the Cathedral some miles
away. Then the small but model airport of excellent facilities with its fine runway: the wind socks and the flags
over the terminal building, and of course the soldiers on
guard, and the policemen in readiness by the gates, also
The Protector's sacred name as the first writing to be read.

There were two gates: one marked for transients who
would reboard their plane, the other for those remaining
in the city. Manuel Andrada intended to remain. Even
before the plane had stopped, with the other passengers
still seated, he rushed forward to take his place by the door.
The stewardess recalled him suddenly appearing beside her,
breathing very heavily. Once again he seemed to be in a

stupor. He stared at the blank steel door as though to stare through it.

He may have looked dazed. And yet he did things in the very way that would make the "episode" impossible to suppress. Was this one more blunder? He was to speak his piece, however incoherently, and where it would be overheard by the outraged neutral observers, vacationers from New York and Miami. For when the door at last swung open it was not the stewardess but Andrada who emerged. He had burst past her and down the stairs and was running in the direction of the soldiers and the police. Yes, he was running directly toward them in full hearing of everyone, shrieking, *"Arrest me, arrest me, I am guilty! Deténganme! Arréstenme! Quiero confesar!"* He had reached the soldiers and policemen now; they stared at him as he went on in his shrill voice, shouting, *"I have struck down the honored one, I have killed Villamayor. I am guilty. I have failed in my mission to bring him back to the homeland, I did not bring back the papers. He is lost, he lay bleeding at my feet. I have disobeyed my orders, I demand to be arrested, I want to make confession, I want to speak to a priest. My name is Manuel Andrada, I have killed Villamayor."*

And that was all the vacationers pausing on their voyage to San Juan heard. For the circle of astounded soldiers and policemen had at last closed in. Then it was moving away, the circle, and the brown suit had vanished among the uniforms. This was also all the vacationers saw. During the fifty minutes the plane remained on the ground they were neither allowed to return to it nor to enter the terminal building. They stood there in the terrible heat thrown up by the concrete runway in the afternoon glare.

So they heard the sirens, some ten minutes after that disquieting incident. But they would not have seen the buglike gray cars arriving in angry procession, their thin antennae waving. Manuel Andrada had already vanished from their lives.

AND he had vanished also from ours. We rushed back to Port-au-Prince with the police, leaving Belesprit and Ezile to pack for everyone. We went back to broadcast the denials. Villamayor spoke on the radio transmitter of one of the relief agencies: in that suave insistent voice known well enough in the city of scrawny palms. *He had not been assassinated, he was in excellent health, the confession was the utterance of one deranged.* But Villamayor assumed from the start that these denials would come too late. At the time of his broadcast, and of the cables to the news services, over twenty-four hours had passed since Andrada's most public confession. More than enough time for the Services of Security to act! Through the late afternoon and until the station went off the air we listened to Santa Isabella. But the same weary lulling music went on, record after record, and the meaningless news announcements. There was no reference at all to Villamayor's denial as there had been none, the day before, to Andrada's confession and arrest. The great silence of the land had closed in over Andrada and his crime. Only much later some reference might be made, after the rumors of an airport commotion had reached everyone of any position in the city. Then there might be a brief report in the *Diario* of a later and more coherent confession (this one containing no reference to a "mission" or to lost "papers" or even to Villamayor) followed by trial and "imprisonment for

life." Soon thereafter, as so often in the past, a body might
be found hanging in the jail: "suicide out of remorse."
But for the present there was only silence.

Of course I thought of going to Santa Isabella myself.
But my application for a tourist permit was refused without explanation. I was not at all surprised.

Villamayor in these days remained aloof and saddened,
and he would have nothing to do with Barbara Swenson
and her minions who lingered in Port-au-Prince. He did
tolerate Consuela and Julieta, and he still tolerated me.
We all had rooms in Bernard's hotel. I think he permitted
Consuela to remain because she too, like Andrada, cared
so much . . . because she too had her unsubduable in-
tegrity of the passionate or the mad. But on the very afternoon of his broadcast, immediately after it in fact, he was
ready to cast her off. For she had made the gross error of
throwing a sordid suspicion over Andrada's complex act
of atonement.

"And if he went back only to claim his reward?" she
asked. "Suppose he expected to take from them at once
whatever foul money the assassin gets, and then disappear
before the truth was learned? He knew well enough you
could not answer his confession for many hours: that
explains everything. Was he not sent to assassinate you?
And is this not what he claimed to have done?"

Villamayor looked away from her as from a creature
shamefully incapable of thought.

"On the contrary," he said coldly, "Manuel Andrada
chose the one mode of confession certain to bring him
punishment. Had he made his absurd claim in privacy
. . . who knows? Then perhaps he would have enjoyed
a few hours or days basking in the illusion of official
gratitude. In the end, of course, it would have been the

same. The Services of Security need their killers but the killers also must die. By his clamor at the airport Andrada gave them the best possible pretext. . . ."

I broke in to ask whether he didn't credit Andrada with too much intelligence; or, at least, too much understanding of his own case. But he answered me at once:

"That is not the same thing! Andrada went swiftly to the act of confession, in a most effective way. Confession was obligatory. He did this with the directness of a man who understands everything. And yet of course he didn't understand everything. Why should he pay both for striking me and for not bringing me back? The question is much too hard. It is the ultimate evil of such a tyranny that it demands impossible choices, and makes compassion a crime. Unless one totally submit. . . . I think Andrada at the end was convinced only that he had committed a crime, many crimes in fact. This was at least one thing he could believe. So of course, given this one certitude, he could not live on without punishment. Doubtless in this his attitude was realistic enough."

I felt in Villamayor a restlessness and bitter *dégoût de la vie* during the next days. A disgust with his own life, at least, an obvious longing for change. He had given up working on his book and spent much of his time in uneasy pacing. He might emerge for a swim or to lie on a chaise longue by the pool, then minutes later go inside and get dressed. He was more irritable than I had seen him before. And every day in the late afternoon he went out for a walk, insisting that he wanted to go alone. We would watch the tall erect and slightly limping figure go out the gate at the bottom of the hotel garden and vanish into the swarm of Negroes walking silently in the dust, the white robes and black faces moving with an evenness of stride that suggested a conveyor belt.

The silence of Santa Isabella continued, concerning Andrada's confession and his fate. The small matter of an imprudent agent's punishment required no international explanation or apology; it was too small, too internal an "affair." In the weekly news magazines in the United States, Andrada did have one more small lease on life, before moving into the lasting silence. There the story of the assassin who confesses and of the victim who protests his good health was presented as an item of humor: a moment of absurdity to relieve the grim monotonies of crime, poverty, war. None of these stories spoiled the fun by suggesting what all of us now assumed: that the imprudence had already been punished by death, and the inadequacy put in its place.

The several stories though—first the radio and newspapers, then the brief comments in the weeklies—brought Villamayor back into the limelight he detested. Many letters arrived, including a long one from the guilty José Cabral. There were handwritten letters in impassioned Spanish offering congratulations, divers services and advice, or requesting contributions. The exile leaders had gone back to their homes. But on the sixth day after Manuel Andrada's confession a mysterious visitor arrived from Caracas, wearing dark glasses and in his tie a great stickpin that flashed in the sun. He insisted that Villamayor accompany him in a taxi. An hour later Villamayor returned, his face ugly with annoyance. The visitor had come to "make contact," had spoken of a new Popular Movement backed by Venezuelan oil millionaires, and wanted Villamayor to fly to Caracas at once. But when pressed for names he had been able to mention only three notorious irresponsibles. Then the day after that Barbara Swenson made new overtures through the incorruptible and unexhausted Eduardo Gonzales. We watched them from the other end of Bernard's veranda: the gesticulating Gonzales now and then rising from the table to make his points, and Villamayor with his twisted face cupped dismally in his hands.

With me, Villamayor reverted only once to the subject of The Protector and his pacifying methods . . . which he certainly hated more than ever. We were alone by the pool when suddenly he asked me whether I thought of him as "resigned."

"Do you mean resigned to life? Resigned to having your privacy invaded by strangers who won't go away?"

Villamayor smiled.

"No: I mean do you think of me as 'resigned' concerning Santa Isabella?"

"I'd say you're pessimistic . . ."

Villamayor put his hand on mine. It might have been he was appealing to me to become his witness—which is what I have, after all, become. Villamayor was no freer than the rest of us from incorrigible vanity. And perhaps he had tolerated me this long because he did want that magazine article to be written after all, because he wanted even cold Northerners to understand.

"That is not the same thing," he said quietly. "Let me make my position clear once for all. I will not participate in ill-prepared invasions of Santa Isabella that can lead only to further repression. But this does not mean I am resigned. The small history of Manuel Andrada has made me less resigned than ever."

The statement, in retrospect, has an almost testamentary character and tone. It suggests to me now that he did not want to be misunderstood by those he left behind, as poor Andrada was misunderstood by Consuela. But at the time I was rather stupidly unaware that he intended to leave us behind. Even when he made various financial arrangements on behalf of Belesprit and Ezile—arrangements which I witnessed—I merely supposed he was fulfilling certain social obligations. Was he not grandly handing the girl over to her future spouse, having first enjoyed his *droit de seigneur?* Well, that impression too was unjust. . . . The truth was that Villamayor had not intended this brief attachment, any more than he had intended to evoke the exhausting devotions of Julieta. They had appeared and had loved him, and in his way he had loved them. He could not simply thrust them away.

BUT thrust away he finally did. For one day Villamayor did not return from that solitary late afternoon walk among the throngs of Negroes crowding the street at the foot of our garden. He simply vanished into the shadowed streets, then into the darkness of the Port-au-Prince night, taking no baggage and no manuscripts with him, having said no good-byes. It was the fourth disappearance, to my certain knowledge, of the *homme fuyant* and stubborn repudiator of social fixities. Yet had he not all his life been seeking new selves and new visions, as he moved from the ranch to the town and from the town to the ranch, from Santa Isabella to Europe and back? I was inclined from the first to take an optimistic view. But Julieta at once assumed he had been kidnapped again by the unappeased authorities of Santa Isabella. She appealed to Barbara Swenson and through her to Auguste Bataille.

Then after twenty-four hours a brief letter from Santiago de Cuba removed her worst fears. Villamayor wanted to reassure everyone that he was alive and well. He had made provisions with a bank in Port-au-Prince for a sum of money to be paid to Julieta. And he advised her to return to her sister. Then only this: *"I shall not be in Santiago when you receive this note. I do not wish to be pursued. I trust you will in time forgive me. Stubbornly and selfishly I must now continue alone."*

AND that is all I know: this story must come to its ambiguous end; Villamayor would now continue alone. He too has vanished into a silence, leaving behind him unanswered questions. What would happen to him next, who said he wanted most from life an "unpredictable novelty" and freedom to think his solitary thoughts? He meant such remarks. And yet I think it was precisely when Villamayor talked most of selfishness and solitude that he found himself most committed. His thirst for independence in a world free from compromise drove him straight into the thick of complex, insoluble dilemma. This was ineradicably in his nature: he could not leave people alone. Nor they him. So I imagine him aspiring to lose himself among the poor, in a slum of Havana or Mexico City: an unattached man on whom no demands can be made. And how long would his freedom last? I imagine him entering a dingy café to stand by himself at the bar, among the soldiers and the ruined drifters of the district. Solitude at last! Yet within minutes, I know, he would be deeply engaged in conversation, and passionately involved in the lives around him. Someone would have come to him with a burden he could not refuse.

That is why I cannot believe Villamayor has turned his
back for good on Santa Isabella and its suffering . . . on
his "corrupted, brutalized, vulgar, illiterate country,
parched and enervated and ruined." How well I remember
those passionate and surprising words! And that too is
why I feel I shall some day see Villamayor again . . .
even see his name in the newspapers once more. In any
event I am sure there will be further sinuous perversities,
further pursuits of freedom, further visions of an un-
attainable solitude. And that is in fact how I best imagine
him, fifteen or twenty years hence: an aging but sturdy
man on a crescent beach on some last unspoiled island,
enjoying a swim or perhaps walking the white sand in the
pleasures of intense solitary meditation . . . while in the
background clusters a noisy swarm of new converts and
unsought disciples, not to speak of female companions.
Perhaps among them will be, declaiming on a still imperfect and still unresolved destiny, and lamenting the slow-
ness of the soul's progress toward its home: the white-
haired but ageless Julieta.

So I feel I shall some day see Villamayor. But Andrada
I shall not, I think, see. At times it is very hard for me to
imagine him dead, who had been so full of life: the small
stubborn burning man who cared so much, and who in a
few short weeks went so far. He has not left me the same.
He left none of us the same, and least of all himself. So
now as I write I dream of various ways he might have
survived, thrown up safe by some whim or error of a
vicious bureaucracy or through an underling's rash act of
compassion. They who take up the sword shall perish by
the sword. And they who stumble upon and take up compassion, furious but helpless in the presence of their own
suddenly revealed humanity, and at the risk of their lives?

Should they too not be permitted to survive? Yes, I like to think an emaciated and blinking Andrada will emerge into the terrible sunlight of Santa Isabella after a few years of prison: to kneel and touch patriotically the dust at his feet. I wish I could persuade myself to interpret thus the silence of the authorities. But was it not really too much to forgive, especially of a humble one who had no famous poems to be memorized, and no fortune to confiscate? The ultimate and grossly deliberate error —the surrender of the incriminating manuscripts moments before boarding the plane—must have made forgiveness impossible. Andrada would have had to receive the punishment he so carefully sought.

That is why there are these other times when all my wishful thinking seems in vain. At these times I know in my heart that somewhere my queer friend lies at peace, punished, and dead, in his brown suit and buried some feet into the soil he loved; and will not wake again.

NOTE

SOME OF THE MATERIAL for this novel was gathered in the course of a trip to Cuba, Haiti and the Dominican Republic, in the summer of 1959. I went to these places, on a magazine assignment, to investigate the planning of vest-pocket invasions and revolutions. In Havana I talked with the loyal and the subversive, with Haitians plotting an invasion, and (within twenty-four hours of each other) with Castro's executioner, a trainer of his guerrilla forces, and his director of the National Library. My novel is nevertheless in no way intended to reflect present or past conditions in Cuba. My "Santa Isabella" (for all its resemblances to the Dominican Republic of Trujillo) is a fictional country, and two of my Haitian cities will be found on no map. Specifically: the story of Villamayor is not intended to suggest a solution to the mystery of Dr. Jesús de Galindez, presumed to have been killed by Dominican authorities.

Much of this novel was written during my tenure as a Fellow at the Center for Advanced Study in the Behavioral Sciences at Stanford, California.

A.J.G.